Experiencing European Integration

Experiencing European Integration

Transnational Lives and European Identity

Theresa Kuhn

OXFORD
UNIVERSITY PRESS

OXFORD
UNIVERSITY PRESS

Great Clarendon Street, Oxford, OX2 6DP,
United Kingdom

Oxford University Press is a department of the University of Oxford.
It furthers the University's objective of excellence in research, scholarship,
and education by publishing worldwide. Oxford is a registered trade mark of
Oxford University Press in the UK and in certain other countries

© Theresa Kuhn 2015

The moral rights of the author have been asserted

First Edition published in 2015
Impression: 2

Published in the United States of America by Oxford University Press
198 Madison Avenue, New York, NY 10016, United States of America

British Library Cataloguing in Publication Data
Data available

Library of Congress Control Number: 2014943392

ISBN 978–0–19–968891–3

Printed and bound by
CPI Group (UK) Ltd, Croydon, CR0 4YY

To Bram

Preface

Having lived, studied, and worked in seven European member states, I have experienced the advantages of European integration first-hand. As an Austrian student in Germany, I was happy to give up my two wallets—one for Schillings, one for Deutschmarks—when the euro was introduced. I cheered each time when international roaming fees for mobile phones were decreased once again. I was frustrated by the amount of additional paperwork that still needs to be done to register a binational marriage, and I was probably among the first Europeans to know their twenty-digit IBAN number by heart. At the same time, I understood that some of my friends led less transnational lives but were nonetheless confronted with European legislation and international competition, and often did not see the point of it. This sparked my interest in transnational experiences and their impact on orientations towards European integration, and ultimately motivated me to write this book.

These cross-border interactions and networks not only influence people's attitudes and identities; in my case, they helped tremendously in advancing and improving my book. I would therefore like to thank the people and institutions that supported me in this endeavour and made it a much more pleasurable and rewarding experience.

First of all, I would like to express my gratitude to my supervisor at the European University Institute (EUI), Martin Kohli. He gave me a lot of freedom, never failed to encourage me, and regularly pushed my research in the right direction. In numerous discussions, Mark Franklin supported my research much more than his role as Second Reader asked him to do. Jack Citrin at the University of California at Berkeley was kind enough to invite me to the Institute of Governmental Studies as a visiting fellow in 2010 and served as an external jury member of my thesis. I am indebted to him and to Juan Díez Medrano for detailed feedback and suggestions on my dissertation. The lunch breaks on the terrace of EUI's Badia Fiesolana provided ample opportunities to discuss my research. I would particularly like to thank Rainer Bauböck, Laurie Beaudonnet, Michael Keating, Christel Koop, Jeroen Moes, Thomas Paster, and Carolien van Ham for challenging my ideas and helping improve my work. Elias Dinas, Sergi Pardos Prado, and Jonas Radl expertly and patiently acted as my personal 'Stata help desk' by always getting the code right.

The 'State of the State' Fellowship Programme at the University of Oxford provided a unique opportunity to extend this research into a book manuscript. This programme was organized by the Universities of Bremen, Göttingen, and Oxford, and I would like to thank the two main coordinators, Lothar Probst at Bremen and Radoslaw Zubek at Oxford, for their support and encouragement. Nuffield College and the Department of Politics and International Relations provided a stimulating research environment where I could live and breathe social science on a daily basis. I am indebted to my mentors, Geoff Evans and Sara Hobolt, for giving detailed feedback on my work in progress and for inspiring me to become a better researcher. I would also like to thank my colleagues, in particular Faisal Ahmed, Lucy Barnes, Eline de Rooij, Catherine de Vries, Elias Dinas, Anja Neundorf, Ola Onuch, Sergi Pardos Prado, and Daniel Stegmueller. Avril Keating and Heike Klüver took the time to read and comment on entire chapters of this book.

Tanja Börzel and Thomas Risse gave me the excellent opportunity to visit the KFG 'Transformative Power of Europe' at Freie Universität Berlin and to benefit from insightful discussions with other fellows there. Liesbet Hooghe and Gary Marks provided invaluable feedback on my work and gave general advice on how to manage a transnational career in academia. Florian Stoeckel has read and commented on several chapters of this book and has also become a great co-author. At FU Berlin's sociology department, I particularly thank Sören Carlson, Monika Eigmüller, Jürgen Gerhards, Marta Kozlowska, Jochen Roose, and Sophia Schubert. Michael Zürn hosted me at WZB Berlin Social Science Center, where discussions with Pieter de Wilde, Marc Helbling, Christian Rauh, and Céline Teney sharpened my thinking about the topic.

In 2011, Catherine de Vries kindly shared her office at the University of Amsterdam, many lunch breaks, and her academic experience with me. Thanks to Ettore Recchi, I got involved in the FP7 project 'The Europeanisation of Everyday Life: Cross-Border Practices and Transnational Identities among EU and Third-Country Citizens'. The intellectual exchange with him and the other scholars in the project has left its mark on my research.

Audiences at several conferences and workshops have provided valuable comments and criticism that have helped to improve the book. In particular, I would like to thank Christine Arnold, Laura Cram, Amandine Crespy, Steffen Mau, Hans-Dieter Klingemann, Hanspeter Kriesi, Virginie van Ingelgom, and Jonathan White.

As is shown in Chapter 4 of this book, transnational interactions are highly dependent on economic resources. The work on this book was made possible by generous grants of the Austrian Federal Ministry of Science and Research, the European University Institute, and the Volkswagen Foundation.

I would like to thank the people who worked with me at Oxford University Press: Dominic Byatt, Lizzie Suffling, and Olivia Wells. I am deeply grateful to

the two anonymous reviewers whose suggestions improved this book pro-
foundly. The book draws on two of my previous publications: 'Individual
Transnationalism, Globalization and Euroscepticism: An Empirical Test of
Deutsch's Transactionalist Theory', *European Journal of Political Research* 50(6)
and 'Europa ante Portas: Border Residence, Transnational Interaction and
Euroscepticism in Germany and France', *European Union Politics* 13(1).
I thank the two journals as well as Sage and Wiley for allowing me to use
that material here. Barry McKeon put the stylistic and editorial finishing
touches to this manuscript.

My deepest gratitude goes to my parents, Barbara and Michael Kuhn, who
instilled both a passion for transnational mobility and for academic research
in me. They and my siblings Maria, Susanne, Stefan, and Verena never failed
to visit me at my various homesteads and regularly reminded me of the world
outside the academic 'bubble'.

Finally, I would like to say 'dank je' to Bram Lancee for his love and
unfailing support, and for tolerating my life on the move and work under
pressure. Over the past seven years, he has become a true expert in transnational relations, both in theory and in practice. With gratitude, I dedicate
this book to him.

Amsterdam
May 2014

Contents

List of Figures

List of Tables

List of Abbreviations

AUT	Austria
BEL	Belgium
BLG	Bulgaria
CYP	Cyprus
CZE	Czech Republic
DEU	Germany
DNK	Denmark
EB	Eurobarometer
EP	European Parliament
ESP	Spain
EST	Estonia
EU-15	15 member states that had joined the EU by 1995
EU-25	25 member states that had joined the EU by 2004
EU-27	27 member states that had joined the EU by 2007
EU+12	European member states having joined in 2004 and 2007
FIN	Finland
FPÖ	Freiheitliche Partei Österreichs (Austrian Freedom Party)
FRA	France
GBR	United Kingdom
GDR	German Democratic Republic
GRC	Greece
GSOEP	German Socio-Economic Panel
HUN	Hungary
IRL	Ireland
ISSP	International Social Survey Programme
ITA	Italy
LTU	Lithuania
LUX	Luxembourg

LVA	Latvia
MEP	Member of European Parliament
MLT	Malta
NLD	The Netherlands
NMS	New member states
NUTS	Nomenclature of Territorial Units
OLS	Ordinary least squares
ÖVP	Österreichische Volkspartei (Austrian People's Party)
POL	Poland
PRT	Portugal
ROM	Romania
SPÖ	Sozialdemokratische Partei Österreichs (Austrian Social Democratic Party)
SVK	Slovakia
SVN	Slovenia
SWE	Sweden

1

Introduction

Europe is about founding a new kind of community—one not constrained by historical legacies, or geographic limits—one without borders or barriers.

—Neelie Kroes, Vice-President of the European Commission

There is a growing frustration that the EU is seen as something that is done to people rather than acting on their behalf.[1]

—David Cameron, Prime Minister of the United Kingdom

European integration has had a fundamental impact on people's everyday lives. The creation of a common market and the opening of national borders have spurred a wide range of new economic, political, and social opportunities beyond the nation state (Bartolini 2005: 21). European citizens are free to obtain their academic degree in Germany, earn their money in London, invest it in Luxembourg, and retire in Spain. In other words, Europeans now have manifold possibilities to interact across the borders of EU member states.

It is exactly this development that Karl Deutsch's (Deautsch et al. 1957) transactionalist theory expected to trigger public support for European integration and to foster a common European identity. In the aftermath of World War II, Deutsch and his colleagues advised the establishment of 'security communities' where strong cross-border bonds of common identification and trust would eliminate the risk of war. To do so, states ought not only integrate their elites and institutions, but also set a framework for increased cross-border transactions and networks among their publics. The proliferation of transactions was expected to stimulate psychological learning processes among the people involved. According to the authors, these processes would lead individuals to lower their out-group boundaries, appreciate the newly established polity, and eventually adopt a collective identity.

---

[1] Neelie Kroes, 'A vision for Europe', World Economic Forum, Davos January 2014; David Cameron, speech on the future of Europe, January 2013.

This prominent 'pre-theory' of European integration (Haas 1970) was widely acclaimed in political science, international relations and nationalism studies (Puchala 1970a, 1970b; Sinnott 1995; Adler and Barnett 1998a; Schlueter and Wagner 2008). Recently, there has been a revived interest in transactionalist theory in (above all, sociological approaches to) European integration studies (see, among others, Delhey 2005; Fligstein 2008; Cram 2009; Favell and Guiraudon 2009; Sigalas 2010a; Klingemann and Weldon 2013).

Transactionalist theory has also left its mark in European policymaking. Along with the prominent Erasmus student exchange programme (Petit 2007; Sigalas 2010a), a wide array of other Europe-wide and binational programmes, such as European regional and research funds, have been established to foster a common European identity and support for further integration by bringing Europeans together to work, study, and live.

Despite the positive reception of transactionalist theory in academic research and policymaking, little empirical research exists on the relationship between transnational interactions and orientations towards European integration. On the one hand, this reluctance might be due to the fact that for a long time, the consequences of European integration have been studied mainly from economic, legal, and political-institutional perspectives. In contrast, sociologists have arrived 'late at the EU studies ball' (Ross 2011: 215). Only in the past decade have scholars begun to study the societal consequences of European integration. Researchers have asked, for instance, whether European integration upsets existing patterns of inequality in national societies (Beckfield 2006; Whelan and Maître 2009), or whether there are European social fields (Fligstein 2008), public spheres (Koopmans et al. 2010), or a collective identity (Bruter 2005; Checkel and Katzenstein 2009; Risse 2010) in the making.

Furthermore, empirical research on the impact of transactions on EU support is hampered by the limited availability of data on transnational interactions among the public. Thus, the very few systematic attempts to test Deutsch's theory in empirical research do so either by indirectly linking transactions to EU support via other indicators (Fligstein 2008) or focus on interactions among specific groups such as Erasmus students (Sigalas 2010a, 2010b; Wilson 2011), border residents (Rippl et al. 2010; Roose 2010), or intra-European migrants (Favell 2008; Recchi and Favell 2009). Other authors attempt to test transactionalist theory at the aggregate level (Delhey 2007).

In his seminal contribution *Euroclash*, Fligstein (2008) combines findings on proliferated European cross-border interactions at the institutional, corporate, and individual level with those on the development of a collective European identity. Similarly, Díez-Medrano (2008) searches for the development of European social groups in the face of Europeanizing behaviour and experiences. In more general terms, Mau and colleagues (2008) analyse the impact of transnational interactions and networks on cosmopolitan attitudes among Germans, finding a strong correlation between the two.

Other studies concentrate on identity and value change among certain groups which are strongly involved in cross-border exchanges. Focusing on Erasmus exchange students in the United Kingdom and in continental Europe, Sigalas (2010a, 2010b) studies the effect of international student mobility on European identity and membership support. Similarly, Wilson (2011) conducted a panel study among French, English, and Swedish Erasmus students. The authors in the volume of Recchi and Favell (2009) offer a comprehensive account of the small but growing group of intra-European migrants, who they expect to be the harbingers of European identity formation. Gustafson (2009), in turn, focuses on collective identity change among frequent travellers. Other authors expect intra-European border districts to be 'laboratories of social integration' (Dürrschmidt 2006: 245), analyse collective identities among border residents (Meinhof 2003; Rippl et al. 2010), and shed light on the prospects of cross-border sociation (Roose 2010).

While these contributions have been essential in advancing our knowledge of the Europeanization of national societies, there is a persistent lack of systematic and empirically grounded insight into transnational interactions and networks among the *entire* European population, and their *direct* link to citizens' orientations towards European integration.

This research gap is even more problematic as empirical findings belie the optimistic expectations of transactionalist theory. Figure 1.1 shows the development of net EU membership support and transnational personal contacts and information flows for the EU-15 between 1973 and 2007. Net membership support refers to the percentage of respondents indicating that EU membership is a 'good thing' minus the percentage of respondents deeming it to be a 'bad thing' in each member state, averaged over the EU-15, as measured in the Eurobarometer surveys.[2] The data on transnational personal contacts and information flows are derived from the KOF index of globalization (Dreher et al. 2008). This index provides a comprehensive measure of economic, political, and social globalization for 158 countries, and is discussed in further detail in Chapter 2. The data used in Figure 1.1 refer to information on international telephone contacts and international mail, the percentage of foreign people living in a country, internet users, and trade in newspapers among other things. As shown in Figure 1.1 for the EU-15, transnational personal

---

[2] Note that observations for Spain and Portugal start in 1980, for Greece in 1981, and for Austria, Finland, and Sweden in 1995. Observations were averaged across countries.

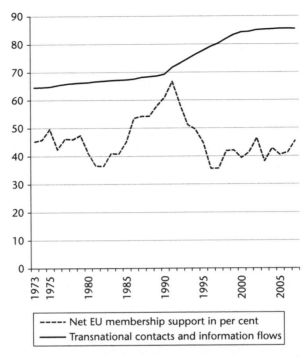

Figure 1.1. Transnational contacts and information flows vs. net membership support, EU-15

Sources: Eurobarometer (1973–2007), Dreher et al. (2008)

contacts and information flows steadily increased between 1973 and 1992, and rapidly proliferated in the wake of the Maastricht Treaty (Treaty on European Union, European Union 1992) until the year 2000. However, just at the time when transnational personal contacts and information flows gained momentum, net EU membership support decreased, reaching a historical low of 36 per cent in the year 1996. While it did recover from this shock, it has not considerably increased since then.[3] This development strongly challenges the Deutschian assertion that increased transnational interaction results in a collective identity and public support for further political integration.

---

[3] The data shown in Figure 1.1 stop in 2007, when the data used in the empirical analyses of this book were collected. While more recent data are available and document a sharp decrease in EU membership support, they have to be interpreted in light of the European sovereign debt crisis. Taking these data into consideration might overstate the discrepancy between general EU support and transactions. The implications of the crisis are discussed in Chapter 8.

1.1 The Puzzle: The Discrepancy between Being and Feeling European

This brings me to the puzzle motivating this book: while transnational networks and activities have indeed proliferated over the past decades, they have not been accompanied by an augmentation in European identification and political support for European integration among the European public. We see, on the one hand, a remarkable increase in transnational interactions in the European Union: northern Europeans spending their retirement at the Mediterranean coast; university students from all over Europe studying for a semester in London, Amsterdam, or Prague; Germans employing a Polish caretaker; Austrians getting their teeth fixed for a better price in Hungary, and Scandinavians buying Italian coffee in their local supermarket are all part of an integrating Europe and seem to reflect the 'Unity in diversity' that is desired by European policy makers. However, this cosy image of European integration does not tell the entire story. Especially since the signing of the Treaty on European Union in 1992, instances of eurosceptic attitudes and behaviour have abounded (Eichenberg and Dalton 2007; Hooghe and Marks 2009a; Lubbers and Scheepers 2010). Public discontent about Europe is not only well documented by the twice-yearly Eurobarometer surveys, but is also evidenced by the successful anti-European campaigning of some political parties, mainly at the left and right fringes of the political spectrum (De Vries and Edwards 2009). While certainly relating to a broader range of motivations than just euroscepticism (Hobolt 2009), the negative constitutional referendum outcomes in France and the Netherlands in 2005 and in Ireland in 2008 testify to a constraining dissensus (Hooghe and Marks 2009a) rather than the permissive consensus (Lindberg and Scheingold 1970) that was expected by politicians and scholars alike. Equally surprising is the fact that numbers on European collective identity have remained relatively stable over the past decades (Díez Medrano 2010b), and that European identity is neither stronger nor more widespread than regional identities in other regions of the world (Roose 2012b). In short, why, in the face of increased transnational interaction and networks across Europe, do we not observe more public support for European integration and a stronger collective identity in Europe?

A number of research questions are instructive in finding the answer to this puzzle. First, although there is an increase in transnationalism at the macro-level, one has to ask how transnational interactions and networks are distributed across society in Europe today. Are they widespread, or just a niche-phenomenon, restricted to a very select group of Europeans? Closely related to this is the question: who are the highly transnational Europeans? Do we find a clear pattern in terms of country of residence, age, socio-economic background? Additionally, it is essential to further scrutinize the relationship between individual transnationalism and orientations towards European integration. Do more transnational interactions indeed imply more EU support and European identity, in line with transactionalist theory? If so, which aspects of individual transnationalism matter most? Further, what are the consequences of increased transactions for the people who do not interact across borders?

1.2 The Argument: Three Qualifications to Transactionalist Theory

The central argument of this book is that, in line with Deutsch's expectations, there is a significant relationship between transnational interactions and orientations towards European integration *at the individual level*, but that transactions are (1) socially stratified, (2) their effectiveness depends on their purpose and scope, and (3) they can foment negative externalities among Europeans who are not transnationally active themselves.

To develop this argument, it is necessary to differentiate between transactions at the individual and at the aggregate level. The book therefore develops the concept of individual transnationalism, that is, people's ties, interactions, and mobility across borders. There is empirical support for the expectation that individual transnationalism is significantly related to a more European mindset. While not directly establishing an empirical link between transactions and orientations towards European integration, Fligstein (2008) shows that the same social groups that are more likely to interact across borders are also more likely to support European integration. In more general terms, Mau and colleagues (2008) show that transnationally active individuals endorse cosmopolitan ideals. Rother and Nebe (2009) find that the majority of intra-European migrants identify as Europeans. They are also more knowledgeable and supportive of European integration than the overall population. While there is little evidence that participating in an Erasmus exchange strengthens European identity (Sigalas 2010a), this can be explained by a ceiling effect: students in higher education are a highly selective group that are from the outset highly pro-European (Kuhn 2012b). Thus, at the individual level, transactionalist theory seems to pan out in reality. However, this is not the end of the story, and the following three qualifications help explain the discrepancy between transactions and attitudes at the macro-level.

First, social structures filter those who take part in transnational interactions (Marks 1999). Research suggests that the foundations for transnational behaviour are laid as early as in adolescence and are strongly determined by parents' socio-economic background and the opportunities provided at school (Gerhards and Hans 2013). Only a highly skilled and young minority regularly interact across borders (Fligstein 2008). Thus, the transactionalist hypothesis is relevant only with respect to a small, *avant-garde* section of the public, while most Europeans are not prompted by transnational interactions to develop support for European integration. Consequently, it is not sufficient to model EU support as a function of the *aggregate* level of transnational interactions as this conceals the unequal distribution of transactions across society. Rather, one ought to study the effect of transactions at the individual level.

Next, it is important to assess when and how transnational interactions are linked to a change in attitudes and identities. There are good reasons to believe that the effectiveness of transactions in triggering EU support is contingent on a number of factors, such as their purpose and scope. These aspects influence how Europeans experience and frame their interactions. A study on cross-border interactions in Germany and France found that sociable interactions are more effective in structuring EU support than purely instrumental interactions (Kuhn 2012a). The book corroborates these findings for the entire EU, suggesting that political efforts to increase mainly instrumental transactions do not achieve the expected effect. This finding has important theoretical implications, as it suggests that questions of group identity rather than utilitarian considerations underlie the link between transactions and EU support.

Moreover, not all transnational interactions in Europe are genuinely European. Rather, they can limit themselves to the binational level, or reach beyond the borders of Europe. Consequently, people might not cognitively link their interactions to European integration. It should be noted that transactionalist theory posited that increased transactions within a security community would decrease the propensity to interact with the rest of the world (Inglehart 1968: 121–2). In contrast, we observe a more global transnationalization of European societies that includes the diffusion of ideas and people from outside Europe. Transactions that go beyond European borders are less effective in generating EU support than intra-European transactions. It is plausible that people who mainly interact with non-Europeans develop more global feelings of attachment. They might even criticize the EU for establishing a 'fortress Europe' which represents an obstacle to their transactions. Furthermore, people who primarily interact with one other country (such as their neighbouring country) might frame their interactions in a binational rather than European context. Therefore, transnational interactions that do not have a genuinely European scope might fail to yield the expected change in public orientations towards European integration.

Finally, one ought to consider the effect of transactions on people who do not interact across borders themselves. While still representing a majority in the European Union today, these people are likely to feel overwhelmed by the influx of new ideas, people, and products into formerly rather homogenous national societies, and by the ensuing social and economic tensions.

Moreover, they might feel excluded from the transnationalization of their environment. In other words, transnational interactions might generate negative externalities in social and political terms. Rather than observing more widespread and uniform EU support, we witness a divide between winners of transnationalization who favour further integration, and its losers who opt for the closing of national borders (Kriesi et al. 2008).

In sum, one should not expect all interactions at all levels of society to promote EU support and collective identity formation. Rather, to understand how transnationalism is connected to orientations towards European integration, one has to consider (1) who is taking part in interactions, (2) whether interactions are instrumental or sociable, (3) whether they are binational, European, or extend beyond the borders of Europe, and finally, (4) what their consequences are for Europeans that are not transnationally active themselves.

1.3 Contribution to Current Research

This book places itself in the field of political sociology of European integration, but reaches out to a broader readership in several ways. First, the book extends regional integration theory by clarifying the relationship between increased transnational interactions and orientations towards European integration. Deutsch remained vague with respect to what underlies the expected 'learning effects', and under which conditions they are successful (Haas 1970; Eilstrup-Sangiovanni 2006). This issue has not been solved by contemporary scholars following a Deutschian approach (Díez Medrano 2008; Fligstein 2008). The book fills this lacuna by proposing two mechanisms that explain how transactions foster EU support and European identification. On the one hand, utilitarian cost–benefit considerations might play a role: highly transnational Europeans are likely to endorse European integration because they are ultimately the people who benefit from integration on a daily basis. Frequent travellers are likely to welcome policies such as the Schengen area or the common currency because they make their lives easier and because they offer a wealth of new opportunities (Sandholtz and Stone Sweet 1998). On the other hand, transnational interactions are expected to make Europeans more cosmopolitan. By interacting across borders, individuals are expected to become aware of international interdependence, to approximate their behaviour and beliefs, and to lower intergroup boundaries (Mau et al. 2008). This should also influence their orientations towards European integration.

Second, the book extends social theory by developing the concept of individual transnationalism as individual ties, interactions, and mobility across borders, thereby distinguishing between the dimensions of transnational background, transnational practices, and transnational human capital. It helps to overcome the issue of methodological nationalism that continues to dominate current sociological research (Beck and Beck-Gernsheim 2009). The book further contributes to research on transnationalism by emphasizing its social stratification and by studying potentially adverse effects of macro-level transnationalization on orientations towards European integration. While there is growing interest in the social stratification of transnational 'capital' (Gerhards and Hans 2013), little empirical evidence exists thus far. Relying on some of the few existing survey data that refer to individuals' cross-border practices, the book takes stock of the extent and scope of individual transnationalism across Europe and analyses its distribution across age groups, socio-economic groups, and countries. The book shows that the extent to which Europeans are transnationally active depends mainly on the opportunity structure provided by institutions, as well as on their resources. Finally, the book fills a gap in the literature by analysing the impact of transnationalism on EU support and European identity, thereby also examining the intervening effect of transnationalization at the country level. While transactionalist theory has been tested indirectly (Fligstein 2008), or for specific groups, such as Erasmus students (Sigalas 2010a, 2010b; Wilson 2011), this is the first direct empirical test of transactionalist theory for the entire European population.

Beyond the scope of the questions outlined above, this book is of relevance to political scientists and sociologists for several reasons. First, the book speaks to the nascent sociological debate on the emergence of a European society (Kohli 2000; Outhwaite 2008; Favell and Guiraudon 2011). From a sociological perspective, it is crucial to determine whether European institutional integration is accompanied by *societal integration* (Bach 2000). Interaction and interdependence constitute important building blocks of society (Roose 2010: 17). The scale and scope of EU-wide transnational networks and interactions may therefore indicate to what extent we can speak of a European society.

Second, both the extent of EU-wide transnational interaction and the level of public support for European integration have direct implications for the *democratic legitimacy of the European Union* (Recchi and Kuhn 2013). Citizens' consent to be governed and their belief in the rightfulness of the political regime constitute a pillar of political legitimacy (Weber 1962; Beetham 1991; Titunik 2005). In fact, according to Weber (1962), a system of political dominance is to be considered as legitimate only when those subjected to it believe the claim to political power to be valid. Thus, the scope and persistence of euroscepticism is a potential challenge to the democratic legitimacy of the European Union. One may even go further and argue that the extent to which Europeans engage in transnational interactions and networks is crucial to the EU's legitimacy. In fact, an often-overlooked condition of political legitimacy is the overlap between political and social spaces (Held 1995; Zürn 2000; Anderson 2002). Only when the social and political borders of a political system are congruent can all actors in a system of governance have the opportunity to actively take part in the decision-making process and input legitimacy is rendered. Moreover, congruence between political and social spaces is necessary for output legitimacy, in that it limits externalities from decisions that have been made outside one's territory (Zürn 2000: 189).

This (potential) lack of democratic legitimacy has direct implications for the *further development of European integration* (Hooghe and Marks 2009a). As Almond and Verba (1963) have argued, a supportive political culture is a necessary condition for the stability of the political system. Throughout history, low levels of political support have led to governmental crises and sometimes challenged the entire political system. In the case of the EU, low levels of political support have undoubtedly slowed down the integration process, as demonstrated by the negative referendum outcomes in France and the Netherlands that hindered the signing of the European constitutional treaty. The reason for the increasing salience of public opinion in European politics is not necessarily due to crumbling political support, but is also due to the fact that 'legitimate decision-making has shifted from an insulated elite to mass politics' (Hooghe and Marks 2009a: 13).

Meanwhile, whereas European integration was long perceived as an isolated process with no impact on *domestic politics*, it has become clear that it has the power to restructure national political conflict (Kriesi 2007). As shown in the growing literature on EU issue voting (Tillman 2004; De Vries 2007, 2010), people's attitudes towards European integration influence their voting decisions in national elections. As De Vries (2010: 89) summarizes, 'there is increasing evidence demonstrating the impact of EU issues on vote choice in national elections' (see also Gabel 2000; Tillman 2004). What is more, national politicians increasingly position themselves for or against European integration—British Prime Minister Cameron's EU referendum plan is an important recent example. Through this link, public support for European integration also becomes highly relevant to researchers primarily interested in national politics in Europe.

1.4 The Research Strategy

In order to empirically scrutinize the theoretical argument of this book, I use statistical analyses of two Eurobarometer survey waves: Eurobarometer 65.1 (European Commission 2006) and Eurobarometer 67.1 (European Commission 2007). Fieldwork for Eurobarometer 65.1 was conducted in the EU-25 in 2006, and for Eurobarometer 67.1 in the EU-27 in 2007 (see

Table 1.1. Survey data used in empirical analysis

	Eurobarometer wave 65.1	Eurobarometer wave 67.1
Year of fieldwork	2006	2007
Countries covered	EU-25	EU-27
Main independent variable	Individual transnationalism index	Individual transnationalism index
Dependent variable	EU membership support	European identification

Table 1.1).[4] On behalf of the European Commission, Eurobarometer has been monitoring public opinion on European integration for over four decades. Eurobarometer provides a unique wealth of first-hand information on issues such as EU membership support, European identification, and people's opinions on European policymaking (Bläser 2013). On the other hand, the surveys have been criticized for not abiding by survey design rules in terms of ordering and wording of the questions (Höpner and Jurczyk 2012).[5] While bearing this criticism in mind, this book draws on Eurobarometer 65.1 (2006) and Eurobarometer 67.1 (2007), as they are the only cross-national surveys that include both a wide range of questions regarding European cross-border interactions and networks and items referring to EU support. Moreover, given that Eurobarometer surveys are extensively used to analyse attitudes towards European integration (Kittilson 2007), comparison with other scholarly research is possible. The data allow the operationalization of individual transnationalism, that is, people's cross-border ties, interactions, and mobility as a multifaceted concept that entails the three dimensions of transnational background, transnational interactions, and transnational human capital. The two dependent variables of this book refer to two related but distinct aspects of citizens' orientations towards European integration: EU membership support and European identification. Each of the two Eurobarometer surveys used includes only one of the two dependent variables. Hence, analyses using Eurobarometer 65.1 model EU membership support, and analyses of Eurobarometer 67.1 predict European identification.

The survey data are combined with a variety of macro-level indicators. To capture the effect of macro-level transnationalization, I employ the KOF index of globalization, which provides a comprehensive measure of economic, political, and social transnationalization for 158 states (Dreher et al. 2008). As discussed in more detail in Chapter 2, several sophisticated measures of macro-level transnationalization exist (Lockwood and Redoano 2005;

---

[4] Eurobarometer 67.1 was also conducted in Croatia, but these observations have been omitted from the analyses in this book.

[5] Höpner and Jurczyk (2012) go as far as to question the political independence of Eurobarometer and suspect that it is used to draw an overly positive image on European integration.

Foreign Policy 2007; Raab et al. 2008), but the KOF index is the only one that covers both the geographical scope and the time points analysed in this book, and that goes beyond purely economic measures of transnationalization. Additionally, the analyses include a variety of structural indicators controlling for country-level (Eurostat 2006a–2006e, 2007a–2007e) and district-level differences (INSEE 2005, 2006, 2007; Statistical Offices of the Federation and the Länder 2006a–2006c).

Two major European events took place in the years preceding the surveys used in the empirical analysis. In 2004, the EU witnessed its biggest enlargement round both in terms of population and territory, opening up to ten new member states in the East. In several Western European countries, this historical landmark sparked widespread fear of massive immigration and (ab-)use of social rights. Moreover, in 2005, the French and Dutch populations rejected the European Constitution in referenda. These two events have to be kept in mind when evaluating the results of the empirical analyses.

1.5 Overview of the Book

The book is divided into eight chapters. Chapters 2 and 3 set the theoretical framework by conceptualizing transnationalism and by developing the link between individual transnationalism and EU support. Chapters 4 to 7 place this theory under empirical scrutiny. The concluding chapter collates the findings and implications of this book.

Chapter 2 summarizes how European integration has set the stage for increased cross-border transactions and then conceptualizes transnationalism, in particular distinguishing between macro-level transnationalism and individual-level transnationalism. Macro-level transnationalization, as captured by the KOF index of globalization (Dreher et al. 2008), is distinguished into economic, social, and political dimensions. It is shown that there are considerable differences among European member states with respect to their level of transnationalization. Individual-level transnationalism is conceptualized as a tri-dimensional phenomenon, consisting of the dimensions of transnational background, transnational practices, and transnational human capital. The remainder of Chapter 2 presents the operationalization of individual transnationalism in Eurobarometer survey waves 65.1 and 67.1.

Chapter 3 further develops the theoretical framework by linking individual transnationalism to public orientations towards European integration. It proposes two mechanisms that underlie the relationship between individual transnationalism and EU support and European identity: when people interact across borders, they might become aware of the material benefits of European integration. They might also change their self-concept and adapt a more inclusive collective identity and cosmopolitan mindset. Building on Deutsch's transactionalist theory, the chapter develops a set of hypotheses on the conditions under which individual transnationalism leads to attitude change. The core argument can be summarized as follows. First, due to the highly stratified distribution of transnational interactions across society, relatively few Europeans are actually triggered to adopt a European mindset by interacting across borders. Second, not all European interactions automatically foster EU support and European identity; their effectiveness depends on their purpose and scope. Third, increased transnational interactions can cause negative externalities with respect to the people who are not transnationally active themselves. The chapter concludes by outlining how this argument is translated into empirical research.

Chapter 4 tests a central hypothesis of this book: the more transnational an individual, the more likely he or she is to support European integration. It does so by analysing the link between individual transnationalism and EU membership support (EB 65.1, 2006) and the likelihood of identifying as European (EB 67.1, 2007). The chapter also provides analyses for each dimension of individual transnationalism (transnational background, practices, and human capital), and for each EU member state separately. Findings strongly support hypothesis 1 by showing that individual transnationalism has a very powerful and highly significant effect on EU support and European identity. What is more, each of the three dimensions of individual transnationalism significantly increases the likelihood of pro-European orientations.

The subsequent three chapters scrutinize Deutsch's transactionalist theory by providing empirical evidence for the three qualifications developed in Chapter 3. **Chapter 5** highlights the social stratification of individual transnationalism. The findings show that individual transnationalism is by no means a mainstream phenomenon. Only a minority of Europeans interact across borders on a regular basis, with the majority remaining (mainly) within the confines of their nation state. In all models, high education, high socioeconomic status, and younger age are strong predictors of transnational behaviour. Results suggest profound differences among citizens from different member states. Subsequent analyses test the effect of a country's degree of transnationalization, measured by the KOF index of globalization, as well as its economic prosperity and geographical and population size. People from wealthier countries are more transnational. To a lesser extent, economic globalization is positively related to individual transnationalism. Also, a country's size is inversely related to the transnationalism of its citizens.

Chapter 6 deals with the second qualification of Deutsch's transactionalist theory, namely that transnational interactions differ with respect to their effect on EU support. It does so by examining the purpose and scope of transnational interactions. Sociable interactions, such as socializing with other Europeans, are shown to play a greater role in predicting public orientations towards European integration than purely instrumental ones such as trade. Considering that the lion's share of intra-European transactions is instrumental by nature, this finding helps to explain why we find little EU support in spite of increasing levels of transactions. Moreover, it suggests that questions of collective identity rather than purely utilitarian considerations underlie the relationship between individual transnationalism and EU support. Subsequent analyses show that intra-European interactions are more effective in fostering EU support than interactions that go beyond European borders. This finding suggests that intra-European transactions trigger orientations that are genuinely European rather than more open or cosmopolitan in general. Assuming that people who live at intra-European borders primarily interact with the people across the border, Chapter 6 then zooms in on intra-European border regions and shows that transnational interactions among border residents have a smaller impact on EU support than among the rest of the population. In sum, the evidence suggests that to effectively trigger EU support, transactions ought to be genuinely European, that is, they take place within the EU, but also with more than one member state.

Chapter 7 focuses on the negative externalities of increased transactions on people who do not interact across borders themselves. Multilevel analyses show that in highly transnationalized countries, individual transnationalism has a greater impact on EU support than in less transnationalized countries. In other words, higher degrees of macro-level transnationalization exacerbate the relationship between individual transnationalism and orientations towards European integration. In highly globalized countries, people who rarely interact across borders are even more likely to be eurosceptical than in less globalized countries. This finding suggests that in highly globalized societies, the integration-demarcation divide found by Kriesi and colleagues (2008) is even more pronounced as people who do not interact across borders might feel overwhelmed and marginalized by the transnationalization of their environment.

The concluding chapter (**Chapter 8**) pulls together the findings of this book and tells a coherent story about the (incomplete) transnationalization of European societies. It then widens the perspective to discuss the prospect of European identity formation in the wake of the European sovereign debt crisis. From a more critical stance, it asks what kind of European identity is actually desirable, and it discusses potential risks that are inherent in European identity building. Implications for current research and policymaking and possible pathways for further studies are discussed.

2

Transnationalism

Over the past few decades, European societies have witnessed a rapid growth of cross-border interconnectedness, while national borders have become less salient. As trade taxes and tariffs have been reduced or even eliminated, cross-border exchanges of goods and services have proliferated in unprecedented ways (Dreher et al. 2008). Moreover, innovations in communication technology and transport have smoothed the progress of global interconnectedness (Harvey 1990). However, there is no consensus as to the scope of these transformations, and some authors even argue that there is nothing new to them (Bentley 1996). In the European context, European integration has been a major driver of this process. Regardless of the causal links between globalization and European integration, their impact on domestic societies today cannot be denied. Both globalization and European integration have transformed substantially the life chances and realms of the mass public and have led to a 'transnationalization of the masses' (De Swaan 1995).

Consequently, this chapter aims at capturing the transnationalization of European societies. The first section of this chapter discusses how European integration has set the stage for increased transactions in Europe. While the entire integration project can be seen as a major impetus for cross-border transactions, two aspects are of especially high relevance to citizens: first, the development of free movement of people and European citizenship rights, and second, European policies that promote everyday cross-border transactions.

The second and third section of this chapter develop a concept of transnationalism by distinguishing between the processes at the macro-level and at the individual level. Scholars differentiate between transnationalism *from above* and transnationalism *from below* (Guarnizo and Smith 1998). Transnationalism from above refers to the interactions at the macro-level, that is, between nation states, regions, international organizations, and corporations. Transnationalism from below, on the other hand, addresses the interactions occurring on the individual level, such as cross-border employment mobility

(Mau 2007: 53). Even though these two levels are closely intertwined, it would be a conceptual shortcut to interpret individual-level transnationalism as a mere instance of macro-level transnationalism, or the latter as nothing but the aggregation of the former. It therefore seems useful to conceptualize and measure transnationalism at each of these two levels separately. At the macro-level, I first review existing conceptual approaches before presenting the concept of macro-level transnationalism. Subsequently, I distinguish among the political, economic, and social dimensions of macro-level transnationalism, and discuss the KOF globalization index (Dreher et al. 2008), which is used to operationalize macro-level transnationalism. Finally, using data from the KOF index, some empirical findings on macro-level transnationalism in the EU member states are presented. Individual transnationalism, that is, individual cross-border ties, mobility, and interactions, is conceptualized as a tripartite phenomenon, entailing transnational background, practices, and human capital. This concept is operationalized in the form of the individual transnationalism index using Eurobarometer survey data.

2.1 Setting the Stage for Increased Transactions in the European Union

It is fair to say that setting the stage for cross-border mobility and transactions is at the heart of the European integration project. Both positive and negative integration steps (Scharpf 1999) have removed obstacles to transnational interaction in the EU. Consequently, European integration has multiplied the opportunities to interact across national borders. As Bartolini puts it (2005: xii), European integration can be seen as 'a process of territorial and functional boundary transcendence, redefinition, shift, and change that fundamentally alters the nature of the European states'. Consequently, Europeans have gained access to a wide array of economic, political, and social opportunities beyond the borders of their nation state. Referring to the theorizing of Hirschman (1970) and Rokkan (2000), Bartolini (2005) speaks of 'exit options' that European citizens have acquired in the wake of European integration. In contrast to earlier times, when people had to decide whether to completely exit the nation state by migrating to another country, or to remain within its confines, Europeans nowadays can opt for 'partial exits' by accessing certain resources in another member state while remaining within their own country (Bartolini 2005: 7). While giving a full account of all the initiatives taken to provide these exit opportunities is beyond the scope of this book, two steps deserve further examination: free movement and European citizenship rights, as well as EU policies promoting cross-border interactions. These are discussed in the following pages.

2.1.1 *Free Movement and European Citizenship*

Throughout the European integration process, Europeans have obtained a set of economic, political, and social rights that now form an integral part of European citizenship. Already the Treaty establishing the European Economic Community (European Union 1957) introduced the principle of the 'four freedoms': the free movement of goods, services, capital, and labour across the member states. This was intrinsically related to the objective of establishing a common market. In the early years of European integration, major steps were achieved by removing tariff and non-tariff barriers to the free movement of goods, as well as by abolishing restrictions on labour mobility. The 1985 White Paper envisaging the completion of the Single Market (European Commission 1985) spelled out a roadmap to achieve this goal by removing physical, technical, and fiscal barriers; subsequent treaty changes, most notably in the Single European Act (European Union 1986) and the Treaty on European Union (European Union 1992), were further important steps towards facilitating the four freedoms in the European Union. In addition to treaty changes, judicial activism by the European Court of Justice promoted free movement across the European Union (Stone Sweet 2004). Another important step in facilitating free movement is the Schengen system, which abolishes internal border controls. Originally signed between France, Germany, and the Benelux countries outside of the EU framework in 1985, it was incorporated in the Treaty of Amsterdam (European Union 1997). Today, twenty-six states are part of the Schengen system (Hix and Hoyland 2011). Finally, the introduction of the euro in seventeen member states has made travelling and trading among these countries even easier. Nonetheless, the Monti Report proposing a new strategy for the Single Market (Monti 2010) underlines that the EU is still far from being a truly integrated market.

What do the 'four freedoms' entail in a nutshell? To ensure *free movement of goods*, tariff and non-tariff barriers have been removed, and national regulations and standards have been dismantled. This is primarily achieved by harmonizing national standards and by the principle of mutual recognition, that is, the practice of recognizing other member states' regulations as equivalent (Schmidt 2007). With the aim of establishing an integrated financial market, *free movement of capital* enables people and companies to carry out financial operations, such as opening bank accounts, in other member states. *Free movement of services* entails the freedom of establishment, that is, the right to permanently 'set up shop' in another member state. It also means that companies and individuals have the right to provide services in other member states without having to be established there.

Of all the four freedoms, *free movement of people* is the most important for the purpose of this book.[1] Intended to facilitate the creation of the internal market (Aradau et al. 2010), it was initially limited to the active workforce (Eigmüller 2013) and subject to national immigration laws (Favell and Recchi 2009). However, throughout the European integration process, free movement across member states was gradually extended to an increasing share of the European population, and it eventually became a set of rights that European citizens can claim (Maas 2008). In fact, it now forms an integral part of European citizenship. As stipulated in Article 20 of the Treaty on the Functioning of the European Union (European Union 2008), European citizenship provides all nationals of European member states with 'the right to move and reside freely within the territory of the Member States'. It is important to note that this right is mentioned even before all other European citizenship rights, such as voting rights in the member state of residence, diplomatic protection of other member states, and the right to petition the European Parliament. This emphasizes the important role of the right of free movement in the European Union (Triandafyllidou and Maroufof 2013). In fact, Maas argues that 'free movement can be seen as the bedrock upon which the entire construction of European rights has been built' (Maas 2008: 583). Aradau and colleagues (2010) go as far as to claim that European citizenship is activated only through transnational mobility. In addition to having the right to move to and reside in another member state, Europeans are entitled to a set of economic rights across the European Union, such as the right to work, the right of access to work, and the right of equal treatment at the work place (Goudappel 2010: 57).[2]

In short, following the logic of market integration, European citizens have access to a wide array of economic exit options. In comparison, political and social exit options are less well developed. As is well known, the social dimension of European integration is relatively weak in comparison to its economic dimension. The Treaty of Rome (European Union 1957) left social policy largely in the hands of the member states (Majone 1993). Nonetheless, throughout the integration process, it became increasingly evident that labour market mobility across member states requires a minimum of social coordination. It was established that European citizens working in a different member state should be treated equally to the nationals of that country (Hantrais 2000: 201).

---

[1] For a more exhaustive account of the development of people mobility rights in the European Union, see Favell and Recchi 2009.

[2] It should be kept in mind that free movement was originally granted only to the active workforce and was intended as a means to ensure an integrated labour market. Still today, people living in a different member state for more than three months have to be either engaged in economic activity, actively seeking work, studying, have sufficient economic resources and sickness insurance, or be a family member of a person who falls into one of these categories.

Therefore, above all in cases where social policy touches upon labour law, European citizens have access to a number of social exit options such as the accumulation of social security rights acquired in different member states (Threlfall 2003). These innovations ensured 'that the new exit options opened by the Common Market were actually matched by corresponding entry opportunities' (Ferrera 2004: 104). Additionally, policies such as patient mobility show that the attainment of social rights in other member states is no longer limited to citizens who are active in the workforce. Nonetheless, it is clear that there are still important differences in the access to social benefits between nationals and mobile Europeans, and between European migrants who work and those who do not. For example, pension rights cannot always be accumulated in different member states (Favell and Recchi 2009: 8). Moreover, granting social benefits to all EU citizens is the subject of heated political and legal debate. For example, after a long political struggle in Germany over the question of whether intra-EU migrants qualify for German non-contributory unemployment benefits (Hartz IV), in 2013, the German Federal Social Court asked the European Court of Justice for a preliminary ruling on that issue (Die Zeit Online 2013).

Finally, European citizenship grants nationals of member states a number of political rights that they can invoke in other member states. First, European citizens are entitled to active and passive voting rights at municipal and European Parliamentary elections in their country of residence as long as they fulfil the same eligibility criteria as nationals of that country (Goudappel 2010: 92). Additionally, European citizens have the right to petition the European Parliament and to call upon the European Ombudsman. It is important to note, however, that voting rights do not apply to participation in national and regional elections, no matter how long one has been living in a different member state (European Commission 2013a: 32). Using Hirschman's (1970) terminology, one can thus say that exit options from one member state are complemented with limited voice options in another member state.

It is important to note that not all people living in the European Union enjoy full freedom of mobility. First, owing to the concerns of some old member states, authorities have sometimes implemented transition arrangements of a maximum of seven years for some new member states following accession rounds (Holland et al. 2011). This was the case for Spanish and Portuguese citizens when they joined the European Community in 1986, for citizens of eight member states that joined in 2004, as well as for Romanians, Bulgarians, and Croatians. While these limitations to free movement apply only for the duration of a couple of years, it is worth noting that third-country nationals living in the European Union do not enjoy European citizenship and the corresponding mobility rights, no matter how long they have been living in the EU (Maas 2008).[3] Third-country nationals make up a significant share of the European population. In 2012, over twenty million citizens of non-European countries were registered in the European Union, accounting for 4 per cent of the overall population (Eurostat 2012). The population of third-country nationals is thus larger that the population of some European member states, such as the Netherlands or Portugal. Thus, a significant amount of people permanently living in the EU is excluded from European free movement rights.

2.1.2 *Policies Encouraging Transnational Interactions*

In addition to free movement and European citizenship, a wide array of European policies actively promote everyday transnational interactions across the European Union. These initiatives represent, as Krotz (2007) puts it, the 'parapublic underpinnings' of European integration. While it is not the aim of this book to provide an exhaustive analysis of these policies, a number of them deserve further discussion.

Probably the most widely known instrument to trigger transnational inter-actions and mobility is the Lifelong Learning Programme of the European Commission. Next to the Erasmus exchange programme in higher education, which is seen as its 'flagship initiative' (Pépin 2007), the European Commission promotes educational exchange among schools (Comenius), during vocational training (Leonardo da Vinci), and in adult education (Grundvig).[4] The Erasmus exchange programme has had a remarkable career. When it was first initiated in 1987, 3,244 students went on an exchange abroad. These numbers increased each year, and in the academic year 1999/2000, more than 100,000 students benefited from an Erasmus grant. By 2011, over 2.3 million students had undertaken an exchange abroad (European Commission 2011). Policy makers have even more ambitious plans for the coming years. The member states have agreed that by 2020, at least 20 per cent of all higher education graduates in the EU should have spent an extended study or train-ing period abroad. To this end, remaining national and regional obstacles to student mobility shall be removed. In the framework of the new Erasmus+ programme, the Commission plans to send around two million students abroad between 2014 and 2020 (European Commission 2013b).

In the framework of the Europe for Citizens Programme, the European Commission supports town-twinning projects (Falkenhain et al. 2012).

---

[3] As an exception, third-country nationals who are married to an EU national enjoy some EU citizenship rights, see Goudappel 2010: 158.

[4] For the period 2014–2020, these programmes, as well as Youth In Action and five international programmes are embedded in the Erasmus+ programme.

Town twinning refers to initiatives of (transnational) lasting cooperation between cities. Since the end of World War II, a considerable number of twinning initiatives have emerged. Most of these initiatives are bottom-up, and their motivations and objectives are quite diverse (Clarke 2009; Krotz and Schild 2012). While the number of newly established twinning initiatives is currently falling slightly, there exists a dense net of cooperation across the European Union. Even though town twinning originated outside the European Union framework, the European Commission supports these partnerships as it sees them as falling in line with its broader aim of fostering European citizenship and identity (European Commission 2008; Falkenhain et al. 2012).

Finally, with its Youth in Action Programme, the European Commission 'promotes mobility within and beyond the EU's borders, non-formal learning and intercultural dialogue' (EACEA 2013) among young people. With youth exchanges, the European Voluntary Service, and other initiatives, young Europeans aged between 13 and 30 years old have the opportunity to visit another European country and to interact with fellow Europeans. Between 2007 and 2011, close to 725,000 people participated in the Youth in Action Programme (European Commission 2013c). While not all initiatives involve intra-European cross-border contacts, over 231,000 young Europeans embarked on a (transnational) youth exchange, and a total of 8,625 young Europeans took part in the European Voluntary Service abroad (European Commission 2013c).

While far from being exhaustive, the examples discussed in the above section show that not only mobility and citizenship rights, but also a number of policies implemented by the European Commission and its agencies actively promote transnational exchange and mobility among European citizens. Additionally, a considerable number of nongovernmental organizations, private non-profit foundations, and think tanks pursue similar goals. In addition to these genuinely EU-wide programmes, a wide array of binational initiatives exist that promote contact between two member states, for example between France and Germany (Krotz 2007). Consequently, Europeans have the opportunity to become transnationally active through various channels. Given these institutional developments, the following section develops the concept of transnationalism by distinguishing between macro-level and individual transnationalism.

2.2 Macro-level Transnationalism

Both the proliferation of cross-border interconnectedness and the weakening of national borders have sparked considerable attention in scholarly literature. Several theoretical concepts, such as globalization (Giddens 1990; Held et al.

1999), denationalization (Beisheim et al. 1999; Zürn 2005), internationalization (Chomsky 1994), and world society (Meyer et al. 1997; Meyer 2005) aim
at capturing these processes (for a review, see Mau 2007: 19–48).

The following section discusses the concepts of globalization and Europeanization and then presents macro-level transnationalism as the guiding concept
of this book. Macro-level transnationalism is operationalized using the KOF
index of globalization (Dreher 2006; Dreher et al. 2008). Finally, the chapter
discusses existing research and provides empirical evidence on the development and current state of macro-level transnationalism in the European Union.

2.2.1 Globalization, Europeanization, or Both?

Since the 1980s, the rapid intensification of cross-border interaction and
connectedness is usually referred to as globalization. Probably the most
often cited definition of globalization was proposed by Held and colleagues
(1999: 16), who define it as 'a process ... which embodies a transformation in
the spatial organization of social relations and transactions ... generating
transcontinental or interregional flows and networks of activity, interaction,
and the exercise of power'. While it is difficult to identify a clear starting point
for these processes, authors agree that they were driven by policies favouring
free markets, and facilitated by innovations in transport and communication
technologies. This has decreased national autonomy and mitigated the significance of territoriality (Smith 2001: 3). As a result, globalization is thought
to alter the way in which people interact and in which societies are organized
(Bauman 1989).

Some authors contend that increased cross-border connectedness is a
regional rather than a global phenomenon, and that it is concentrated on
the triangle between Europe, North America, and East Asia (Rosamond 2005;
Thompson 2005). Moreover, according to Thompson (2005: 53), globalization
research downplays 'the still central role that discrete national economies play
in organising and governing the international economic system'. Critics
further argue that the concept of globalization is not empirically applicable.
Also for this reason, authors suggest the use of a more concrete and better
measurable concept than the one of globalization (Rosamond 2005).

The concept of Europeanization fulfils this criterion. Europeanization refers
to domestic change that is caused by EU-level politics (Radaelli 2000). The
term Europeanization has been coined with respect to political and institutional transformations, the core question being how national legislation is
influenced by, and adapts to, the European legal and political system (Radaelli
2000; Börzel 2002; Falkner 2003). Only recently, researchers have applied the
concept of Europeanization to the *social change induced by European integration*.
From this perspective, Europeanization can be understood as 'a widening of

the scope of the national citizens' economic and political activities that directly or indirectly result from the economic and political institutions of the European Union' (Díez Medrano 2008: 5). In a similar vein, Mau and Verwiebe (2009: 270) refer to 'horizontal Europeanization' as 'contacts, interactions and social relations across different European countries as well as pan-European mobility'.

As was discussed in the preceding section, European integration has facilitated transnational contacts and mobility among the public by removing intra-European borders and by implementing policies that encourage cross-border transactions. The concept of Europeanization might therefore be proposed as the guiding concept of this study. However, the concept of Europeanization as social change induced by European integration might be too narrow a frame for the present study. In fact, when looking at societal change in Europe through the lens of Europeanization, one runs the risk of underestimating or even ignoring other factors causing this change, such as global market integration, or regional integration that is triggered by other institutions, such as the OECD (Beisheim et al. 1999). Hence, scholars engaged in research from this perspective may overstate the transformative power of European integration by ascribing the intra-European increase in economic and socio-cultural exchanges solely to European integration (Beck and Grande 2004: 289 ff.).

This brings us to the link between European and global trends of integration, which is vividly debated in the scholarly literature. On the one hand, authors view European integration mainly as a response to globalization that aims at cushioning its impact. In line with this reasoning, Wallace (1996: 17) argues that European integration 'can be seen as a distinct west European effort to contain the consequences of globalisation'. In fact, European policy makers tend to legitimize further European integration by pointing towards the challenges of globalization or American supremacy (Beck and Grande 2004: 45). Other authors contest this view. They argue that European integration intensifies globalization, and may even be one of its causes (Ross 1998; Fligstein and Mérand 2002). Finally, Schmidt (2003) sees European integration simply as a 'regional variant of globalization'.

Is it actually feasible to distinguish analytically and empirically between Europeanization and globalization? Castells' (2000a: 348) oft-cited observation that 'European integration is, at the same time a reaction to the process of globalisation, and its most advanced expression' suggests that it is impossible to conceive of one without the other. What is more, one might ask whether it is useful to distinguish the two phenomena, especially in the context of this research. What is of interest here are the consequences of globalization and European integration on people's everyday lives, and how people react to it in their attitudes and identities. These consequences remain the same, no matter their main source. One could even go as far as to say that, given the difficulties in distinguishing between the two phenomena, citizens' evaluations of European integration (the main dependent variable in this book) will automatically entail evaluations of globalization as well—if social scientists are unable to draw a clear line between them, how should citizens be able to do so?

The concept of macro-level transnationalism solves this problem by avoiding the direct establishment of an exclusive causal link to either genuinely global or purely European processes of transnationalization. Several other aspects make it very useful for this book. As signalled by its name, it does not entirely discard the importance and structuring capacity of the nation state. Rather, it focuses on processes that undermine national borders. The territorial dimension is therefore not expected to become completely insignificant. Finally, it accounts for the fact that some societal groups and regions still act exclusively or at least primarily on a local or national level (Mau and Mewes 2007). For this reason, this book uses the concept of macro-level transnationalism, and follows Vertovec's (1999: 447) definition as 'multiple ties and interactions linking people or institutions across the borders of nation states'.

2.2.2 Dimensions of Macro-level Transnationalism

When analysing macro-level transnationalism, authors agree to distil different dimensions of this phenomenon. Whereas most scholars distinguish between the economic, political, and social dimension of transnationalism (Hofmeister and Breitenstein 2008), Raab and colleagues (2008) break the social dimension further down into a socio-technological dimension and a cultural dimension.[5] This last distinction is not of further interest to this book, however. While these dimensions are interdependent, considerable variance exists between them with respect to the degree of transnationalism. The following section briefly discusses each dimension.

The *economic dimension* of macro-level transnationalism refers to the transnationalization of markets and is shaped by economic organizations and corporations, but also by economic policies and bilateral and international economic agreements. Frequently, the economy is seen as the centrepiece of transnationalization. In fact, the current economic crisis reveals how far international interaction and mutual interdependence have advanced in the financial sector. Nonetheless, economic transnationalism is still constrained

---

[5] Note that these authors actually speak of dimensions of globalization rather than transnationalism. However, for reasons that will be explained in Section 2.2.4, it seems reasonable to draw on their contribution also with respect to transnationalism.

by tariff and non-tariff trade barriers, especially in countries outside the triad of North America, East Asia, and Europe.

The *political dimension* of macro-level transnationalism relates above all to the transfer of national sovereignty to the supranational level, the embeddedness in the international community, and to the diffusion of government policies. According to Sklair (1991, 2001), it is strongly influenced by the so-called transnational capitalist class. This class is constituted of transnational corporations, globalizing professionals, bureaucrats, and politicians as well as the media (Sklair 2001: 17). It fuels further transnationalization by influencing the political decision-making process.

The *social dimension* of macro-level transnationalism comes closest to the aggregation of individual-level transnationalism by capturing social transnational interaction, that is, everyday cross-border communication and mobility of the population. However, some scholars also include the spread of (Western) values, culture, and standards in this dimension (Dreher et al. 2008; Raab et al. 2008). On the one hand, this refers to instances of 'McDonaldization' (Ritzer 2004), that is, the spread of Western popular culture such as the worldwide proliferation of shopping malls, fast food chains, and other commercial entities[6] (Ritzer 2004). On the other hand, it entails the expansion of democratic principles, human rights, and gender equality (Meyer et al. 1997).

2.2.3 Operationalization of Macro-level transnationalism

To operationalize macro-level transnationalism, it is sensible to draw on existing empirical measures of this phenomenon. In recent years, there have been several sophisticated attempts to quantify the degree to which each country is transnationalized, such as the A.T. Kearney/Foreign Policy Magazine globalization index (Foreign Policy 2007), the KOF index of globalization (Dreher et al. 2008), or GlobalIndex by Raab and colleagues (2008).

Early attempts to measure macro-level transnationalism focused on the economic dimension. For instance, 90 per cent of the World Market Research Centre G-Index (Randolph 2001) is based on economic indicators, while the remaining 10 per cent refers to technology. Another pioneering attempt to measure international interconnectedness is the A.T. Kearney/Foreign Policy globalization index (Foreign Policy 2007) that measures political engagement, technology, personal contact, and economic integration for sixty-two countries. Nonetheless, the lion's share of the weighting is assigned to economic integration and technology. Such primarily economic measures

---

[6] McDonaldization refers not only to transnationalization. Ritzer notes that the rules and logic of fast food chains are increasingly applied to other sectors (such as higher education), both in the USA and beyond.

are of limited use for the present study which aims to grasp the social and political aspects of macro-level transnationalism as well. In light of this, the index developed by the Centre for the Study of Globalization and Regionalization (CSGR) (Lockwood and Redoano 2005) is more useful because it also accounts for the social and political dimension of transnationalization. Likewise, GlobalIndex (Raab et al. 2008) has the explicit aim of providing a sociological index of globalization. While the operationalization of the political dimension roughly coincides with the one developed by Lockwood and Redoano (2005), the cultural dimension is complemented by data on human rights, gender equality, and increasing urbanization and sectoral change. Whereas both of these indices (Lockwood and Redoano 2005; Raab et al. 2008) could be valid operationalizations of macro-level transnationalization for the purpose of this book, they cannot be used for this study due to data constraints. On the one hand, Raab and colleagues (2008) do not cover the new member states, which are also of interest here. On the other hand, the CSGR index (Lockwood and Redoano 2005) only covers data up to the year 2004. In contrast, the individual data that will be used for the empirical analysis were collected in 2006 and 2007. Taking into consideration that transnational interaction and contacts have increased remarkably in the course of the last decade, data from 2004 might not provide the most accurate picture. This is even more the case for the new member states that joined in 2004 and 2007.

In short, most indices of macro-level transnationalism are of limited use for this book because they either do not sufficiently capture the cultural and political aspects of transnationalization or because they are not available for the time points and countries that will be analysed. In contrast, the KOF index of globalization has neither of these disadvantages and is therefore used to operationalize macro-level transnationalism.

2.2.4 KOF Index of Globalization

Before discussing the KOF index in further detail, a justification is warranted: having discussed the conceptual advantages of speaking of macro-level transnationalism rather than of globalization or Europeanization, it might come as a surprise that this concept is operationalized with an index of globalization. This reflects the fact that the concept of globalization is considerably more common than transnationalism. Moreover, when considering the criticism against research in the globalization paradigm (globalization being a vague term, ignoring global inequalities in interconnectedness, and being difficult to use empirically), it becomes clear that an index that aims to quantify the level of transnationalism for each country separately solves these problems. It therefore seems sensible to use this index.

Table 2.1. Dimensions and indicators of macro-level transnationalism

Dimensions		Indicators
Economic	Actual flows	Trade (% of GDP) FDI, flows (% of GDP) FDI, stocks, (% of GDP) Portfolio investment (% of GDP) Income payments to foreign nationals
	Restrictions	Hidden import barriers Mean tariff rate Taxes on international trade (% of current revenue)
Social	Personal contact	Telephone traffic Transfers (% of GDP) International tourism Foreign population (% of total population) International letters (per capita)
	Information flows	Internet users (per 1,000 people) Television (per 1,000 people) Trade in newspapers (% of GDP)
	Cultural proximity	Number of McDonald's restaurants (per capita) Number of Ikea (per capita) Trade in books (% of GDP)
Political		Absolute number of embassies in country Absolute number of membership in international organizations Personnel to UN Security Council missions (per capita) Absolute number of international treaties signed

Source: Dreher (2006), updated in Dreher et al. (2008).

Table 2.1 shows the dimensions and indicators used in the KOF index of globalization (Dreher 2006; Dreher et al. 2008).[7] Following the aforementioned distinction between economic, political, and social transnationalism, Dreher and colleagues operationalize the *economic dimension* by two sub-indices. The first one refers to *actual flows* and comprises information on trade, foreign direct investment, and portfolio investment. Data on income payments to foreign people and capital are included as well. The other sub-index accounts for *restrictions* on trade and capital by including hidden import barriers, the mean tariff rate as well as the percentage of taxes on international trade (Dreher et al. 2008: 43).

The *social dimension* consists of three categories. The first one, *personal contact*, is 'intended to capture the direct interactions among people living in different countries' (Dreher et al. 2008: 44) by including international telecommunication traffic, international mail traffic, the degree of international tourism as well as the percentage of foreigners living in the country. Furthermore, the index accounts for remittances and government transfers

[7] For further information on the exact weights of each indicator (determined using structural equations modelling), see Dreher et al. 2008.

from the country. The category *information flows* aims at capturing the potential flow of ideas and images by measuring internet users, the percentage of households disposing of television and the trade in international newspapers. The third category, *cultural proximity*, comes close to 'McDonaldization' (Ritzer 2004) by including international trade in books, the number of McDonalds restaurants and of IKEA chain stores per capita.

The *political dimension* includes the number of embassies in a country, the number of international organizations the country is member of, and the number of UN Security Council peace missions in which the country was engaged. Finally, it accounts for the number of bi- or multilateral treaties that the country has signed since 1945 (Dreher et al. 2008).

2.2.5 Macro-level Transnationalism in the European Union

Figure 2.1 depicts data on the three dimensions of the KOF index for the EU-15 from 1970 (for the twelve new member states from 1993 onwards due to data availability) until 2007, when the empirical study presented in this book was conducted. The figure reveals a sharp upward trend in macro-level transnationalism in the EU as measured by the KOF index of globalization. In the EU-15, the greatest increase has taken place in the social sphere, rising from forty-eight index points in 1970 to eighty-four index points in 2007. Political transnationalization in the old member states increased slowly at first, and then dropped over the 1980s until it reached its lowest point in 1989. Between 1990 and 1993, it gained momentum again. This development certainly mirrors the

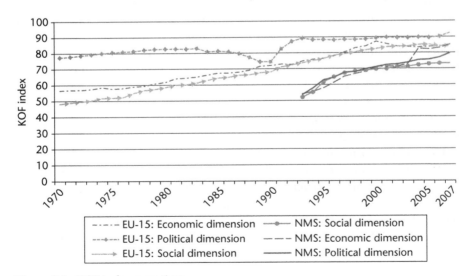

Figure 2.1. KOF index over time
Source: Dreher (2006), updated in Dreher et al. (2008)

end of the Cold War and the advent of the Maastricht Treaty in 1992. From the mid-1990s, political transnationalization in Western Europe has stagnated. Not surprisingly, transnationalization has proliferated in the new member states since 1993. Most notably, economic transnationalization has skyrocketed since the beginning of the new millennium. This is clearly caused by their EU membership accession in 2004.

Figure 2.2 shows the KOF index of globalization for the twenty-seven member states in 2007. The most transnationalized member states are Belgium (scoring 92.59), Austria (92.51), and the Netherlands (91.9). They are at the same time also among the most globalized countries worldwide. At the other end of the spectrum is Romania (KOF index of 71.51), which had joined the EU just that year, as well as Latvia (71.61) and Malta (74.42), which joined in 2004. Of all EU-15 countries, the least globalized country is Greece (KOF index of 75.83).

Figure 2.3 shows the KOF indices for economic, political, and social transnationalization for the twenty-seven member states in 2007. The countries vary especially with respect to the political dimension. This variation is likely to reflect the fact that smaller countries might have a smaller number of embassies, and that member states take part in international organizations and institutions, such as NATO, to varying degrees. Moreover, there is also considerable variance across the three dimensions within certain countries.

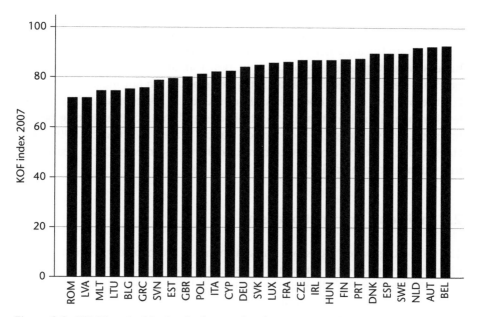

Figure 2.2. EU-27 ranked by level of macro-level transnationalism in 2007
Source: Dreher (2006), updated in Dreher et al. (2008)

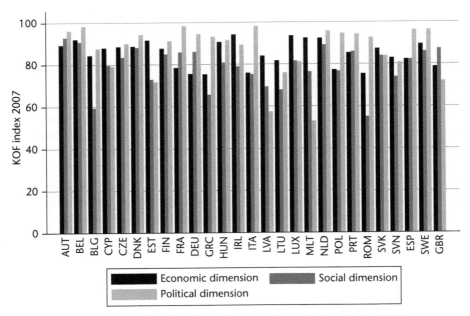

Figure 2.3. Economic, political, and social transnationalization in the EU-27
Source: Dreher (2006), updated in Dreher et al. (2008)

For instance, Luxembourg scores very high with respect to the economic and political dimension, but much less so in terms of social transnationalism.

To sum up the argument so far, in the past few decades, European societies have witnessed processes of economic, political, and social transnationalization that stem from global market integration and from European integration. For the purpose of this book, this phenomenon is conceptualized as macro-level transnationalism, that is, 'multiple ties and interactions linking people or institutions across the borders of nation states' (Vertovec 1999: 447). Having discussed macro-level transnationalism, the next section deals with individual transnationalism.

2.3 Individual Transnationalism

The following pages focus on transnationalism from below, which is here identified as individual transnationalism. It would be too simplistic to conceptualize transnationalism at the individual level as simply the disaggregation of macro-level transnationalism. Individuals differ considerably in the extent to which they are transnationally active. Predominantly, transnationalism is conceptualized as a 'twin-concept' to diaspora, that is, a dispersed ethnic community that maintains its boundaries towards other ethnic groups and remains oriented towards its homeland (Brubaker 2005). Studies following this approach have, for example, analysed migrant workers' remittances to their kin in the country of origin and their impact on economy and society (Glick Schiller and Fouron 2001; Horst 2004). In the context of European integration, ample attention has been given to intra-European migrants (Favell 2008; Recchi and Favell 2009; Roeder 2011) or exchange students (Carlson 2013). In short, these studies focus on highly transnational groups. By contrast, the approach taken here is to analyse transnationalism among the entire population.

Individual transnationalism can be understood as individual ties, interactions, and mobility across borders of nation states. It includes all sorts of interactions that extend beyond national borders, such as personal relations to foreigners and people living abroad, the use of international media, and so forth. Hence, this concept of transnationalism is also applicable to individuals that remain in their country of origin but are confronted with a transnationalization of their realm by, for example, interacting with foreigners or using foreign media.

2.3.1 *Dimensions of Individual Transnationalism*

I conceptualize individual transnationalism as a tri-dimensional phenomenon, entailing (1) transnational background, (2) transnational practices, and (3) transnational human capital. These three dimensions are displayed in Figure 2.4. Before discussing each dimension in further detail, it is worth noting that this approach differs from Mau and colleagues (2008), who conceptualize individual transnationalism as long-term stays and short-term visits abroad as well as personal cross-border relations. Thus, their conceptualization of individual transnationalism does not account for an individual's personal background, such as having dual citizenship. Neither do they take into account consumption of international media or foreign language use. However, in my view, these aspects are crucial to understanding whether or not someone is transnational.

In the first place, *transnational background* refers to traits of the personal background, such as dual citizenship or the fact of being born outside the country of residence. This dimension therefore relates to the growing and increasingly heterogeneous group of (intra-European) migrants (Favell 2008; Recchi 2008b).

The dimension of *transnational practices* comes closest to Deutsch's concept of transactions by referring to active engagement in contact with non-national actors. This dimension consists of long-term stays and short-term

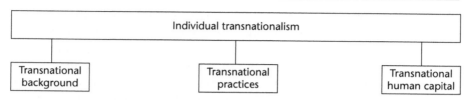

Figure 2.4. Dimensions of individual transnationalism

visits abroad as well as transnational interactions. In line with Roose (2010: 55), I distinguish between instrumental and sociable interactions. Instrumental interactions are motivated by the prospect of (material) benefits gained by interaction and mainly refer to transnational economic activities such as foreign direct investment or trade. Sociable interactions have an aim in themselves, such as socializing and friendships. This dimension is relatively close to the concept of transnational social capital (Rippl et al. 2010) in the form of cross-border personal contacts, participation in transnational activities, and transnational trust.

Finally, *transnational human capital* refers to types of human capital that are supposed to facilitate transnational interactions and mobility (Koehn and Rosenau 2002). Without doubt, foreign-language skills are a crucial resource if one is to be transnationally active, especially in the multilingual European context (Fürstenau 2004; Gerhards 2012). According to Gerhards (2012), two aspects add to an individual's transnational human capital: first, the number of foreign languages spoken, and second, whether these foreign languages are actually understood and spoken by a large share of the global population.

It should be noted that individual transnationalism is linked to cognitive openness towards transnationalism, that is, the awareness of non-national actors or the interest in transnational actors and phenomena. This dimension is close to Vertovec's (1999) notion of transnationalism as a type of consciousness of multi-locality.[8] However, it seems sensible not to include this dimension in the conceptualization of transnationalism as there should be a clear distinction between transnational background and behaviour on the one hand and attitudes on the other hand. After all, the aim of this book is to test the impact of transnationalism on attitudes toward European integration, which are likely to entail a cognitive openness towards transnationalism. Thus, accounting for cognitive aspects in the concept of transnationalism would run the risk of endogeneity.

---

[8] Vertovec (1999) identified six different forms of transnationalism: a social morphology, a type of consciousness, a mode of cultural reproduction, an avenue of capital, a site of political engagement, and the reconstruction of place and locality.

2.3.2 Operationalization of Individual Transnationalism

To recapitulate from the above section, individual transnationalism is defined as individual ties, mobility, and interactions across national borders. It is conceptualized as a three-dimensional phenomenon, comprising transnational background, transnational practices, and transnational human capital.

The remainder of this section discusses how this concept is operationalized for the purpose of empirical research. The analyses presented in this book rely on two Eurobarometer survey waves—Eurobarometer 65.1 (European Commission 2006) and Eurobarometer 67.1 (European Commission 2007). Fieldwork for Eurobarometer 65.1 was conducted in the EU-25 in 2006, and Eurobarometer 67.1 was fielded in the EU-27 in 2007.[9] They are the only cross-national surveys that include both a wide range of questions regarding European cross-border interactions and networks and items referring to EU support. They are hence used to analyse the extent to which Europeans interact across borders, and how this may be linked to their orientations towards European integration. Each survey wave includes only one of the two dependent variables. Hence, data of Eurobarometer 65.1 (2006) are used to model EU membership support, whereas data of Eurobarometer 67.1 (2007) predict European identification.

Table 2.2 gives an overview of the indicators used to operationalize individual transnationalism in this book. It should be noted that the operationalization of individual transnationalism in Eurobarometer survey 65.1 slightly differs from the one developed in Eurobarometer survey 67.1. The questions referring to transnational networks and mobility asked in these surveys overlap, but are slightly different. Thus, it is not possible to use one and the same operationalization of each dimension of individual transnationalism throughout this book. However, the indicators seem to be sufficiently similar to allow for comparisons. Moreover, as is shown in Chapter 5, the variables that have the strongest effect on either operationalization of individual transnationalism are very similar, which suggests that they measure the same latent concept.

The first dimension shown in Table 2.2, *transnational background*, is operationalized by the fact of being born abroad and by having at least one foreign-born parent. This operationalization is consistent across all analyses in this book.

The dimension of *transnational practices* refers to long-term stays and short-term visits abroad as well as sociable and instrumental forms of interactions and virtual contacts. In Eurobarometer 65.1, long-term stays abroad are

---

[9] Eurobarometer 67.1 was also conducted in Croatia, but these observations have been omitted from the analyses in this book.

Table 2.2. Operationalization of individual transnationalism

Dimension		Indicators	Item in EB65.1	Item in EB67.1
Transnational background		Nationality other than the country of interview	Q1	Q1
		Parent(s) born outside the country of interview	D42	D42
Transnational practices	Long-term stays abroad	Lived in another EU country to work, study, or retire for 3 months or more	QD14	
		Moved to another European/non-European country in past 10 years		QD1
	Short-term visits abroad	Visited another EU country in past 12 months	QA5.1	
		Travelled abroad at least 3 times in past 3 years, for work or for leisure		QA10
	Sociable interactions	Socialized with people from another EU country in past 12 months	QA5.3	
		Having friends who are from other European countries		QA10
		Having friends who are from other non-European countries		QA10
	Instrumental interactions	Shopping trip to another EU country in past 12 months	QB2	
		Having a job that involves contact with organizations or people in other countries		QA10
	Virtual communication	Communicating with people in other countries via the Internet or email		QA10
Transnational human capital	Foreign-language skills	Preparedness to buy a product in another EU language	QB21	
	Foreign-language use	Read newspaper, book, or magazine in foreign language in past 12 months	QA5.2	
		Often watching TV programmes or movies in foreign languages		QA10
		Sometimes reading newspapers in foreign languages		QA10
		Enjoying reading foreign books in their original language		QA10

Source: Eurobarometer 65.1 (2006), Eurobarometer 67.1 (2007).

captured by the fact of having lived in another EU country to study, work, or spend retirement there for at least three months. In Eurobarometer 67.1, respondents are asked whether they have moved to or from another EU or non-EU country in the past ten years. An item asking whether respondents have visited another EU member state in the past twelve months in Eurobarometer 65.1 measures short-term stays in the models predicting EU support. Eurobarometer 67.1 captures this aspect by the fact of having travelled abroad at least three times in the past three years, either for work or for leisure.

Sociable interactions include all forms of interactions that are intrinsically motivated (i.e. not due to expected gains). In the analyses using Eurobarometer 65.1, sociable interactions are captured by having socialized with people from another EU country in the past twelve months, whereas in Eurobarometer 67.1, they are operationalized by having friends from other European and non-European countries. This operationalization is more restrictive with respect to the quality of interactions, but more inclusive with respect to the scope of interaction partners covered.

In contrast to sociable interactions, instrumental interactions are motivated by the expected returns of interacting (Roose 2010). Eurobarometer 65.1 includes a special topic referring to the internal market and therefore asks respondents about their cross-border shopping habits. According to Roose (2010), purchases are among the purest forms of instrumental interactions. Consequently, in the analyses of Eurobarometer 65.1, instrumental interactions are measured by having gone on a shopping trip to another EU country in the past twelve months. In turn, Eurobarometer 67.1 asks respondents whether their job involves contact with organizations and people from other countries. This item operationalizes instrumental transactions in the models predicting European identity. In the analyses using Eurobarometer 67.1, an item referring to virtual communication is also included in the transnationalism index. This item asks respondents whether they often communicate with people from other countries via the internet or email.[10]

When turning to *transnational human capital*, it is best captured in terms of foreign-language skills (Fürstenau 2004; Gerhards 2012). Eurobarometer 65.1 asks whether respondents are able to purchase goods and services in another EU language. This is a straightforward operationalization of foreign-language skills as human capital that enables people to interact across borders. Thus, it is used to represent transnational human capital in the models that predict EU support. Foreign-language proficiency can also be measured indirectly in terms of actual use of foreign languages such as the consumption of foreign-language media. While not everyone who is capable of speaking a foreign language will necessarily do so, the use of foreign languages requires a certain degree of proficiency. Therefore, the fact of having read a foreign-language newspaper, book, or magazine in the past twelve months serves as an additional indicator of transnational human capital in the models predicting EU support.

Three items referring to foreign-language media use in Eurobarometer 67.1 capture this dimension of transnationalism in the models analysing European identity: the habit of watching TV programmes or movies in foreign languages, reading—at least sometimes—newspapers in a foreign language, and

---

[10] The categorizations of sociable vs. instrumental interactions and short-term vs. long-term interactions are not mutually exclusive. Instrumental and social interactions can take place both over a long and short time span. However, the wording of the questions does not give detailed enough information to make such distinctions.

Table 2.3. Distributions of items used in transnationalism index, Eurobarometer 65.1

Variable	Per cent
Foreign nationality	1.82
At least one parent born abroad	10.51
Lived in another member state to work, study, retire for 3 months or longer	7.47
Visited another EU country	
Never	59.04
Once or twice	24.56
On several occasions	16.40
Socialized with people from another EU country in past 12 months	
Never	56.06
Once or twice	18.14
On several occasions	25.80
Trip to another EU country primarily for shopping in past 12 months	
No	86.50
Once or twice	7.82
Several times	5.68
Read a book, newspaper, or article in another language than mother tongue in past 12 months	
Never	70.89
Once or twice	11.07
Several occasions	18.04
Prepared to purchase goods and services in another EU language	
Totally disagree	41.94
Tend to disagree	20.71
Tend to agree	22.79
Totally agree	14.57

Source: Eurobarometer 65.1 (2006).

enjoying reading books in a foreign language. To be sure, the last item in particular is not an ideal operationalization of foreign-language skills, as it entails evaluative aspects and refers to 'high culture'—not everyone who has learned foreign languages necessarily appreciates reading books in their original language. However, lacking any data that directly refer to foreign-language skills in Eurobarometer 67.1, these items serve as a measure of transnational human capital to predict European identity.

Table 2.3 and Table 2.4 show the percentages of each answer category for the variables used in the transnationalism indices. As can be seen in the tables, the distributions are highly skewed. In all questions asked, less than half of the respondents reported participating in any form of transnational practice or having some indicator of transnational background or human capital. In some cases, such as with respect to having lived abroad (Table 2.3), or having a job that involves international contact (Table 2.4), this number is even lower than 10 per cent. These distributions suggest that transnationalism is a niche phenomenon in Europe—an idea that will be explored in further detail in Chapter 5.

Table 2.4. Distributions of items used in transnationalism index, Eurobarometer 67.1

Variable	Per cent
Foreign nationality	2.01
At least one parent born abroad	10.33
Moved from/to another EU country in past 10 years	7.95
Which, if any, of the following statements apply to you?	
Travelled abroad at least 3 times in past 3 years, for business or for leisure	28.65
Friends from other European countries	28.31
Friends from non-European countries	16.35
Job involves contact with organizations or people in other countries	9.31
Communicating with people in other countries via the internet or email	14.47
Often watch TV programmes or movies in foreign languages	28.85
Sometimes read newspapers in foreign language	12.35
Enjoy reading foreign books in their original language	9.36

Source: Eurobarometer 67.1 (2007).

In the analyses, the above items are combined onto a single scale, the individual transnationalism index. In Eurobarometer 65.1, some of the items used are binary, whereas others are Likert scales. Therefore, a factor analysis based on a modified correlation matrix was applied, combining Pearson's correlation for the Likert items with polychoric correlation for the binary variables.[11] With a mean of .23 on a scale running form 0 to 1, this scale is highly skewed towards low levels of individual transnationalism. The transnationalism index in Eurobarometer 67.1 (2007) has a mean of .15 on a scale from 0 to 1, which again indicates that the majority of people are not particularly transnational.[12] Chapter 5 further analyses the distribution of individual transnationalism across society.

2.4 Conclusion

Political integration, economic cooperation, and social interactions on a regional and global scale have led to the 'transnationalization of the masses' (De Swaan 1995) and have substantially transformed people's everyday lives in Europe. This transformation has triggered considerable interest from scholars who study it both 'from above' and 'from below'. This book pursues a double perspective by conceptualizing transnationalism at the individual level and at the macro level. Individual transnationalism relates to individual ties, interactions, and mobility across national borders. This includes the

---

[11] I thank Dave Armstrong, currently at the University of Wisconsin-Milwaukee, for very helpful advice and for providing me with the code.
[12] Reliability analyses and inter-item analyses show that both scores are reliable and internally consistent.

dimensions transnational background, transnational practices, and transnational human capital. Macro-level transnationalism, on the other hand, captures the extent to which a country is embedded in cross-border transactions and networks in the political, economic, and social spheres.

It is important to reiterate that while individual and macro-level transnationalism are closely connected, they do not necessary run parallel to each other. Nor is transnationalization a linear, unidirectional process. Both at the individual and at the macro-level, considerable differences exist regarding the degree to which people and countries are embedded in transnational networks. What is more, discrepancies between the individual and macro-level can generate considerable tensions. The following chapter theorizes on the link between individual transnationalism and EU support.

3

Linking Transnationalism to Citizen Orientations towards European Integration

The enterprise of regional integration studies would be improved enormously if we knew when, how, and why actors 'learn' to behave differently than they did in the past.[1]

—Ernst Haas

This chapter further develops the theoretical framework of the book by establishing a link between individual transnationalism on the one hand and European identity and support for European integration on the other. To this aim, the following pages first discuss the dependent variables of the book, that is, European identity and EU support. The chapter then reviews Deutsch's transactionalist theory (Deutsch 1953a; Deutsch et al. 1957; Deutsch et al. 1967), as well as its reception and further development in current research. Deutsch and colleagues suggested establishing 'security communities' by integrating elites and institutions. This would set the framework for increased transnational interactions among ordinary citizens which in turn would lead to mutual trust, a collective identity, and support for the newly created security community. These propositions inspired a plethora of EU policies that aim at bringing Europeans closer together, such as town-twinning projects or educational exchanges (Falkenhain et al. 2012).

While highly relevant, transactionalist theory has left some crucial questions unanswered: we know very little about why and how transactions should affect public orientations towards European integration. It is very pertinent to ask which mechanisms underlie the relationship between increased transactions and changing orientations towards European

[1] Haas 1970: 643.

integration. This chapter proposes two main potential mechanisms that link transnationalism to attitudes and identity, namely changes in group boundaries and utilitarian cost–benefit calculations. Highly transnational Europeans are expected to support European integration because they have adopted a more inclusive concept of group identity, and because further institutional integration is in their interest. Another important question relates to the conditions that have to be met for transactions to effectively promote EU support and European identity. This chapter develops a set of hypotheses on the conditions under which transactions are expected to lead to attitude and identity change.

The core argument of this chapter can be summarized as follows. First, while there is a clear relationship between individual transnationalism and orientations towards European integration at the individual level, transnational interactions are highly stratified across society. Consequently, few Europeans are actually triggered to adopt a European mindset by interacting across borders. Second, not all transnational interactions are necessarily successful in promoting EU support and European identity. Their effectiveness depends on their purpose and scope. Third, increased transnational interactions can generate negative externalities with respect to the people who do not become transnationally active themselves. These arguments advance scholarly knowledge on the effectiveness of transnational contacts in promoting a European mindset and help explain the discrepancy between increased cross-border transactions and low public support for European integration and European identity at the aggregate level.

3.1 Public Orientations towards European Integration

Before these questions can be dealt with in more detail, it is important to clarify what the dependent variable of this study is. In his theory, Deutsch spoke of a 'we-feeling', of mutual trust, and of support for the security community (Deutsch 1954 [1970]: 36). In other words, by interacting across borders, Europeans are expected to change their orientation towards European integration. This book focuses on two crucial aspects of this phenomenon. First, it emphasizes people's collective European identity, and second, it studies the extent to which Europeans support the European integration process. These two aspects are closely intertwined, but entail different phenomena (Cram 2012: 73).

Collective identity as a social science concept is as contested as it is acclaimed, and some authors argue that it should not be used at all (Brubaker and Cooper 2000; Abdelal et al. 2009). The concept of European identity has been dealt with at length elsewhere (Kohli 2000; Checkel and

Katzenstein 2009; Kaina and Karolewski 2013), and this book does not endeavour to add a new conceptualization to this discussion. Authors agree that collective identity entails at least three distinct dimensions: cognitive, evaluative, and affective (Citrin et al. 2001). The cognitive dimension relates to whether people see themselves as part of a community or not. In the European context, the relevant question is whether people categorize themselves (i.e. identify) as European. The evaluative dimension relates to the criteria that underlie this categorization. With respect to political communities, these criteria are most commonly based either on a civic understanding of community, or on an ethnic-cultural understanding (Shulman 2002; Bruter 2004). The third dimension refers to the affective attachment to a community, in other words, whether one identifies not only *as* part of, but also *with* the collective (Cram 2012: 72). In view of multiple collective identities (Díez Medrano and Gutiérrez 2001) that sometimes compete with each other, Bellucci and colleagues (2012) include salience as an additional dimension—to what extent does one collective identity trump the other?

Consequently, European identity can take quite different forms: people might see themselves as European, but not feel any attachment to Europe; they might perceive the European collective as a community based on civic principles or as tied together by cultural or ethnic proximity, or a common heritage. Finally, their feeling of European identity might not have any behavioural consequences because other collective identities might be more prevalent. Thus, studying one of the three dimensions alone does not tell us much about the other two. Nonetheless, the cognitive dimension seems to be the most fundamental one on which the two others are based. If individuals do not identify themselves as European, they do not include it in their self-concept, and consequently, the second and third dimension refer to a collective of which they do not feel a part. Therefore, the analyses presented in this book focus on the cognitive dimension of European identity.

On the other hand, support for European integration entails citizens' evaluation of the integration process. Easton (1975: 436) defines support as 'an attitude by which a person orients himself to an object either favorably or unfavorably, positively or negatively'. In this sense, support can be understood as a range of attitudes emanating from positive as well as negative evaluations. The author identifies three hierarchical object levels of support: political authorities, the regime, and the political community. Additionally, Easton (1975: 436 ff.) opposes specific to diffuse support. Diffuse support relates to general orientations that remain very stable and robust over time. It is rather close to the concept of identity discussed above. Specific support results from rational evaluations of authorities' performance and output and is subject to short-term fluctuations.

Hence, this book focuses on two forms of public orientation towards European integration. On the one hand, it studies (the cognitive dimension of) European identity by looking at people's identification as European. On the other, it looks at public support for European integration by focusing on the question of whether people think that EU membership is a 'good thing' or not. These orientations are connected to each other, but they differ in some fundamental ways. EU membership support is an output-oriented evaluation of the costs and benefits of membership that may fluctuate with the performance of European institutions, whereas European identification relates to whether people include the European collective into their self-concept.

To be sure, this is a relatively thin understanding of two highly complex phenomena that have received much attention in scholarly literature. However, this choice is warranted for two reasons. First, identification as European and EU membership support are the most commonly accepted and most widely used ways to study public orientations towards European integration (see, among many others, Gabel 1998b; Citrin and Sides 2004; Eichenberg and Dalton 2007; Risse 2010). Comparison with existing studies is therefore warranted. Second, in contrast to the plethora of contributions that endeavour to understand what European identity and EU support entail (Niedermayer and Westle 1995; Fuchs et al. 2009c; Favell et al. 2011), this book seeks to contribute to current research by focusing on how transnational interactions can change these orientations. The focus is therefore much more on the independent variable—transnationalism—which so far has received little systematic attention in scholarly research. While a wide array of empirical data on EU support and European identity exists, the extent to which individuals interact across borders is relatively uncharted territory. I am bound by the few existing data that capture individual transnationalism in cross-national opinion surveys and therefore have to make do with the few measures of orientations towards European integration that are included in these surveys.

3.2 Deutsch's Transactionalist Theory

Transactionalist theory, or communications theory, was one of the dominant pre-theories of European integration (Haas 1970). It was coined by the scholars surrounding Karl W. Deutsch (Deutsch 1954 [1970]; Deutsch et al. 1957; Deutsch et al. 1967), who, in the aftermath of World War II examined how to avoid future international conflicts by successfully integrating nations with each other. A German-speaking native of Prague who emigrated to the United States at the dawn of World War II, Deutsch was interested in this question not only from a purely social scientific perspective, but also as a policy maker and political advisor to the United States. He also participated in the International Secretariat of the founding conference of the United Nations in San Francisco (Markowits 2012).

Deutsch based his argument on his extensive research on nation building (Deutsch 1953a; Deutsch and Foltz 1963). He found that existing national communities were held together by a high degree of cohesion, mutual trust, and a feeling of collective identity generated by social, political, and economic transactions on the elite and mass levels (Deutsch 1953a). A nation, in Deutsch's (1953a: 70) view, is a 'community of social communication' whose members are more inclined to interact with one another than with people outside this community.

What would tie people together *within* nations, Deutsch reasoned, should also tie them together *across* nations. Therefore, Deutsch and colleagues (1957) aimed at applying the same mechanisms of communication and interaction to the international level. Consequently, the authors proposed to establish 'security communities' where war between states is no longer possible due to strong bonds of common identification and trust. The latter are generated by increased transactions, that is, 'various types of exchanges, including symbolic, economic, material, political, technological, and so on' (Adler and Barnett 1998b: 41).

In a security community, according to Deutsch and associates, 'there is real assurance that the members of that community will not fight each other physically, but will settle their disputes in some other way. If the entire world were integrated as a security community, wars would be automatically eliminated' (Deutsch et al. 1957: 5). Deutsch and colleagues distinguish between *amalgamated* security communities, which largely follow the model of nation states, and *pluralistic* ones, which, similarly to the EU, retain independent units of government (Deutsch et al. 1957: 6). The latter are considerably more likely to succeed than the former because the level of political integration ought to be followed by an equal level of societal integration, which is hard to achieve (Senghaas 2012).

Adler and Barnett (1998b: 30) further develop the concept of security communities and define pluralistic security communities as 'a transnational region comprised of sovereign states whose people maintain dependable expectations of peaceful change'. They distinguish between loosely and tightly coupled pluralistic security communities. While loosely coupled pluralistic security communities only have to achieve the minimal definitional properties of pluralistic communities mentioned above, tightly coupled pluralistic security communities refer to a 'system of rule that lies somewhere between a sovereign state and a regional, centralized government; that is, it is something of a post-sovereign system, endowed with common supranational, transnational, and national institutions and some form of a collective security system' (Adler and Barnett 1998b: 30). This definition captures the institutional make-up of the European Union and therefore renders trans-actionalist theory highly relevant to the study of European integration (Jones and Van der Bijl 2004) in general and to this book in particular.[2]

To establish such security communities, states are advised to institutionalize and encourage increased transactions, in other words, transnational communication, networks, and mobility among their citizens (Deutsch et al. 1957; Deutsch 1969). Deutsch's understanding of transactions was very broad. In a non-exhaustive list of 'transactions relevant for mapping a potential political community', Deutsch (1954 [1970]: 70) includes political transactions, transactions in public and private finance, personal mobility, redistribution of commodities, direct and mass communications as well as indirect and informal communications.

Transactions are expected to prompt social learning processes, that is, 'active process[es] of redefinition or reinterpretation of reality—what people consider real, possible, and desirable on the basis of new causal and normative knowledge' (Adler and Barnett 1998b: 43). Deutsch and associates (1957) expected these learning processes to serve as a wellspring of a common identity and trust among the population and to lead them to support the newly established political community. To be effective, transactions have to fulfil a number of conditions. The most important ones seem to be the following: transactions should embrace multiple aspects of life, such as flow of capital and labour, scientific cooperation, cultural exchanges, inter-marriage etc. In other words, promoting cross-border interactions in only one sphere, such as the economic one, is not enough. Next, they ought to be consistent and thus predictable from a long-term perspective—in other words, they should be institutionalized (Deutsch 1969: 102). Moreover, they ought to be accompanied by compatible values in terms of common decision-making (Deutsch et al. 1957: 123).

Deutsch was well aware that these changes would not happen from one day to the next. His own empirical research (Deutsch 1956; Deutsch and Eckstein 1961) showed that in the 1950s, national societies and economies were in fact less integrated than before. Contrary to general expectations, international trade and mail in many industrial societies had actually decreased rather than increased, especially when contrasted with the simultaneous increase in domestic transactions (Deutsch et al. 1957: 120, 206) and gross national product (Deutsch and Eckstein 1961). Against the backdrop of 'eurosclerosis' and the Luxembourg compromise, he acknowledged that European integration had come to a halt (Deutsch 1969: 34). Nonetheless, Deutsch praised the achievements that had been made thus far:

---

[2] For a detailed list of indicators of tightly coupled pluralistic security communities, cf. Adler and Barnett 1998b: 57.

In the first 20 years since World War II a Europe of nation-states has been rebuilt. It *is* a Europe of nation-states in spite of the fact that some of its units, such as the Federal Republic of Germany, are in some ways different from their predecessors. However, it is at the moment considered wholly illegitimate to prepare war against any fellow Western European country....For the first time in many centuries Western Europe is now a pluralistic security community (Deutsch 1969: 35; emphasis in original).

What is more, Deutsch had high expectations of European integration in the medium term:

After 1975...a generation, which was young when integration was first proposed after World War II, will come into power in Europe. All their lives, these people will have seen increasing efforts, if not achievements towards a European union.... When they do come to power, they may then take Europe another substantial step toward integration (Deutsch 1969: 35).

In Deutsch's view, international governance is at the same time very challenging and promising. The challenge lies in governing a vast, heterogeneous, and increasingly complex community and in ensuring compliance and political support. The promise lies in the elimination of war and, consequently, increasing wealth, initiative, and inventiveness (Deutsch 1954 [1970]: 27)

Stone Sweet and Sandholtz (1998: 7) take up some of these ideas in what they call a 'transaction-based theory of European integration'. While focusing on the mode of governance rather than on collective identity, they argue that separate national legal regimes result in significant transaction costs to transnationally active members of society. Consequently, increased societal transactions and communication across borders generate public demand for supranational governance (Stone Sweet and Sandholtz 1998: 11). According to the authors, European cross-border transactions are therefore the catalyst of European integration (Stone Sweet and Sandholtz 1998: 4).

Many studies in the transactionalist legacy focused primarily on transactions, learning processes, and changes in attitudes and identities among elites rather than among the public (Deutsch et al. 1967; see, for example, Adler and Barnett 1998a; Eberwein and Ecker-Ehrhart 2001). One might thus argue that transactionalist theory is not suitable for the analysis of mass support of European integration. However, mass-level transactions and the consequential learning processes are at the heart of transactionalist theory: for instance, Deutsch (1954 [1970]: 70) cites the ratio between domestic and international mail, international trade, and the use of foreign mass media (see also Deutsch 1960). He further emphasizes the mobility of persons as 'essential for amalgamation and helpful for pluralism' (Deutsch et al. 1957: 151) and enquires about public opinion towards free movement. Puchala (1981: 151) notes that 'Deutsch has never really conceived of international relations strictly as interactions among states. Rather, his writings have constantly pictured a world of peoples, communities, or identitive groups.' Adler and Barnett (1998b: 44) agree that, while they focus on the elite level, the same mechanisms are possible at the mass level and are crucial to the development of collective identities.

To sum up the argument, transactionalist theory conjectures that increased transnational interactions and networks between citizens of formerly confined nation states result in a sense of community, trust, and support for further supranational integration.

3.3 Underlying Mechanisms: Interests and Identity

While transactionalist theory has received widespread scholarly attention in international relations (Scheingold 1971; Puchala 1981; Adler and Barnett 1998a), European studies (Sinnott 1995; Sandholtz and Stone Sweet 1998; Fligstein 2008), and research on nationalism (Smith 1998), it also has been criticized for its lack of precision and clarity (Inglehart 1968; Nye 1968; Haas 1970; Connor 1972) and for its wanting theoretical accuracy (Marks 1999).

For example, Deutsch remained relatively vague with respect to what exactly underlies the relationship between transactions and EU support. To be sure, he expected transactions to trigger learning processes, which in turn would promote regime support (Deutsch et al. 1957: 37). However, Deutsch was not clear regarding what the mechanism is that links transactions to attitudinal change. To fill this gap in the literature, this book proposes two mechanisms that link transnational activity to public orientations towards European integration. The first mechanism relates to changes in collective identity, while the second one implies utilitarian considerations.

First, by interacting across borders, individuals change their perceptions on how 'alien' members of other countries are, and eventually include them in their in-group. In other words, highly transnational people adapt their perceptions of who is part of their 'imagined community' (Anderson 1991). As Jones and Van der Bijl (2004: 332) put it, '[t]he assumption is that that interaction breeds familiarity, which in turn promotes the "we-feeling" or attitudinal sympathy that Deutsch believed to be a key to success'. This idea resonates with the conjecture of social constructivism (Berger and Luckmann 1966; Adler 2002) that by interacting with each other, people exchange their views of themselves and of their environment and thus approximate each other's perceptions and norms (Wendt 1994; Adler and Barnett 1998b). A necessary condition for this to happen is that individuals expect positive consequences of this change.

Similar ideas have been put forward by intergroup contact theory in social psychology (Allport 1954; Pettigrew 1998; Howard 2000; Pettigrew and Tropp 2006). Intergroup contact theory asserts that when individuals interact with members of other groups, they become aware of the common ground they share with each other. They thus tend to lower their cognitive distinctions between in- and out-group and might eventually adopt a collective identity (Howard 2000). While originally developed for the study of racial and ethnic relations, this theory has been shown to be applicable to other group contacts as well (Pettigrew and Tropp 2006).

Allport (1954) identified four necessary conditions for successful intergroup contact. First, the individuals interacting with each other ought to have equal status in the situation. Second, they have to pursue a common goal, such as playing in the same sports team or musical orchestra. Moreover, their interaction should be supported by institutions and should highlight common interest. In a more recent study, Pettigrew (1998: 76) added to this list the condition that intergroup contact bears the possibility of developing intergroup friendships.[3] For this to happen, contact must be intensive and recurring.

The conjectures of intergroup contact theory have been widely tested among international exchange students. Sassenberg and Matschke (2010) find that German exchange students in the United States integrated the (American) host society into their self-concept. In contrast, using a unique longitudinal analysis among Erasmus exchange students in the United Kingdom and continental Europe, Sigalas finds limited and mixed evidence that the Erasmus exchange experience leads to stronger European identification (Sigalas 2010a), but no evidence that it increases support for European integration (Sigalas 2010b). Comparing British, French, and Swedish Erasmus students to stationary university students in a panel study conducted in 2007 and 2008, Wilson (2011) finds similar results. He analyses students' attachment to Europe, European identification, propensity to vote for a pro- or anti-European candidate, and their position towards further political integration. While he finds exchange students to be significantly more pro-European than stayers, this difference already existed before they went abroad. Importantly, Wilson finds no observable change in attitudes during their sojourn.

However, university students might not be the best group to test whether transnational experiences strengthen public support for European integration and European identity. In fact, university students are among the most pro-European members of society: their young age and higher education are

---

[3] One could argue, however, that this is a criterion rather than a condition of successful intergroup contact.

strong predictors of EU membership support and of identifying oneself as European. Therefore, the mixed findings regarding their attitude change after an Erasmus exchange might be due to a ceiling effect: university students are already so likely to be pro-European that an Erasmus exchange abroad cannot add much to their support (Kuhn 2012b).

Consequently, it makes more sense to study the effects of transnational interactions among the overall population rather than among this highly selective group of university students. While there is no empirical research that directly assesses the relationship between transnationalism and EU support among the entire European population, some studies exist that focus on the effect of cross-border interactions on cosmopolitan attitudes. Analysing a representative survey among the German population, Mau and colleagues (2008) provide support for intergroup contact theory. Their analysis finds that highly transnational people subscribe to more cosmopolitan attitudes. Equally, Gustafson (2009) shows that Swedish frequent travellers have more cosmopolitan worldviews than the overall Swedish population. These findings are of interest here because there is a certain overlap between cosmopolitanism and orientations towards European integration. Cosmopolitan attitudes are not only marked by the appreciation of other human beings irrespective of their national origin (Vertovec and Cohen 2002), but also by awareness of the increased interconnectedness of political communities and the readiness to legitimize the transfer of authority to the supranational level (Held 2002: 58). These dimensions of cosmopolitanism can also be found in attitudes towards European integration. In this sense, a positive evaluation of European integration entails cosmopolitan attitudes in the way that it refers to the legitimization of a supranational polity and the acceptance of increased interaction with members of other European countries (see also Risse 2010: 61).[4]

How does national identity link to orientations towards European integration? National and European identity are not necessarily mutually exclusive. Some Europeans feel strongly attached to both the national and the European community. In contrast, some people exclusively identify as members of their nation state, and these people are also significantly less supportive of European integration (Carey 2002; Citrin and Sides 2004; Hooghe and Marks 2004; Fuchs et al. 2009a). This relationship can also be captured in terms of a perceived threat to national integrity (McLaren 2002, 2006). As McLaren (2002: 554) puts it, 'people see the nation-state as the appropriate point of reference for identity and the EU as undermining the integrity of the nation-state'. Feelings of threat come in a variety of guises. McLaren (2006)

---

[4] Nonetheless, some ideas of European integration are less cosmopolitan than is often assumed (Haller 2008).

emphasizes cultural threats posed by immigration, whereas Christin and Trechsel (2002) explain eurosceptic attitudes by the perceived threat to national interest. In a similar vein, xenophobic attitudes (De Master and Le Roy 2000), the propensity to categorize out-groups (De Vreese et al. 2008), and anti-immigrant attitudes (Lubbers and Scheepers 2007) have been linked to eurosceptic attitudes.

To sum up the argument, in order to develop support for European integration and to acquire a European identity, people need to be able to accommodate a more open group affiliation than the national one into their social identity. As is argued here, one way that this might come about is by interacting across borders.

The second mechanism underlying the learning effects that Deutsch expected relates to utilitarian considerations. Interest-led cost–benefit analyses of European integration have long been the primary explanation for attitudes towards European integration (Anderson and Reichert 1995; Gabel and Palmer 1995; Gabel 1998b, 1998c). Whether individuals lose or benefit from European integration is usually understood as dependent on their socio-economic status and their social location, that is, their human capital, occupation, income, foreign-language skills, or proximity to neighbouring countries. Individuals highly endowed with capital and income benefit from new investment opportunities arising from economic integration, while low wage earners are dependent on a crumbling national welfare system. Moreover, highly skilled Europeans profit from an integrated labour market. In line with this argument, more educated and wealthy individuals have been shown to display more utilitarian support for European integration (Gabel and Whitten 1997; Gabel 1998a).

While socio-economic status is one way to capture personal benefits from European integration, they can also be measured more directly by emphasizing individual transnationalism. As argued by Sandholtz and Stone Sweet (1998), the European integration process removes transaction costs that usually arise from interactions. For instance, when purchasing goods from other member states, Europeans no longer have to face import tariffs. Equally, the introduction of the common currency has rendered intra-European trade much less complicated. Travellers benefit from the Schengen Treaty, which abolishes intra-European border controls and thus makes travelling easier. Another example of how European integration leads to reduced transaction costs is the recent EU regulation imposing a limit on international roaming fees for the use of mobile phones abroad.

Many Europeans benefit from these advantages only during their two-week summer vacation. In contrast, such policies have a great impact on the everyday lives of Europeans who interact across borders on a regular basis. By interacting across borders in order to, for example, buy property abroad, pursue an academic degree, set up a business, or buy cheaper products, transnationally active people directly benefit from the new opportunities generated by European integration. They experience the advantages of an integrated Europe in their daily lives and are likely to perceive European integration as a source of additional opportunities. Their 'learning process' that Deutsch was expecting to observe can thus be explained by the awareness and exploitation of new opportunities emerging in the wake of European integration. In contrast, others 'remain "nationalized"; they see their life chances as depending on the territorialized systems of social sharing, identity and political participation rights and on the monopolistic production of related public goods by national and local authorities' (Bartolini 2005: 399).

In short, highly transnational individuals are expected to be more supportive of European integration than individuals who do not frequently interact across borders. Not only are they the ones who directly benefit from European integration by seizing the opportunities arising from European border removal—their transnational interactions are also likely to render them more open-minded towards non-nationals and to support regional integration. This leads to the formulation of the following hypothesis:

Hypothesis 1: The more transnational an individual, the more she or he is likely to support European integration and to identify as European.

3.4 Transactionalist Theory Revisited

Since I first came to these shores over 30 years ago, Britain has become much more European. You've built the Channel-Tunnel, you got used to mixer taps, duvets and double glazing. Even your cooking has improved. Yet, your public opinion and politics is more Euro-sceptic than ever.[5]

—Radoslaw Sikorski, Polish Minister of Foreign Affairs

Following transactionalist theory, we should observe soaring levels of EU support that go hand in hand with the upsurge in transnational interactions. As is evidenced in Figure 1.1 in the introductory chapter, cross-border networks and mobility have proliferated tremendously over the past decades. Moreover, the conditions under which Deutsch expected transactions to trigger learning processes are fulfilled: transactions are not limited to a certain sphere but are multi-dimensional, covering aspects as diverse as binational marriages, tourism, and foreign direct investment. They are institutionalized by a plethora of European and national policies and initiatives that guarantee and actively promote free movement across Europe (Krotz 2007; Petit 2007;

---

[5] Radoslaw Sikorski, The Blenheim Palace Speech (on the UK and Europe), September 2012.

Falkenhain et al. 2012). Nonetheless, as discussed in more detail in the introductory chapter, European integration has become an increasingly politicized (Hooghe and Marks 2009a; De Wilde and Zürn 2012) and controversial issue (Harmsen and Spiering 2004; Haller 2008; Fuchs et al. 2009b). Low public EU support documented in the Eurobarometer surveys, (Eichenberg and Dalton 2007; Lubbers and Jaspers 2011), the anti-European campaigning of some political parties (Krouwel and Abts 2007), mainly at the fringes of the political spectrum (De Vries and Edwards 2009), as well as negative EU referendum outcomes (Schild 2005; Hobolt 2009) testify to a constraining dissensus (Hooghe and Marks 2009a) rather than the permissive consensus (Lindberg and Scheingold 1970) that was expected by politicians and scholars alike. In short, what Polish Minister of Foreign Affairs, Radoslaw Sikorski (2012), cogently observed in a speech on the UK and Europe (see the quote at the start of this section), is accurate for many Europeans, maybe in a less accentuated manner: 'being' and 'feeling' European often drift apart.

In fact, Deutsch's transactionalist theory needs to be further developed and qualified in order to convey an adequate picture of European society. Not all transnational interactions in Europe are successful in promoting EU support. The core argument of this book is that, while generally effective, transactions are concentrated among a small elite, that their effectiveness is contingent on their purpose and scope, and that they create negative externalities among the immobile parts of society. In Puchala's (1981: 158) words, Deutsch's model of political unification 'is incomplete, not inaccurate'. Consequently, the following section theorizes the conditions under which transnational interactions lead to increased EU support among the European public.

3.4.1 *Individual or Societal Transnationalization?*

There is no room for doubt that transnational interactions have increased in the past decades. This was shown in Figure 1.1 and is well documented by longitudinal research on globalization (Lockwood and Redoano 2005; Dreher et al. 2008; Raab et al. 2008). Global migration stocks have increased from 92 million in 1960 to 165 million in 2000 (Özden et al. 2011). A large proportion of these transactions are genuinely intra-European and do not extend beyond the continent (Fligstein and Mérand 2002). In fact, migration to Western Europe comes mainly from other European countries (Özden et al. 2011). König and Ohr (2013) have shown for the EU-15 that intra-EU movement of goods, services, labour, and capital has grown over the past decades. Besides these aggregate data, systematic empirical evidence of the extent and scope of individual transnationalism across time is scant. The following paragraphs refer to some primary and secondary data in order to illustrate this trend. Among the few empirical accounts of individual transnationalism in

Europe, Mau and Büttner (2010) find that cross-border networks and activities have proliferated over the past two to three decades. This is especially the case for youth exchanges, student mobility, tourism, and regional cross-border cooperation.

With respect to intra-European migration, it is worth noting that the figures are (still) very low: between 2003 and 2012, the share of intra-European migrants has slightly risen from 1.3 per cent to 2.7 per cent of the total EU-27 population. In the EU-15, the share of mobile Europeans is marginally higher, totalling 1.6 per cent of the EU-15 population in 2003, and 3.2 per cent in 2012 (Juravle et al. 2013). Thus, the number of intra-EU migrants living in the EU is still lower than the number of migrants from non-EU countries (Eurostat 2012). This low number, however, is partly due to the fact that many intra-European movers refrain from registering in their country of destination and consequently do not appear in the official statistics. Moreover, when considering different member states separately, the picture changes slightly. For example, the share of Romanians living in the EU-15 has increased from 1 per cent to 7 per cent of the total Romanian population. Likewise, 4 per cent of Bulgarians live in an EU-15 member state. Intra-EU migration has not only proliferated but also taken on new, hybrid forms, such as regular commuting between the countries of destination and origin, etc. (Schneider and Meil 2008). Among these new migrants are the small but growing group of 'Eurostars'—highly educated, free-moving professionals (Favell 2008)—as well as lifestyle and retirement movers, mostly North-Europeans resettling in Southern Europe (King et al. 2000; Benson 2010).

At the same time, short-term visits to other (European) countries have increased remarkably. Comparing Eurobarometer survey data for the EU-10 in 1985 and 2007, Díez Medrano (2010a) finds that short trips abroad have proliferated over this twenty-two-year period. While in 1985, only 19 per cent of the population of the first ten EU member states had travelled abroad at least three times in the preceding three years, 31 per cent had done so in 2007.[6] Similar increases in short-term trips abroad are further documented by surveys on travel behaviour that are conducted every ten years among the German population: while in 1964, only 15 per cent of the West German population had undertaken a tourist trip abroad, 30 per cent had done so in 1974 and 36 per cent in 1984. In the reunited Germany, 52 per cent (1993) and 54 per cent (2003) of the German population had visited another country as a tourist (Recchi and Kuhn 2013).

However, this upward trend in transnationalism does not necessarily imply that all members of society actively take part in this development. According

---

[6] The exact question wording and categories offered were not identical in the two surveys. See Díez Medrano 2010a: 28.

to Hofmeister and Breitenstein (2008: 481), 'the degree to which a society or nation is engaged in transnationalization processes can be quite different from the degree to which an individual within that society is engaged'. Drawing on a variety of primary data, Fligstein (2008) concludes that only a small group, comprising 10–15 per cent of the European population, regularly operate on a transnational level and have strong transnational networks. According to his estimates, about 40–50 per cent of Europeans do not speak a foreign language and remain within the national realm. The rest of the population is couched between these two poles, occasionally interacting on a transnational level for professional or private reasons (Fligstein 2009: 250). As we will see in further detail in Chapter 5, these numbers are roughly corroborated by the empirical data used in this book.

In short, individual transnationalism has not (yet) become a mass phenomenon in Europe. What is more, it appears to be highly stratified by social class (Mau and Mewes 2009). To be sure, when comparing Eurobarometer survey data from 1985 and 2007, Díez Medrano (2010a) finds short-term visits abroad to have most notably increased among those with a low level of education, and argues that the decreasing cost of travel opportunities has disproportionately benefited the lower class. Nonetheless, even today the extent to which people take part in short-term visits abroad varies along socio-economic lines (Díez Medrano 2010a), and this is likely to be the case for other aspects of transnationalism as well. In fact, studies among middle-school pupils show that their likelihood to have embarked on a school exchange or a similar transnational experience is highly dependent on their parents' socio-economic background and the opportunity structures provided by their schools (Frändberg 2009; Gerhards and Hans 2013). Equally, German university students' participation in academic exchange programmes is remarkably stratified along socio-economic lines, and these differences have been increasing rather than decreasing (Finger 2011; Lörz and Krawietz 2011). Similar observations have been made with respect to foreign language skills (Gerhards 2012).

Consequently, the transactionalist hypothesis is relevant only with respect to a small, *avant-garde* group of the public, while most Europeans fail to be prompted by transnational interactions to alter their orientations towards European integration. As transnational interactions are concentrated among a minority, the increase in aggregate transactions does not have to generate increases in aggregate EU support. This idea is captured in the following hypothesis:

Hypothesis 2: Individual transnationalism is stratified by socio-economic background.

This implies that to understand how transactions and public orientations towards European integration are linked, it is not sufficient to model attitudes towards European integration as a function of the aggregate level of transnational interactions, as this conceals the unequal distribution of transactions across society. Rather, one ought to study the effect of transactions at the individual and the macro-level.

3.4.2 When Interacting across Borders is not Enough

While the first qualification of transactionalist theory referred to the unequal distribution of transactions, the second qualification relates to their unequal effectiveness. Not all transnational interactions are the same. One would expect some interactions to be more formative for orientations towards European integration than others. In fact, Hay (2009: 538) warns against 'depict [ing] all European social interaction as positive, and as leading to positive identification with Europe'. Rather, some interactions might be ineffective in triggering EU support, or they might even generate boomerang effects. Díez-Medrano (2008: 8) argues that when Europeans interact with each other, they often do so as members of their respective national communities rather than as fellow Europeans. In fact, certain institutional frameworks aimed at promoting European exchange contribute to the reification of national identities and stereotypes. The Eurovision Song Contest and the UEFA European Football Championship might be pan-European events, but they are ultimately competitions between national communities (Baker 2008).

Therefore, while the previous section asked who the transnationally active Europeans are, this sections asks: what are the reasons for, and the scope of, transnational interactions? One can classify interactions with respect to their purpose and scope, and develop hypotheses on their respective effect on EU support. To begin with, it is important to consider the main purpose of transnational interactions. People may interact across borders for very different reasons. As the contributions gathered in Recchi and Favell (2009) show, migration within Europe—a prime form of transnational interaction—encompasses far more than the traditional labour market mobility and is motivated by a plethora of reasons. Europeans may (temporarily) move to another member state in the pursuit of better universities, better food, or better weather. They may follow their partner, seek a nice place for their retirement, or come for cheaper rent (Favell 2008; Santacreu et al. 2009).

It would be a moot point to try and grasp the whole range of motivations behind transnationalism. Rather, it makes sense to rely on a fundamental distinction between sociable and instrumental interactions, as proposed by Roose (2010). As discussed in the conceptualization of individual transnationalism in Chapter 2, instrumental interactions are genuinely inter-est-led and include practices such as cross-border shopping, trade, or business trips. On the other hand, sociable forms of interactions are intrinsically motivated and include practices such as socializing with other Europeans.

This distinction between instrumental and sociable interactions largely corresponds to the two main mechanisms underlying the relationship between individual transnationalism and EU support that were discussed above. On the one hand, highly transnational individuals are supposed to endorse European integration because they are ultimately the people who benefit from integration on a daily basis. Frequent Euro-travellers are likely to welcome policies such as the Schengen area or the common currency because they ease their lifestyles and because they offer a wealth of new opportunities (Stone Sweet and Sandholtz 1998). On the other hand, trans-national interactions are expected to make Europeans more cosmopolitan. By interacting across borders, people are expected to become aware of inter-national interdependence and to lower intergroup boundaries (Mau et al. 2008). They are thus more likely to legitimize European integration and to accommodate Europe into their collective identities. This latter mechanism relates to sociable forms of interactions that are done for the sake of interact-ing as such.

Which one of these two mechanisms is more powerful? The answer to this question contributes to the prominent scholarly debate as to whether utilitar-ian cost–benefit calculations or questions of social identity prevail in explain-ing EU support (McLaren 2002; Hooghe and Marks 2004). Considering that European policymaking emphasizes instrumental interactions, such as labour mobility or trade, it is crucial to know whether these forms of interactions result in support for the EU and a European identity.

If identitarian aspects explain the link between individual transnationalism and orientations towards Europe, we may expect that sociable forms of interactions have an especially strong role in structuring EU support. If, on the other hand, the effect of transnationalism on EU support is driven by interest-led considerations, then instrumental interactions should be of greater relevance. I therefore formulate the following competing hypotheses:

Hypothesis 3a: Instrumental interactions have a stronger effect on orientations towards European integration than sociable interactions.

Hypothesis 3b: Sociable interactions have a stronger effect on orientations towards European integration than instrumental interactions.

One can go a step further and consider the possibility that some interactions might well alter people's attitudes and identities, but not necessarily in the direction that is expected by transactionalist theory. Theoretical consider-ations and empirical findings suggest that transnational interactions and networks can also (a) generate binational rather than supranational identifications, (b) lead to genuinely cosmopolitan attitudes challenging the borders of the EU, or (c) reify national identities. The following paragraphs briefly discuss each of these scenarios and their theoretical underpinnings.

First, transnational interactions might lead to binational rather than European orientations. Whether this is the case depends primarily on whether transactions are framed and experienced in a binational or European way. If interactions are framed as binational, it might not even occur to the people involved to link their transnationalism to European integration. European framing could be facilitated by embedding transnational interactions in an institutional framework at the EU level such as Interreg or Erasmus. If people are aware that their transnational interaction is promoted (or even financed) by the European Union, they might be more inclined to link it to their appraisal of European integration.

In contrast, binational framing is likely if transactions are concentrated on a particular country rather than extending themselves to the entire EU. This can happen between two states with a long tradition of binational exchanges and cooperation, such as Denmark and Sweden (Rother and Nebe 2009), which have a common historical legacy and/or cultural affinity that render interaction easier than with other countries (Roose 2012a). This is even more the case if these interactions are financed and managed in the framework of some binational cooperation, such as the German-French broadcasting channel ARTE (Krotz 2007). Finally, people living close to an intra-European border are likely to interact primarily with the citizens and institutions of their neighbouring country (Rippl et al. 2010), especially if there is some sort of institutionalized cross-border cooperation programme (Klatt and Herrmann 2011). Under these circumstances, it is very likely that people frame their interactions in a binational rather than European context. They might relate their transactions to support for the EU to a lesser extent than people whose transactions are genuinely European. Consequently, people interacting mainly on a binational rather than a wider European scope might develop weaker European orientations than people whose transnational interactions include several member states or the entire EU.

It is assumed that people who live close to an intra-European border experience their daily cross-border exchanges in a binational, rather than European, framework. There are good reasons to believe that border residents interact with people and institutions in the neighbouring country on a regular basis. Without incurring high transaction costs, people living close to an intra-European border can cross the border to work in the neighbouring country, profit from cheaper or better products and services, or simply enjoy a nice dinner in a different atmosphere. In many cases, transnational exchanges in border districts existed long before the unification of Europe. In the minds of border residents, the neighbouring country might therefore be more salient than the EU. In line with this argument, Roose (2010) has shown that people who live on or near intra-European borders tend to develop binational rather than European identities. It therefore seems sensible to differentiate between Europeans living close to an intra-European border and those living further away, and to expect the following relationship:

Hypothesis 4: Transnational interactions in intra-European border districts have a weaker effect on orientations towards European integration than transnational interactions in areas further away from the border.

When developing their theory in the 1950s, Deutsch and colleagues expected increased transactions within Europe to happen as a relatively isolated process in an otherwise rather static international environment. In fact, their model implied that the density of interactions would drop significantly at the borders of a security community (Inglehart 1968: 121–2). This becomes clear when recalling that Deutsch identified a (national) community by its increased level of interactions. Thus, when encouraging increased transactions across borders, he implied that these transactions overcome national borders but not the external borders of the security community itself.

From today's perspective, this assumption is unrealistic. In the wake of global market integration and massive immigration from non-European countries, intra-European transactions go hand in hand with transactions that reach beyond the borders of the European Union. Europeans holiday in Northern Africa, do business with South-East Asia, and study in the United States. In fact, in 2011, Switzerland and the USA were the two top emigration destinations for Germans (Statistisches Bundesamt 2013: 46), and between 2008 and 2011, more than half of all migrants from Spain went to a non-European country (Benton and Petrovic 2013).

The effects of these global experiences are likely to be different from the effects of purely intra-European transactions. First, people interacting with institutions and individuals outside of Europe might not link their transnational activity to the European Union at all. Savage and colleagues (2005) found that British citizens tend to have stronger links to the Commonwealth than to continental Europe and thus develop collective identities that transcend European borders. What is more, people interacting within a global context are likely to hold genuinely cosmopolitan identities and perceive themselves as citizens of the world. This can even lead to criticism of 'fortress Europe': as intra-European boundary removal has been accompanied by the strengthening of external borders, people frequently travelling to countries outside the EU might perceive stricter European border control as an obstacle to their transnationalism. Thus, when analysing the effect of individual transnationalism on EU support, it is necessary to differentiate between interactions that limit themselves to the European realm and those that go beyond European borders. This idea is captured in the following hypothesis:

Hypothesis 5: Intra-European transnational practices are more effective in fostering EU support than transnational practices that reach beyond European borders.

Finally, while contact theory emphasizes the positive aspects of increased intergroup contact, conflict theory (Blumer 1958; Blalock 1967) highlights the other side of the coin. According to these authors, intergroup contact may trigger some boomerang effects, especially if the requirements of effective intergroup contact discussed above are not met. Research in social and intercultural psychology has put forward a wide range of psychological mechanisms hindering constructive cultural contact, such as in-group favouritism (Tajfel 1981), similarity attraction (Byrne 1969), stereotyping (Katz and Braly 1933; Fiske 2000), and the persistence of primary socialization. Failed cultural contact can lead to a 'culture shock' and reify in-group/out-group distinctions and prejudices (Hofstede 1994; Ward et al. 2001). It thus alienates members of different groups rather than bringing them together. In fact, Schmitt and colleagues (2003) show that exchange students who feel rejected by their host society develop a genuine identity as international exchange students, contrasting themselves with their host society. Sigalas (2010a) finds in a study on the impact of the Erasmus year abroad that the European attachment of Erasmus students in the United Kingdom actually decreased rather than increased.[7] Similar findings have been made in research on interethnic relations within the neighbourhood. In a study on ethnic diversity in US neighbourhoods, Putnam (2007) concludes that immigration and ethnic diversity reduce social capital and trust. The study of Lancee and Dronkers (2011) also finds support for this conclusion in the case of the Netherlands.

These examples suggest that the impact of transnationalism on attitudes and identities is neither uniform nor straightforward. In fact, it seems more appropriate to speak of a polarization of attitudes. As Roudometof (2005) claims:

The proliferation of the different levels of transnationalism around the globe leads to a bifurcation of attitudes among the public. Faced with the reality of transnational experience, members of the public might opt for an open attitude welcoming the new experiences or they might opt for a defensive closed attitude seeking to limit the extent to which transnational social spaces penetrate their cultural milieu (Roudometof 2005: 127).

---

[7] This development, however, might also be a consequence of students' assimilation to the generally low levels of political support toward European integration in the United Kingdom.

3.4.3 *Negative Externalities of Increased Transactions*

This leads us to the third qualification proposed to complement Deutsch's transactionalist theory: negative external effects of increased transactions with respect to those Europeans who do not—or rarely—interact across borders. As has been argued above, individual transnationalism is not (yet) a mainstream phenomenon in Europe. Many Europeans remain within the confines of their nation state and hardly interact across borders. How are they affected by the transnationalization of their realm, and how do they react to it? This question is discussed in the following section.

Hypothesis 1 stipulates that a person's level of transnationalism has a positive impact on their orientation towards European integration. One may be tempted to translate this hypothesis to the macro-level by arguing that the higher the degree of macro-level transnationalization in a society, the more transnational and thus more pro-European are its members. Following this logic, one would expect that in highly transnationalized countries, everyone—thus also the people who rarely, if ever, interact across borders—is more pro-European than in less transnationalized countries.

However, a number of empirical findings contradict these expectations. In a longitudinal analysis of the impact of economic, political, and social globalization on EU support, Rossbach (2010) found mixed results: while economic globalization had indeed a positive effect on EU support, he found no effect for social globalization and a negligible impact of political globalization on EU support. Using cross-sectional analyses of survey data of the ISSP and the World Values Survey in sixty-three countries, Ariely (2012) detects a negative relationship between a country's level of globalization on the one hand, and patriotism and the willingness to fight for one's country on the other. However, he finds no significant effect of globalization on national identity or on nationalism. He concludes that the link between globalization and attitudes is complex and multi-dimensional (Ariely 2012). It is also interesting to consider recent developments in Ireland and the Netherlands, two of the most transnationalized countries worldwide. The negative referendum outcomes in the Netherlands (2005) and Ireland (2008) as well as the rise of the Dutch populist right catering to globalization 'losers' (Kriesi and Frey 2008: 181) strongly suggest that parts of the population reject the transnationalization of their realm. Indeed, an analysis of Eurobarometer data of the EU-15 from 1994 to 2004 finds that euroscepticism increased most notably in the Netherlands (Lubbers and Scheepers 2010). In line with these findings, Haller and Roudometof (2010) observe the (re-)emergence of nation-based localism as a reaction to the effects of globalization on people's everyday lives.

How can one make sense of these seemingly contradictory developments? According to Kriesi and associates (2008), globalization gives rise to a new structural conflict along a demarcation–integration divide. Globalization has provoked deep-seated structural changes in domestic societies (Burgoon 2001). While beneficial to some, they are threatening to others. The internationalization and rising importance of markets, political deregulation, and increased interconnectedness have directly or indirectly led to intensified competition and rising needs for flexibility, and have strengthened existing patterns of inequality (Buchholz et al. 2009). This development leads some members of society to turn against the opening of cultural, economic, and political borders. What is more, transnationalization challenges existing national patterns of solidarity and allegiance (Kriesi et al. 2008; Kriesi 2009). European welfare states have to redefine who is part of the national society, and eligible for welfare state services and transfers (Burgoon 2001). In the wake of the transnationalization of their life, individuals are forced to question their identities (Buchan et al. 2009). According to Haller and Roudometof (2010: 279), '[i]ndividuals feel more intensely the need to develop preferences and attitudes vis-à-vis the growing cultural hybridity and syncretism characteristic of the world we are living in'. Consequently, Haller and Roudometof (2010) expect globalization to provoke a whole range of attitudes and identities ranging from cosmopolitan to parochial orientations rather than a uniform shift to cosmopolitanism. While contradictory at first sight, euroscepticism and the reification of national identities seem to be a consequence of European integration and globalization.

Therefore, simply translating the individual hypothesis to the macro-level would run the risk of committing an ecological fallacy by making inferences about individuals based on aggregate data (Snijders and Bosker 1999). In this sense, Beck (2002: 29) warns against committing the 'cosmopolitan fallacy' of believing that 'we are all going to become cosmopolitans' simply because individuals today experience the transnationalization of their realm. There are good reasons to believe that the ensuing conflict between demarcation and integration is stronger the more globalized a society. Negative consequences of globalization, such as increased social insecurity, relocation of companies, and mass migration, are likely to be stronger the higher the level of globalization in a country. Consequently, one can expect that globalization exacerbates the effect of individual transnationalism on EU support.

Thus, it is likely that in more transnational countries, the integration–demarcation cleavage is more pronounced. I expect that in highly globalized countries, highly transnational individuals are even more supportive of European integration, and that people that are not transnationally active oppose European integration even more strongly than in countries that are less globalized. Therefore, it is important to consider an individual's degree of transnationalism in interaction with the degree of globalization at the macro-level in order to predict their attitude towards European integration.

In statistical terms, we can hence expect a positive interaction effect of globalization and individual transnationalism. The next hypothesis therefore reads as follows:

> **Hypothesis 6**: The more transnational a country, the stronger the relationship between individual transnationalism and EU support.

3.5 Conclusion and Outlook

The central aim of this chapter was to establish a theoretical link between individual transnationalism and EU support, and to theorize the conditions under which transactions in fact are successful in generating EU support. To do so, the chapter started out by discussing Deutsch's (Deutsch et al. 1957) transactionalist theory. In a nutshell, transactionalist theory posits that security communities such as the EU trigger increased transnational interactions and networks, which in turn give rise to a common we-feeling, trust, and support for further political integration.

Having discussed the reception and criticism of this theory in the scholarly literature, the chapter proposed two potential mechanisms underlying the relationship between transnationalism and EU support. The first mechanism refers to questions of group identity. In short, people interacting across borders are likely to lower their group boundaries (Allport 1954; Brown 2000; Pettigrew and Tropp 2006). Thus, people highly engaged in transnational interactions and mobility are expected to support European integration and to adopt a European identity due to a more cosmopolitan worldview. The second mechanism entails utilitarian considerations. By interacting and moving across national borders, individuals benefit from the extra-national resources made available by European integration (Sandholtz and Stone Sweet 1998; Bartolini 2005; Kriesi et al. 2008). On this line of reasoning, the higher probability of EU support among highly transnational people also reflects their gains from European integration. Following transactionalist theory (Deutsch et al. 1957), Hypothesis 1 therefore predicted that the more transnational an individual, the more (s)he is likely to show support for the EU and European identity.

Subsequent hypotheses aimed at qualifying this relationship. Hypothesis 2 emphasized the unequal participation in transnational interactions across society. It was further argued that the likelihood that transnational interactions will trigger EU support depends on their purpose and scope. Two competing hypotheses expected instrumental (Hypothesis 3a) or sociable interactions (Hypothesis 3b) to matter more, respectively. Assuming that border residents mainly interact with the neighbouring country and thus interpret their interactions as binational rather than European, Hypothesis 4 expected transnational interactions in border districts to have a smaller impact on orientations towards European integration than transnational interactions happening elsewhere. Hypothesis 5 claimed that intra-European interactions are more effective in triggering pro-European orientations than interactions reaching beyond Europe. Finally, expecting increased interactions to generate negative externalities on people who do not become transnationally active themselves, Hypothesis 6 predicted that macro-level transnationalism polarizes the relationship between individual transnationalism and EU support.

The following four chapters put these hypotheses under empirical scrutiny. Using data from the Eurobarometer survey (2006, 2007), Chapter 4 tests the first hypothesis that individual transnationalism is significantly related to EU support and European identity. Chapter 5 tests the second hypothesis that individual transnationalism is stratified across society. Focusing on the dimension of transnational practices, Chapter 6 examines Hypotheses 3a, 3b, 4, and 5 that relate to the differential effects of transnational interactions. Finally, Chapter 7 analyses the interaction effect of individual transnationalism and globalization on EU support (Hypothesis 6). The concluding chapter (Chapter 8) pulls all these findings together and discusses the implications for theory building and policymaking.

4

Being and Feeling European

The Effect of Individual Transnationalism on EU Support and European Identity

> *The Erasmus idea should be compulsory, not only for students, but also for taxi drivers, plumbers and others. Spending time in other countries within the European Union is the way to integrate.*[1]
>
> —Umberto Eco

Having presented the theoretical framework in the preceding chapters, the focus of the book now shifts to the empirical analysis. The aim of this chapter is to empirically test Hypothesis 1—that individual transnationalism has a significant effect on EU support and European identity. As was outlined in further detail in Chapter 3, highly transnational individuals are expected to be more supportive of European integration for two main reasons. First, they are in fact the people who directly benefit from intra-European boundary removal on a daily basis. European integration and the ensuing removal of borders and barriers thus match their interests. Second, when interacting with people and institutions from other European member states, highly transnational individuals are likely to alter their group boundaries and to develop a European identity.

To test the hypothesis that highly transnational people are more pro-European, the following section recapitulates the operationalization of individual transnationalism and then turns to the statistical models. First, the effect of individual transnationalism on EU membership support is analysed. Second, the models predicting European identity are presented. Further analyses focus on how the effect of individual transnationalism varies across

---

[1] Quote from interview with Umberto Eco, *La Stampa*, English online version, 2012, cited in Kuhn 2012: 994.

countries. The chapter concludes by discussing theoretical and policy-relevant implications of the results.

4.1 Operationalizing Individual Transnationalism

Chapter 2 presents a thorough description of the operationalization of individual transnationalism. To recapitulate, individual transnationalism is understood as a tri-dimensional phenomenon encompassing transnational background, transnational practices, and transnational human capital. Transnational background refers to being born abroad or having foreign parents; transnational practices include short-term and long-term stays in other EU member states as well as interactions with other Europeans; and transnational human capital entails the proficiency and use of foreign languages. The empirical basis for the measurement of individual transnationalism and its effect on EU support and identity stems from Eurobarometer survey waves 65.1 (European Commission 2006) and 67.1 (European Commission 2007) that were conducted in the EU-25 and the EU-27, respectively. In Eurobarometer 65.1, the individual transnationalism scale is constructed from eight items and has a mean of .23 on a scale ranging from 0 to 1. In Eurobarometer 67.1, the scale consists of eleven items and has a mean of .15 on a range from 0 to 1.

4.2 Effect of Individual Transnationalism on EU Membership Support

Eurobarometer 65.1 includes the EU membership support question, which is frequently used as an operationalization of attitudes toward European integration (Anderson 1998; Carey 2002; Eichenberg and Dalton 2007). The exact wording of this item is: 'Generally speaking, do you think that our country's membership is (1) a good thing, (2) a bad thing or (3) neither good nor bad, (4) don't know?' This item serves as the dependent variable. As there is a clearly neutral category, it is recoded as the middle category, while all 'don't know' answers are omitted from the analysis. Given that we are interested here in EU support rather than euroscepticism, the order of the categories needs to be reversed. The recoded dependent variable thus has three ordered categories, 'good thing' having the highest value.

In view of the existing literature on EU support, a number of control variables are included. Respondents' current occupation (managers as reference category) accounts for utilitarian considerations (Gabel and Whitten 1997; Gabel 1998a) that are not directly related to cross-border interactions.

An important predictor of EU support is education (Lubbers and Scheepers 2007; Hakhverdian et al. 2013). Eurobarometer provides information on the age at which respondents have left education. On this basis, a three-category item on education is included in the analysis. A score of 1 refers to having left school at age 15 or lower, 2 refers to having quit education at age 16–19, and 3 refers to having left education at a later stage. The few respondents who have not had full-time education at all are coded as 1. This categorization reflects the age at which pupils move from compulsory education to middle school and from middle school to higher education.[2] Tucker and colleagues (2002) argue that individuals' subjective economic situation is more important than their objective position. Therefore, a five-category item referring to one's self-assessed household situation in two years accounts for self-rated economic prospects. The ability to convince friends and the habit of discussing politics account for the cognitive mobilization hypothesis (Inglehart 1970; Inglehart et al. 1991; Karp et al. 2003).

To capture a potential effect of anti-immigrant feelings on euroscepticism (McLaren 2002; De Vreese and Boomgaarden 2005; McLaren 2007), having indicated 'encouraging immigration of workers from outside the EU' as a measure to solve potential shortages in the workforce is included in the model. Admittedly, this item measures pro- rather than anti-immigrant attitudes. However, it is the only measure referring to immigration in the survey. A ten-category item on left–right self-placement measures political ideology. Given that extreme right positioning is highly correlated with anti-immigrant attitudes (Semyonov et al. 2006), it is likely to pick up further effects of anti-immigration attitudes that are not accounted for by the labour item above. Since in some countries, the effect of ideology is curvilinear rather than linear (Steenbergen et al. 2007; Lubbers and Scheepers 2010), its square is also included. As transnational interactions are more likely to occur in cities (Deutsch 1961), a three-category variable controls for the degree of urbanization of a respondent's residence. Four age groups, the category 55+ as reference, control for age, while a dichotomous variable accounts for being female. Previous findings would suggest controlling for respondents' trust in political institutions (Rohrschneider 2002). Unfortunately, it is impossible to do so because no such item is included in the survey.

As the dependent variable has three ordered categories, ordinal logit models are estimated. All independent and control variables are standardized to run from 0 to 1. The hypothesis tested in this chapter focuses on individual-level predictors. Therefore, dichotomous variables for each country (Germany being the reference country) account for cross-country heterogeneity, and

---

[2] In additional models that are not presented here, dummy variables for each category are included. These models confirm the results shown here.

robust standard errors clustered on the country level are included. This empirical strategy controls for all cross-country variance, such as macro-economic performance or political discourse. In contrast, Chapter 7 emphasizes statistical interaction effects between the individual and the macro-level. Consequently, the results presented in Chapter 7 are based on multilevel models and include macro-level predictors. They show that the individual-level effects of interest here are also robust when estimating multilevel models.

Table 4.1 displays the results of the empirical analyses. To test Hypothesis 1, that highly transnational individuals are more likely to support European integration, Model 1 estimates the effect of individual transnationalism, while Models 2–4 calculate the effect of each dimension of individual transnationalism on EU membership support. As can be seen in Model 1, individual transnationalism has a strong, positive, and highly significant effect on EU membership support. In other words, people who are highly transnational are significantly more likely to endorse EU membership than people who score low on the transnationalism index. Individual transnationalism has the greatest effect in the entire model. This is strong support for Hypothesis 1.

There is, however, one caveat to the results so far: using cross-sectional data, one can only identify correlation rather than causation. In other words, with the data at hand one cannot exclude the possibility that individual transnationalism is caused by orientations towards European integration rather than the other way around, as hypothesized here. Critics of Deutsch's theory argue that it might well be the case that the latter causes the former (Eilstrup-Sangiovanni 2006).

A closer look at the effect of each of the three dimensions of individual transnationalism is informative in this respect. In contrast to transnational practices, a person's transnational background can hardly be caused by their EU support, as the latter is developed later in life while the former is determined at birth. The same applies, to a lesser extent, to transnational human capital, which is often acquired during childhood and adolescence. When each dimension of individual transnationalism is included as a separate predictor of EU membership support in Models 2–4, it becomes clear that each of these dimensions on its own significantly increases the likelihood of EU support. While the dimension of transnational practices has the strongest impact on membership support, the two other dimensions also exert a significant and positive effect. This finding supports the hypothesis that at least part of the causal relation operates from individual transnationalism to EU support.

Table 4.1. Effect of individual transnationalism on EU membership support

	Model 1 b (se)	Model 2 b (se)	Model 3 b (se)	Model 4 b (se)
Individual transnationalism	1.559*** (.098)			
Transnational background		.488*** (.093)		
Transnational practices			1.361*** (.109)	
Transnational human capital				.985*** (.076)
Female	−.173*** (.033)	−.197*** (.033)	−.178*** (.033)	−.183*** (.033)
Age groups (55+ ref.)				
Age group 15–24	.045 (.083)	.122 (.083)	.113 (.083)	.024 (.083)
Age group 25–39	−.127* (.054)	−.083 (.054)	−.094 (.054)	−.136* (.054)
Age group 40–54	−.221*** (.050)	−.212*** (.050)	−.211*** (.050)	−.223*** (.050)
Educational attainment	.614*** (.053)	.780*** (.052)	.692*** (.052)	.638*** (.053)
Occupation (Manager ref.)				
Self-employed	−.237** (.078)	−.287*** (.077)	−.261*** (.077)	−.232** (.077)
White collar	−.229*** (.067)	−.314*** (.067)	−.268*** (.067)	−.253*** (.067)
Manual worker	−.385*** (.061)	−.532*** (.060)	−.451*** (.061)	−.412*** (.061)
Homemaker	−.340*** (.077)	−.469*** (.076)	−.393*** (.076)	−.376*** (.076)
Unemployed	−.514*** (.080)	−.668*** (.079)	−.569*** (.079)	−.555*** (.079)
Retired	−.227*** (.069)	−.395*** (.068)	−.289*** (.068)	−.275*** (.068)
Student	−.263* (.111)	−.299** (.110)	−.250* (.111)	−.293** (.111)
Ideology	.449*** (.065)	.472*** (.065)	.444*** (.065)	.454*** (.065)
Ideology squared	−.113* (.053)	−.123* (.053)	−.117* (.053)	−.111* (.053)
Household situation	.962*** (.094)	1.061*** (.093)	1.021*** (.094)	.977*** (.094)
Attitudes towards immigrants	.524*** (.056)	.576*** (.056)	.563*** (.056)	.531*** (.056)
Convince others	.022 (.055)	.085 (.054)	.037 (.055)	.050 (.055)
Discuss politics	.366*** (.059)	.527*** (.057)	.432*** (.058)	.413*** (.058)
Urbanization	.129** (.041)	.172*** (.041)	.172*** (.041)	.135** (.041)
T1	−.822*** (.110)	−.955*** (.109)	−.415*** (.118)	−.949*** (.109)
T2	1.065*** (.110)	.912*** (.109)	1.464*** (.119)	.931*** (.109)
Log-likelihood	−15,192.5	−15,316.8	−15,247.5	−15,241.7
McFadden's pseudo r-square	.082	.075	.080	.080

Note: Figures are coefficients of ordinal logit models with country-fixed effects, robust standard errors in parentheses. Country coefficients not shown. Two-tailed test, * p < .05, ** p < .01, *** p < .001. n = 16,672.

Source: Eurobarometer 65.1 (2006).

Overall, the coefficients of the control variables are in line with the findings of existing research. Women are significantly less likely to support EU membership than men. This confirms a previously discovered gender gap in attitudes towards European integration (Nelson and Guth 2000). Interestingly, the age group 40–54 is significantly less likely to support EU membership than the oldest age group, while the younger age groups do not significantly differ from the reference category. This may be due to a life-course effect: people in the age group 40–54 tend to be less flexible and more sensitive in terms of economic insecurity as they might still have to support their children and pay off mortgages. Across all models, all occupational groups are significantly less likely to support EU membership than the reference category of managers. Not surprisingly, the strongest negative effect is found for the unemployed. These findings support the theory that people base their EU attitudes on utilitarian cost–benefit analyses (Gabel 1998b).

People placing themselves at the right side of the political spectrum are slightly more likely to support EU membership, while the small negative effect of 'ideology squared' indicates that people holding extreme political attitudes (both on the left and on the right) are more prone to euroscepticism. People who are more open towards immigration are also more likely to support European integration. In line with the hypothesis of cognitive mobilization (Inglehart 1970), the habit of discussing politics is positively associated with utilitarian EU support. Individuals living in more urban areas are more likely to support EU membership than people living in a rural area.

So far, analyses have shown that individual transnationalism significantly increases the probability of EU support, but they are uninformative with respect to the size of this impact. Figure 4.1 sheds further light on this issue. It presents the change in predicted probability for each answer category dependent on the change in individual transnationalism. The predictions are based on Model 1; all control variables are set to the mean or mode. One can infer from Figure 4.1 that highly transnational individuals (here one standard deviation above the mean) are 15 per cent more likely to say that EU membership is good than people who interact less regularly across borders (one standard deviation below the mean). As shown by the confidence intervals, this change is statistically significant. Interestingly, an increase in transnationalism does not only diminish the probability of answering that EU membership is bad, but also the probability of choosing the neutral category: it shrinks from 33 per cent to 23 per cent. This indicates that highly transnational people are not only more positive, but also less ambiguous in their EU support.

All in all, the evidence presented thus far strongly supports the hypothesis that individual transnationalism significantly increases the likelihood of supporting European integration. Not only the overall transnationalism index,

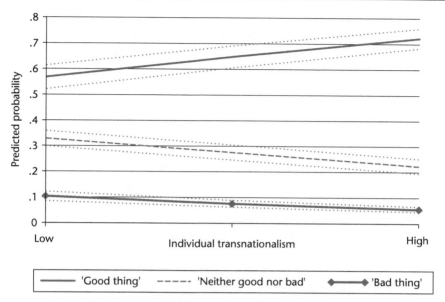

Figure 4.1. Change in predicted probability of EU membership support as individual transnationalism increases
Source: Eurobarometer 65.1 (2006)

but also each of its dimensions has a significant and positive effect on EU membership support.

4.3 Effect of Individual Transnationalism on European Identity

Having analysed EU membership support as the dependent variable in the preceding models, the focus now shifts to European identity. To recapitulate from Chapter 3, European identity is expected to be more stable, and less subject to short-term changes, than EU support. This difference might also matter with respect to the effect of individual transnationalism.

European collective identity entails a cognitive, emotional, and an evaluative dimension (Cram 2012). The analysis here focuses on the cognitive dimension and asks: does individual transnationalism also impact on whether individuals see themselves as Europeans? To answer this question, Models 1–4 in Table 4.1 estimate the effect of individual transnationalism and of each dimension of transnationalism on European identity, using Eurobarometer survey 67.1 (2007) for the EU-27.

The following item operationalizes European identity: 'In the near future, do you perceive yourself as (nationality) only, (nationality) and European, European and (nationality), European only.' The identification item has been frequently included in Eurobarometer surveys, albeit in slightly varying versions (Duchesne and Frognier 1995: 224; see Sinnott 2005: 216 for an overview). The present wording of the question was adopted in 1992 (Sinnott 2005). It is a widely used measure of European identity (Kohli 2000; Citrin and Sides 2004; Fligstein 2008; Risse 2010).

Almost half of all respondents (45 per cent) to Eurobarometer 67.1 hold an exclusive national identity. They consider themselves as national only. Slightly less, 43 per cent, perceive themselves as members of their national community and European, while 7 per cent see themselves as European (first) and members of their national community (second). A diminutive minority of 3 per cent categorize themselves as European only, while 2 per cent of all respondents gave no answer.

It is not of interest here whether respondents belong to the marginal group of people who perceive themselves as first European, then national, or as European only. The key dividing line is whether individuals consider themselves as European in one way or the other, or not at all (Risse 2010: 9), opposing the 'exclusive nationalists' to those who can integrate a European dimension into their identity (Hooghe and Marks 2004). To capture this division, this item is recoded into a dichotomous variable, distinguishing between exclusive national identification ('nationality only') and those who report some sort of European identification. All non-responses are dropped from the analysis. This procedure is in line with previous analyses (Citrin and Sides 2004; Fligstein 2008; Risse 2010). Of the new variable, 46 per cent of the respondents fall into the category of having an exclusive national identification and 54 per cent are coded as having some kind of European identification.[3]

The control variables in this analysis are largely the same as in the models explaining EU membership support. There are a number of exceptions, however. A five-category item relating to how one's household keeps up with bills and credit commitments accounts for respondents' economic situation. Unfortunately, this survey wave does not include any variables referring to cognitive mobilization (Inglehart 1970), nor to immigration attitudes (De Vreese and Boomgaarden 2005). As in the previous analyses, all independent and control variables are standardized to range from 0 to 1. To adequatedly deal with the dichotomous nature of the dependent variable, logit models are applied. Dummy variables for each country and robust standard errors

---

[3] Additional analyses using an ordinal logit model with the un-dichotomized dependent variable were conducted. Results confirmed the findings presented in this chapter.

clustered at the country level account for country-level variance. Multilevel models including higher-level predictors are estimated in Chapter 7.

Next, Table 4.2 presents the results of the logit models predicting European identification. The findings of these analyses largely confirm the findings above. As shown in Model 1, individual transnationalism strongly and significantly increases the likelihood of considering oneself as European. Models 2–4 estimate the effect of each dimension of transnationalism. We can see that each dimension on its own significantly increases the likelihood of perceiving oneself as European. Again, the dimension of transnational practices seems to matter most, but each dimension has the strongest effect in its respective model.

Among the control variables, educational attainment has the greatest impact on the dependent variable. Equally, the better a person's household situation, the more likely (s)he is to identify as European. This indicates that utilitarian considerations also play a role with respect to European identity, which is often portrayed as only relating to 'soft', emotionally driven orientations. The differences between occupational groups are not as clear as in the previous models, however. Now, only retired people, manual workers, and homemakers are signifciantly less inclined than managers to identify as European. In contrast to the previous models, people in the two middle-age groups are now significantly more likely to identify themselves as European than the older reference category. Living in an urban area significantly increases the likelihood of identifying as European.

To capture the substantive effect of transnationalism on EU identity, Figure 4.2 shows the change in predicted probability of European identification relative to an increase in individual transnationalism. The probabilities are predicted on the basis of Model 1, and all control variables are set to their mean or mode. Increasing individual transnationalism from one standard deviation below the mean to one standard deviation above the mean results in a statistically significant increase of European identification of twenty-two percentage points.

4.4 Effect of Individual Transnationalism across Countries

As is shown in more detail in Chapter 5, individual transnationalism varies considerably across countries. Moreover, existing research on public attitudes towards European integration has shown that the integration process is framed quite differently across countries (Díez Medrano 2003). Thus, in different member states, different individual-level predictors are crucial, and sometimes they even have contrasting effects. Therefore, it might well be that the effect of individual transnationalism does not hold in all EU member

Table 4.2. Effect of individual transnationalism on European identification

	Model 1 b (se)	Model 2 b (se)	Model 3 b (se)	Model 4 b (se)
Individual transnationalism	2.850*** (.168)			
Transnational background		1.094*** (.104)		
Transnational practices			1.854*** (.110)	
Transnational human capital				1.256*** (.118)
Female	−.121** (.042)	−.155*** (.043)	−.121** (.043)	−.142*** (.041)
Age groups (55+ ref.)				
Age group 15–24	.163 (.133)	.240 (.145)	.186 (.133)	.204 (.142)
Age group 25–39	.269** (.096)	.316** (.102)	.275** (.094)	.299** (.101)
Age group 40–54	.222** (.077)	.232** (.081)	.217** (.077)	.230** (.079)
Educational attainment	.815*** (.073)	1.030*** (.073)	.864*** (.071)	.911*** (.075)
Occupation (Manager ref.)				
Self-employed	−.104 (.066)	−.186** (.066)	−.110 (.066)	−.159* (.065)
White collar	.014 (.091)	−.124 (.091)	.001 (.091)	−.074 (.088)
Manual worker	−.201** (.077)	−.405*** (.073)	−.204** (.077)	−.329*** (.072)
Homemaker	−.158* (.079)	−.362*** (.070)	−.150* (.076)	−.312*** (.071)
Unemployed	−.208 (.112)	−.392*** (.115)	−.192 (.112)	−.346** (.113)
Retired	−.278*** (.064)	−.496*** (.066)	−.275*** (.063)	−.445*** (.064)
Student	−.078 (.122)	−.115 (.130)	−.033 (.120)	−.159 (.123)
Ideology	−.030 (.103)	−.030 (.109)	−.041 (.102)	−.041 (.104)
Ideology squared	−.177** (.063)	−.148* (.065)	−.166** (.063)	−.156* (.062)
Household situation	.473*** (.122)	.583*** (.121)	.458*** (.123)	.527*** (.123)
Urbanization	.238*** (.052)	.320*** (.061)	.275*** (.054)	.296*** (.059)
Constant	−.351** (.124)	−.177 (.134)	−.337** (.127)	−.136 (.130)
Log-likelihood	−11475.8	−11738.6	−11555.8	−11651.1
McFadden Pseudo r-square	.114	.094	.108	.108

Note: Figures are coefficients of logit models with country-fixed effects, robust standard errors in parentheses. Country coefficients not shown. Two-tailed test, * $p < .05$, ** $p < .01$, *** $p < .001$. $n = 18,882$.

Source: Eurobarometer 67.1 (2007).

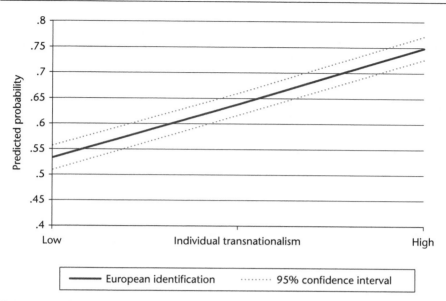

Figure 4.2. Change in predicted probability of European identification as individual transnationalism increases

Source: Eurobarometer 67.1 (2007)

states. So far, analyses covered the pooled data of EU-25 (Eurobarometer 65.1) and EU-27 (Eurobarometer 67.1). Dummy variables for each country and robust standard errors clustered at the country-level accounted for cross-national heteregoneity. To ascertain whether the results are robust across countries, Table 4.3 shows the effect of individual transnationalism on EU membership support and on European identification for each country, thereby controlling for the same variables as above. Considering the small sample size and the fact that the direction of the effect is already known, effect significance is calculated using a one-tailed test. For a better comparison of the coefficients, all statistically significant effects are visualized in Figure 4.3.

In most countries, the positive effect of individual transnationalism on EU membership support and European identification is strong and statistically significant. In the models predicting European identification, the coefficient is significant in all but two countries (Cyprus and Latvia), whereas the effect on EU membership support is insignificant in six countries (Cyprus, Estonia, Italy, Lithuania, Malta, and Poland). To see whether this difference is due to the three control variables that could not be included in the models on European identification (attitude towards immigrants, discussing politics, and convincing others), additional models on EU membership support without these three variables are estimated (results not shown). In this case, the coefficient for individual transnationalism becomes signicant in the case of

Table 4.3. Effect of individual transnationalism across countries

Country	Effect of individual transnationalism on EU membership support (Eurobarometer 67.1)	n	Effect of individual transnationalism on European identification (Eurobarometer 67.1)	n
Austria	1.936***	724	3.04***	812
Belgium	2.734***	835	4.96***	842
Bulgaria			2.59*	581
Cyprus	1.109	301	1.25	295
Czech Republic	1.424**	771	2.72***	879
Denmark	1.427***	838	2.56***	891
Estonia	0.852	550	3.03***	666
Finland	1.870***	816	3.99***	808
France	1.956***	738	3.80***	804
Germany	2.136***	1250	3.55***	1361
Greece	0.915*	793	2.81***	713
Hungary	1.219*	634	3.19***	712
Ireland	2.128*	570	2.62***	651
Italy	0.613	446	4.55***	628
Latvia	2.182***	559	0.87	591
Lithuania	0.882	469	1.30*	477
Luxembourg	2.019*	357	4.64***	349
Malta	1.136	249	1.86*	245
The Netherlands	0.987*	897	2.30***	875
Poland	0.941	595	3.33***	608
Portugal	2.147**	564	3.21***	607
Romania			1.75**	525
Slovakia	1.794***	770	3.66***	818
Slovenia	1.071*	628	3.42***	598
Spain	2.584**	560	1.41*	665
Sweden	1.461***	869	2.63***	919
United Kingdom	1.958***	889	2.50***	989

Note: Figures are coefficients of ordinal logit models predicting EU membership support and logit models predicting European identification. One-tailed test, * $p < .05$, ** $p < .01$, *** $p < .001$.

Source: Eurobarometer 65.1 (2006), Eurobarometer 67.1 (2007).

Poland and Lithuania, while it remains insignificant in the other four countries. It therefore seems that indvidual transnationalism explains European identity slightly better than EU membership support. Taking into consideration that European identity is likely to be more stable than evaluations of a country's EU membership, it is plausible that short-term factors confound the relationship between transnationalism and EU membership support, whereas the relationship between transnationalism and European identity is less affected by them.

When comparing the cross-country pattern of the significant effects on both dependent variables, it appears that they do not go in the same direction. In fact, their correlation coefficient is low: .27. The country where individual transnationalism has the strongest effect on both EU membership support and European identification is Belgium. In Luxembourg, it has a very strong effect on European identification, but its impact on EU membership support is

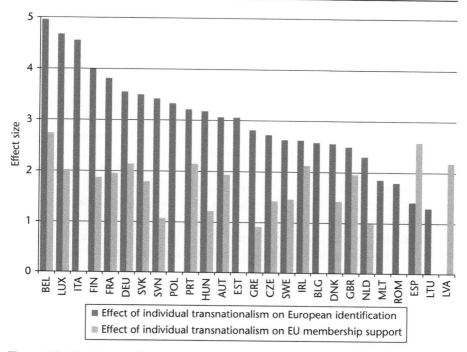

Figure 4.3. Significant effects of individual transnationalism on orientations towards European integration across countries

comparable to several other member states. In Italy, the effect of individual transnationalism on European identification is very large and significant, but it is not significant with respect to EU membership support. On the other hand, Spain is the country where individual transnationalism has the second strongest effect on EU membership support and the second weakest effect on European identification. In Latvia, individual transnationalism has a strong effect on EU membership support, but it does not signifcantly increase European identification. One pattern can be distinguished, however: with the exception of Italy for EU membership support, all the countries where individual transnationalism fails to exert a significant effect are states that have joined in the last enlargement round. This observation suggests that only a couple of years after EU accession, other factors dominate public opinion towards European integration. However, as we shall see in Chapter 7, it is not EU membership duration as such, but rather the level of globalization of a country that determines the extent to which individual transnationalism influences orientations towards European integration.

4.5 Conclusion

After more than half a century of European integration, do we find empirical support for Deutsch's hypothesis that increased transnational interaction promotes support for European integration? This chapter tried to answer this question by analysing the impact of individual transnationalism on European identification and support for EU membership. Individual transnationalism was conceptualized as a tri-dimensional phenomenon encompassing transnational background, transnational practices, and transnational human capital, whereas EU support referred to EU membership endorsement, and European identity entailed identification as European. This chapter has provided an empirical test of Hypothesis 1, that highly transnational individuals are more likely to support European integration and to feel European than people scoring low on transnationalism. It has done so by testing the effect of individual transnationalism (and its three dimensions) on EU membership support and European identification in an analysis of Eurobarometer survey waves 65.1 (2006) and 67.1 (2007) in the EU-25 and EU-27, respectively.

The results of this chapter provide strong support for Deutsch's transactionalist theory that transnational interactions generate a 'we-feeling' and support for further regional integration. In all analyses, individual transnationalism had a strong and highly significant positive effect on the two dependent variables. This relationship remains robust across most European member states.

There are, of course, certain limitations to the conclusions drawn from the analyses presented in this chapter. First, since cross-sectional data only allow between-individual comparisons, one cannot say with full certainty that, as individuals change their degree of transnationalism, they also become more supportive of European integration. Second, there is the possibility of reversed causation. It may well be that individuals are interacting on a transnational level *because* they are pro-European or, more generally, have a more cosmopolitan outlook (Eilstrup-Sangiovanni 2006), and not the other way around, as is argued in this book. To alleviate this criticism, the effect of each dimension of individual transnationalism was estimated separately. By doing so, it was possible to isolate the effect of transnational background (which cannot be predicted by attitudes) on EU support. Transnational background does have a significant positive effect on EU membership support and on European identification, albeit smaller than the effect of transnational practices and transnational human capital. This finding indicates that there is a causal link from individual transnationalism to EU support even though there may additionally be some effect in the other direction in the case of transnational practices and human capital.

One could thus stop here and suggest that Deutsch's theory is correct. However, in view of the development of public opinion on European integration in the past decades, the findings of this chapter raise further questions. Considering the strong and highly significant positive effect of individual transnationalism on citizen orientations towards European integration, why is the upsurge in transnational interactions of the past decades not paralleled by an increase in aggregate EU support and European identity? Why, after half a century of European institution building, have Europeans become more transnational, but not necessarily more European-minded? The following chapters shed light on these questions. Chapter 5 tests Hypothesis 2 of this book by analysing the individual-level and macro-level predictors of individual transnationalism. It shows that individual transnationalism is highly stratified along socio-economic lines and concentrated among a small elite of young, highly educated Europeans from rich countries. In other words, while transnational interactions have certainly increased, they have not spread to the average European citizen. Next, Chapter 6 provides an empirical test of Hypotheses 3–5 by zooming in on the dimension of transnational practices, and argues that not all transactions are successful in generating EU support. It shows that the effectiveness of transnational interactions depends on their purpose and scope. Finally, in line with Hypothesis 6, Chapter 7 goes even further by emphasizing the negative externalities of increased transactions on those Europeans that do not interact transnationally themselves. It shows that in more globalized countries, people with low levels of transnationalism are even more likely to become eurosceptics than in countries that are less globalized.

5

The Social Stratification of Individual Transnationalism in Europe

> *Even if they are less dependent on passports, visas, and residential and labour permissions, most people remain 'nationalized', they see their life chances as depending on the territorialized systems of social sharing, identity and political participation rights and on the monopolistic production of related public goods by national and local authorities.*[1]
>
> —Stefano Bartolini

The preceding chapter provided empirical support for Deutsch's transaction-alist theory by showing that individual transnationalism is positively related to both EU support and European identity. People who frequently interact across national borders are also more likely to endorse EU membership and to see themselves as European. Yet, we do not know the extent of individual transnationalism in the EU.

To better understand whether the expectations about the emergence of a truly integrated European society are being met, it is necessary to answer the following two sets of questions: first, to what extent can we speak of a 'transnationalization of the masses' (De Swaan 1995: 13)? Have transnational mobility and interactions become an everyday practice of most Europeans or are they still out of the ordinary? Do all Europeans take part in transnational interactions to the same extent, or are there pronounced differences across society? In other words, who are the transnationally active Europeans? Second, (how) does this differ across countries? Is transnationalism a genuinely European phenomenon, or does it take place only in certain countries? If the latter is the case, which societies are especially transnational?

It is important to study these issues for several reasons. First, the answer to these questions directly ties into the overarching topic of this book: to what

---

[1] Bartolini 2005: 399.

extent can we confirm Deutsch's seminal transactionalist theory, not only for elites, but also for the general European population? For transactionalist theory to be correct, individual transnationalism needs to have become an integral part of European society rather than a niche phenomenon. In fact, the distribution of transnational activities across society might be the missing piece in the puzzle of increased transnational interactions and relatively low EU support and identification that is the main question motivating this research. Second, this chapter also contributes to the burgeoning field of political sociology of European integration (Favell and Guiraudon 2011; Kauppi 2013) by asking how successful European integration has been in forging true Europeans who overcome national boundaries in their daily lives and in their minds. Third, this chapter provides the first systematic empirical analysis of the individual and country-level predictors of transnational behaviour of the entire European population. While interest in this question has risen in recent years, existing studies focus on particular groups, such as intra-European migrants (Recchi and Favell 2009), university students (Finger 2011; Lörz and Krawietz 2011), or retirement migrants (Casado-Díaz 2006).

The central argument of this chapter is that the extent to which Europeans become transnationally active is strongly stratified across society and is highly dependent on the availability of opportunities and resources. This expectation was formalized in Hypothesis 2 in Chapter 3. The present chapter further elaborates on this idea by developing and testing more detailed hypotheses on how exactly resources and opportunities are linked to individual transnationalism, and how this differs across EU member states. The empirical analyses presented in this chapter provide strong evidence for the argument that individual transnationalism is a niche phenomenon. Importantly, this study shows that the transnationals are predominantly highly educated, young, and in prestigious jobs and that they generally come from richer member states.

The following section discusses existing research on the scale and scope of transnational interactions in the European Union and provides some descriptive findings. Next, a number of hypotheses on the within- and between-country distribution of individual transnationalism are developed. An empirical analysis of Eurobarometer data from 2006 and 2007 puts these hypotheses under empirical scrutiny. The final section of this chapter discusses the implications for the emergence of a European social space.

5.1 Individual Transnationalism in the European Union

Existing research suggests that individual transnationalism is far from being a mainstream phenomenon in Europe. To be sure, opportunities to interact transnationally have increased tremendously over the past few decades, in the EU more than anywhere else. As discussed in more detail in Chapter 2, European integration has rendered intra-European cross-border movements more feasible than ever. Additionally, technological advances in the fields of telecommunications, IT, and transport have considerably decreased transaction costs. Consequently, Europeans can easily communicate across borders, travel abroad, and 'set up shop' in another EU member state.

Notwithstanding these developments, very few Europeans actually take the opportunity to become transnationally active on a regular basis (Fligstein 2008). Andreotti and colleagues (2013) show that members of the urban upper and middle classes are remarkably rooted in their local communities (see also Gustafson 2009). As we shall see in the empirical analyses of this chapter, these people are among the most likely Europeans to interact across borders. From this follows that even the most Europeanized individuals in the EU still lead relatively national lives.

In what follows, I discuss the distribution of various aspects of individual transnationalism, and I show some descriptive statistics. Let us first examine how many Europeans have lived in another EU member state. The decision to go and live in a different member state is the exception rather than the rule among Europeans. In fact, statistics on intra-European migration, a core aspect of transnational interaction, show that less than 3 per cent of EU citizens are registered in another EU country (Juravle et al. 2013). This is also reflected in the Eurobarometer survey data that form the empirical basis of this book. In 2006, only 7 per cent of all EU citizens had *ever* lived in another EU member state to work, study, or retire for a duration of three months or longer (European Commission 2006). To a certain extent, the low number of intra-European migrants is due to the fact that growing economic convergence among European member states and economic growth disincentivizes cross-state migration (Werner 2001; Recchi 2008a).

In contrast to long-term stays abroad, scholars observe a sharp increase in short-term travel (Díez Medrano 2010a) and hybrid forms of mobility in the EU (Schneider and Meil 2008). Nonetheless, the European Union is far from being a fully integrated social space. While political and economic borders have been largely removed, the confines of domestic European societies remain relatively intact.

As shown in Figure 5.1, short-term trips to other EU member states are more widespread than long-term sojourns abroad. This is not surprising because it takes much less effort to travel to a different EU member state for a short trip than to move there for an extended period of time. Nonetheless, these trips have not yet become common practice in the European Union. In 2006, almost two-thirds of the European population had not visited another EU member state in the previous twelve months. About a quarter had done so on

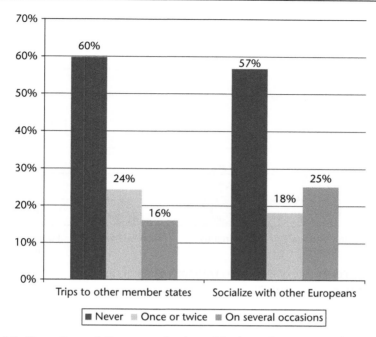

Figure 5.1. Percentage of Europeans having visited another EU member state and having socialized with other Europeans in past year
Source: Eurobarometer 65.1 (2006)

one or two occasions, while only 16 per cent of all Europeans had visited other EU member states on several occasions in the previous year. In sum, these data show that as of yet, neither long-term stays nor short-term visits abroad have become common practice in the European Union.

Considering that our interest here is in a more encompassing phenomenon rather than purely physical border crossing, it is also pertinent to analyse the extent to which people interact transnationally without leaving their country. Even with this broader interpretation of individual transnationalism, the percentage of transnationally active Europeans is not much higher. As can be seen in Figure 5.1, more than half of all Europeans had not socialized with citizens from other EU member states in the previous year. While 18 per cent had done so once or twice, a mere quarter of the European population had socialized with other Europeans on several occasions.

When it comes to international friendships (see Figure 5.2), two-thirds of all Europeans do not have any friends from abroad. While 17 per cent have friends from the EU, 5 per cent have friends from countries outside of the EU. Finally, 11 per cent of all Europeans have friends from both other EU and non-EU countries.

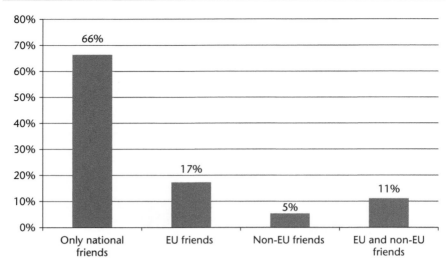

Figure 5.2. Percentage of Europeans with international friends
Source: Eurobarometer 67.1 (2007)

To sum up the argument so far, the figures presented here illustrate that even after over half a century of European integration, most Europeans lead predominantly national lives. This raises the question of who the highly transnational people are, and how they differ from the rest of the population. To this end, the following section develops a set of hypotheses on the individual characteristics of highly transnational people that are then tested in empirical analysis.

5.2 Who is Transnational?

The extent to which Europeans take part in transnational interactions seems to be unequally distributed across society. Europeans differ considerably with respect to individual transnationalism. Some Europeans, such as the ones that Favell (2008) called the 'Eurostars', have adopted a truly European lifestyle and have overcome national borders. In contrast, many others rarely operate on a transnational level, and their daily lives remain largely untouched by European integration. The phenomenon that is of interest here is an individual one—the extent to which a person is transnationally active. It is therefore to be expected that individual transnationalism is to a large extent determined by individual characteristics. What are the traits that make a person more transnational than others? The following section proposes several predictors of transnationalism: socio-economic differences, age, urbanization, and proximity to an intra-European border.

5.2.1 Socio-economic Differences

Transnational interaction has often been portrayed as an elite phenomenon (Sklair 2001; Calhoun 2002; Fligstein 2008). This is reflected in the titles of two influential contributions to scholarly literature. Sklair (2001) speaks of the 'Transnational capitalist class', while Calhoun (2002) ascribes a certain 'class consciousness' to frequent travellers. Indeed, individual transnationalism seems to be highly stratified along socio-economic lines (Mau and Mewes 2009). In a study of intra-European movers, Favell and Recchi (2011) find that upper-class movers are over-represented, while members of the working class are under-represented. They conclude that 'spatial mobility opportunities are still dominantly monopolized by upper and upper middle classes in Europe' (Favell and Recchi 2011: 74). In short, socio-economic status seems to be an important predictor of individual transnationalism. Three aspects determine socio-economic status: a person's level of education, their occupation, and their income. Due to data limitations, the relationship between income and individual transnationalism cannot be analysed here. I therefore develop two hypotheses with respect to educational attainment and occupation.

There are three arguments as to why education should play a role with respect to transnationalism. Highly educated people have (1) greater opportunities, (2) better skills, and (3) more resources to interact transnationally. First, formal education provides manifold opportunities to meet people from other countries or to study abroad. For example, the Life Long Learning Programme of the European Commission offers several avenues to work, study, or travel in a different EU member state while in education. The bulk of this programme targets people who are in higher education (Kuhn 2012b). People who stay longer in education have more opportunities to take part in these programmes (Anheier and Falkenhain 2012).

Second, certain skills ease transnational interaction. Most obviously, foreign language skills are a great asset when interacting across national borders. As Gerhards (2012: 13) observes, people who speak foreign languages 'more easily come into contact with citizens of other countries and also . . . do business and diplomacy, cooperate academically, organize protests across national borders or enter into romantic relations with them'. This is why Gerhards (2012) speaks of transnational linguistic capital. It is not only multilingualism that makes transnational interaction easier—other skills also matter. Koehn and Rosenau (2002) distinguish between transnational analytical, emotional, creative/imaginative, and behavioural competences, as well as functional adroitness. According to the authors, these competences help explain 'why some people are more effective than others in forging meaningful trans-national solidarities, negotiating and benefiting from the intensifying experi-ence of globalization, and waging successful transnational campaigns' (Koehn and Rosenau 2002: 105). While formal education is not the only venue for acquiring these skills, it does provide ample opportunities to do so.

Finally, considering that higher educational attainment increases the chances to find a well-paid job, highly educated people also possess more resources to interact across countries. In line with this reasoning, Mau and Mewes (2009) find in an analysis of the German population that educational attainment is a strong predictor of border-crossing activities. In an empirical study of German secondary school children using the GSOEP data, Gerhards and Hans (2013) find that educational differences manifest themselves as early as the teenage years: German children attending *Gymnasium* (secondary schools that prepare for university) were found to be significantly and consid-erably more likely to embark on a high school exchange than children in other schools.

Consequently, it is to be expected that highly educated people are more transnationally active than people with low educational attainment. I refine Hypothesis 2 formulated in Chapter 3 as follows:

Hyphothesis 2.1: Highly educated people are more transnationally active than people with low educational attainment.

Many transnational interactions and mobilities are motivated by professional reasons. Therefore, above and beyond educational differences, people's occu-pation might channel them into more or less transnational lifestyles. Employ-ees of multinational companies such as Procter & Gamble often work in culturally diverse teams, academics present their work at international con-ferences and are part of an international research community, and inter-national tourism offers many job opportunities. Unfortunately, the data provided by Eurobarometer do not allow for a fine-grained categorization into professions that offer more or fewer opportunities to interact across borders. Therefore, I opt for a less sophisticated analysis by positing that people in more prestigious jobs are more transnational than people in less prestigious jobs, and than people who are not in the workforce. Arguably, a manager of a multinational company has greater transnational exposure than a homemaker or a manual worker. To be sure, the migrant domestic workers who take care of the elderly in West European member states (Van Hooren 2012) and the famous 'Polish Plumbers' suggest something else. However, these migrants are often highly skilled and take up these jobs only temporarily. Moreover, many domestic caretakers have only limited possibilities to leave their workplace and to interact with people from the host country.

This leads me to formulate the following hypothesis:

Hyphothesis 2.2: People in higher-status occupations are more transnationally active.

5.2.2 Age

There are good reasons to expect younger people to be more transnationally active than older people. Both cohort effects and life cycle effects might be at work here. First, younger cohorts grow up in a more transnational society than older ones. Due to this early socialization, living or travelling abroad might come much more naturally to them than to older cohorts. Moreover, career paths and life courses tend to be much less secure today than in the past (Buchholz et al. 2009), and younger generations feel greater pressure to stay physically mobile and flexible in order to advance their careers or to stay employed. Consequently, Edmunds and Turner (2005) argue that the second half of the twentieth century has witnessed the emergence of 'global generations'. In fact, the documented increase of transnational networks and mobility in the past decades (Díez Medrano 2010a) points to a cohort effect, capturing 'stable differences among birth cohorts due to the historical circumstances of their development' (Jung 2008: 583). In other words, the differences across age groups are to some extent part and parcel of a greater trend towards the transnationalization of everyday life. Such a development was predicted by Inglehart's (1977) post materialist hypothesis.

It is possible that in addition to this effect, there is also a life course effect. Younger people are at a stage of their lives where they tend to be more transnational. They tend to have fewer private and professional responsibilities, which makes it easier for them to travel and to move to another country. They might also be more open to new experiences and other cultures and less risk-averse. This might change, however, as they grow older, settle down, start a family, buy a house, and eventually also become less fit and healthy. To be sure, many retired Europeans nowadays experience what could be called a second youth, travelling extensively and even relocating to another country in search of a better quality of life. This phenomenon of retirement migration has in fact been widely discussed in the scholarly literature (King et al. 2000; Gustafson 2001). Moreover, elderly people increasingly migrate to be close to their working children abroad (Warnes and Williams 2007). However, empirical studies have shown that retired people still migrate less than younger people (Bradley and Longino 2009).

To sum up the argument so far, younger people are more likely to be transnationally active not only because they were socialized in a more transnational epoch, but also because they are at a point in their lives where transnational mobility and interaction is more likely to take place. One can therefore expect that the extent to which an individual is transnationally active depends on their age.

Hypothesis 2.3: Younger people are more transnationally active than older people.

5.2.3 *Urbanization*

Besides individual characteristics, the urbanization of the neighbourhood might influence individual transnationalism. Research has shown that trans-nationalism is a primarily urban phenomenon (Sassen 2001; Smith 2001; Favell 2008; Andreotti et al. 2013). This is due to self-selection as well as to opportunities provided in the neighbourhood. Cities tend to attract more foreign people by offering job and recreational opportunities. They also provide a good infrastructure that facilitates transnational contacts and mobility. Therefore, it is to be expected that people who live in more urban areas are also more transnational. They might have moved to the city in order to lead a transnational lifestyle in the first place, for example, by working for a multi-national company. Second, city dwellers might be more exposed to foreign people, ideas, and cultures, and therefore become more readily involved in transnational interactions and mobility. Finally, owing to better facilities, such as international airports or frequent and fast train connections, people in urban areas might find it easier to travel abroad and to interact with citizens of other EU member states. This expectation is captured in the following hypothesis:

Hypothesis 2.4: People living in urban areas are more transnationally active.

5.2.4 *Proximity to a national border*

Finally, a crucial predictor of transnational interactions might be the distance to a national border. Obviously, people living close to a national border have better opportunities to become transnationally active than people living further away. Border residents can cross the border on a daily basis to do some basic shopping in the neighbouring country, to work or go to school there, or to enjoy restaurants and leisure activities. In fact, for intra-European border residents, it might sometimes be easier to run errands across the border than in their own country. These frequent physical mobilities are also likely to result in more frequent virtual interactions with people and institutions from the neighbouring country. In an empirical study of transnational interactions in German border regions, Roose (2010) finds that the interaction patterns of German border residents remain predominantly national. In general, German border residents tend to choose the products, services, and jobs provided in

Germany. They take advantage of the options offered across the border, however, if they are cheaper or of better quality than at home. Thus, while it would be too far-fetched to expect intra-European border residents to be entirely transnationalized, they seem to operate on a transnational level more frequently than people living further away from the border. This idea is captured in the following hypothesis:

Hypothesis 2.5: People living close to a national border are more transnational than the rest of the population.

5.3 Empirical Analysis of Individual Predictors

Hypotheses 2.1–2.5 are tested using a statistical analysis of survey data stemming from the Eurobarometer waves 65.1 (2006) and 67.1 (2007). The data for 2006 cover the EU-25, while the data from 2007 also include Bulgaria and Romania.

The transnationalism indices that have been developed in the previous chapter are now used as the dependent variable, albeit in a slightly altered version: given that transnational background (i.e. being born abroad or having at least one parent who was born abroad) is truly exogenous, it does not make sense to include it into the dependent variable. Therefore, the indices used as dependent variables in this chapter exclusively refer to transnational practices and to transnational human capital.[2] The exact items used for the transnationalism index in Eurobarometer wave 65.1 are slightly different to the ones used in Eurobarometer 67.1, but they are highly comparable. In Eurobarometer 65.1, the transnationalism index has a mean of .28 and a standard deviation of .26 on a scale ranging from 0 to 1, while in Eurobarometer 67.1, the index has a mean of .17 and a standard deviation of .22 on a range from 0 to 1. Both indices are reliable and reflect one latent variable. Since both indices are continuous, OLS regression with dummy variables for each country and country-robust standard errors is used. The country dummies absorb all country-level heterogeneity.

To test the hypothesis that more highly educated people are more transnational, educational attainment is measured using a three-category variable: respondents having left school at age 15 or lower, and those not having had any full-time education are coded 1. People who left school at age 16–19 are in category 2, while category 3 includes all those who left full-time education at age 20 or older. To test Hypothesis 2.2, that people in higher-status jobs are

---

[2] Additional models that are not shown here used the original transnationalism indices as dependent variables and strongly confirmed the findings presented here.

more transnational, the following occupational group variables are included as dummy variables: manager (as reference category), white-collar worker, blue-collar worker, homemaker, retiree, unemployed, and student. Four age groups account for a potential age effect: age group 55 and older serves as the reference category; age groups 15–24, 25–39, and 40–54 are each included as dummy variables. To test the hypothesis that individuals living in more urban areas are more transnational, a three-category variable measuring the urbanization of respondents' residence is included in the analysis.

Finally, the impact of living in a border district is assessed in a separate analysis using data for Germany and France only. These two countries were chosen because they are large enough to sensibly distinguish between border and core districts and because their statistical offices provide reliable contextual data at the district level. To operationalize border residence, a binary variable distinguishes between border and core districts at the level of NUTS-3 regions, that is, the ninety-four continental *départements* in France and over 400 *Landkreise* in Germany. Only districts that directly border another state are included in the category of border districts. This means that coastal districts and German independent cities[3] that are surrounded by a border district are not coded as border districts.[4] Another issue to consider is the special case of Swiss borders. As Switzerland is not part of the European Union, one might argue that transformations induced by European integration do not apply to areas bordering Switzerland, and that they should not be considered in the analysis. However, Switzerland signed the Schengen Treaty in 2004—two years before this survey was carried out. Next to the euro, the Schengen Treaty is likely to be the treaty that has the greatest impact on the everyday lives of border residents thus far, as it makes border control redundant. Therefore, districts bordering Switzerland are coded as border districts as well. This procedure yields twenty-eight German and twenty-one French border districts.

A dichotomous variable (1 for being a female respondent) controls for potential differences between men and women. As discussed in further detail above, the two variables referring to transnational background (being born abroad and having at least one foreign-born parent) have been omitted from the transnationalism index in this analysis as they are truly exogenous. Rather, they are included as control variables. One might argue that certain attitudinal orientations, such as attitudes towards immigrants, could also be

---

[3] German independent cities (*Kreisfreie Städte*) are a particularity of the German administrative system, and in some cases there is some ambiguity with respect to the coding. An example is the city of Trier: the district of Trier-Saarburg forms a circle around it. While Trier does not directly border another country, some parts of the district of Trier-Saarburg are farther from the border than Trier. In the present analysis, they are not coded as border districts.

[4] In an additional analysis, coastal districts and independent cities surrounded by a border district were coded as border districts. The results of this analysis were not substantially different from the results shown here.

related to transnational interactions. However, as they might themselves be influenced by educational attainment (Hainmueller and Hiscox 2007), and by transnational experiences, they are not included in the models.[5]

The analyses of border and core districts in Germany and France control for unemployment rate and GDP per capita at the district level. These data are obtained from the Regional database of the German Statistical Offices of the Federation and the Länder (2006b, 2006c) as well as from the French Institute of Statistics and Economic Studies (INSEE 2005, 2006). Additionally, the ratio of foreign residents in a NUTS-3 district is controlled for (Statistical Offices of the Federation and the Länder 2006a; INSEE 2007). In the German case, a dichotomous variable accounts for living in the former GDR.

Table 5.1 presents the results of the statistical analyses. All models are estimated using OLS with country dummies and country-robust standard errors. This means that all country-level heterogeneity is accounted for. Before discussing the estimated models, it is worth noting that the model including the country dummy variables alone explains 19 per cent of the variance in transnationalism in Eurobarometer 65.1, and 18 per cent of the variance in Eurobarometer 67.1. Thus, slightly less than a fifth of the variance in individual transnationalism in the European Union can be explained by country-level differences (be they composition effects, such as different demographic compositions across countries, or genuine macro-level differences, such as GDP per capita). These differences are studied in further detail in Section 5.4. Models were estimated in a step-wise procedure, that is, by including an additional block of predictor variables in each new model. For the sake of brevity, Table 5.1 presents only the final model including all independent variables. All other models can be found in Table A1 in the appendix. In terms of the explained variance, the model using data from Eurobarometer 65.1 (2006) performs slightly better. It explains 38 per cent of the variance, while the model using data of Eurobarometer 67.1 explains 34 per cent of the variance. To further illustrate the effect of the independent variables that have a significant impact on transnationalism, Figure 5.3 shows the change in transnationalism due to these variables.

The final model shows that educational attainment has a strong, positive, and significant effect on the dependent variable: having a higher educational outcome increases the transnationalism index by roughly 9 per cent[6] in Eurobarometer 65.1 and by 6 per cent in Eurobarometer 67.1. This variable has the strongest effect in both models. The relationship is highly robust

---

[5] Additional analyses also accounted for the effect of political ideology using one's self-placement on the left–right scale. Its effect was negligible in terms of effect size, significance, and explained variance. It has therefore been excluded from the final models.

[6] Given that the transnationalism index runs from 0 to 1, the coefficients can be interpreted in terms of change in per cent.

Table 5.1. Effect of individual-level predictors on individual transnationalism

	EB 65.1 (2006)		EB 67.1 (2007)	
	b	se	b	se
Educational attainment	.087***	(.002)	.054***	(.002)
Occupation (manager ref.)				
Student	−.058***	(.010)	−.024*	(.010)
Manual worker	−.146***	(.006)	−.105***	(.005)
Self-employed	−.048***	(.008)	−.041***	(.007)
White collar	−.084***	(.007)	−.070***	(.006)
Homemaker	−.132***	(.007)	−.106***	(.006)
Unemployed	−.154***	(.008)	−.092***	(.006)
Retired	−.165***	(.007)	−.110***	(.005)
Age groups (55+ ref.)				
Age group 15–24	.065***	(.007)	.030***	(.006)
Age group 25–39	.041***	(.005)	.026***	(.004)
Age group 40–54	.012**	(.005)	.004	(.003)
Urbanization	.020***	(.002)	.022***	(.001)
Foreign-born	.116***	(.014)	.100***	(.011)
Foreign parent	.062***	(.006)	.089***	(.005)
Female	−.035***	(.003)	−.021***	(.002)
Constant	.178***	(.011)	.061***	(.008)
[Country dummies not shown]				
Log-likelihood	3317.8		8508.6	
Explained variance	.38		.34	
n	21,898		24,975	

Note: Figures are coefficients of OLS models with country-fixed effects, robust standard errors in parentheses. Country coefficients not shown. Two-tailed test, * $p < .05$, ** $p < .01$, *** $p < .001$.

Source: Eurobarometer 65.1 (2006) and Eurobarometer 67.1 (2007).

across models and across countries, also when using dummy variables for each category. In all model specifications (see Table A1 in the appendix), the effect size and significance remain high. Separate analyses for each country show that the effect of education is significant at the $p < .001$ level in each country. When including education as the only individual-level predictor of trans-nationalism, the explained variance increases by more than 10 per cent when compared with the model including country dummies only. Taking into consideration that Eurobarometer provides a relatively rough measure of educational attainment, it has very high explanatory power. These findings thus provide strong support for the hypothesis that highly educated Europeans are more transnational.

To further analyse socio-economic differences, occupational indicators are included in the model. All occupational groups are significantly less transnational than managers, which serves as the reference category. This indicates that in addition to an educational effect, different occupations influence whether people lead more or less transnational lives. Retirees, the unemployed, and manual workers are the least transnational. Retired individuals are 17 per cent less transnational in Eurobarometer 65.1, and 11 per cent

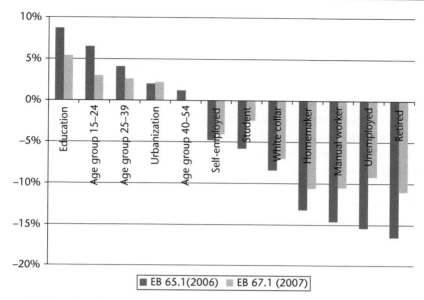

Figure 5.3. Statistically significant change in individual transnationalism due to independent variables

Source: Eurobarometer 65.1 (2006) and Eurobarometer 67.1 (2007)

less transnational in Eurobarometer 67.1. Among respondents in employment, the contrast is most pronounced between managers and manual workers. People in the latter group are roughly 14 per cent less transnational than managers in Eurobarometer 65.1, and about 11 per cent less so in Eurobarometer 67.1. All in all, the findings on occupational differences provide strong and ample support for Hypothesis 2.2 that people in better jobs are also more transnational.

Turning to Hypothesis 2.3, the model estimates the effect of age on individual transnationalism using four age groups: age group 15–24, age group 25–39, age group 40–54, and age group 55 and older (reference category). With the exception of the age group 40–54 in 2007, all younger age groups are significantly more transnational than respondents in the reference group. In fact, respondents in the youngest group are 7 per cent (Eurobarometer 65.1) and 3 per cent (Eurobarometer 67.1) more transnational than respondents who are 55 years and older. It is interesting to consider the results of Model 3 presented in Table A1 in the appendix. This model predicts transnationalism based solely on age, that is, not accounting for education and occupation. In this model, the effect sizes and significance of age are considerably greater than when including education and occupation into the analysis. This suggests that the difference in transnational activity across age groups is mainly due to educational expansion: a greater proportion of younger cohorts is highly educated and thus better able to interact across borders. Moreover, when comparing the explained variance of Models 1, 3, and 4 in Table A1 in the appendix, it becomes clear that age on its own explains far less of the variance in transnationalism than education and occupation. Thus, while there is some empirical support for the hypothesis that younger people are more transnational than older ones, it is not as robust as the effect of socio-economic status. In fact, it seems to be mediated by the latter. This suggests that the age effect is a cohort rather than a life course effect: younger cohorts are more transnational than older ones mainly because they tend to be more highly educated. This suggests that future generations will become increasingly transnational.

Next, the analysis tests the hypothesis that people living in more urban areas are more transnationally active (see Table 5.1). It does so by including the three-category variable that refers to the urbanization of residence. While the effect of urbanization is significant, its effect size is relatively small: holding everything else equal, people in more urban areas are about 2 per cent more transnational. Also, the contribution of this variable to the explained variance in individual transnationalism is less than 1 per cent (see Table A1 in the appendix). Things do not change a lot when the other independent variables are excluded from the model (estimates not shown). In this case, being in a more urban category is associated with an increase in transnationalism of roughly 4 per cent. These models explain about 21 per cent of the variance. Thus, urbanization hardly adds to the explained variance of the models with country dummies only.

To test the hypothesis that people who live close to a national border are more transnational than the rest of the population, additional analyses distinguish between people living in border and core districts in Germany and France. Figure 5.4 shows the mean transnationalism score in German and French core districts and in border districts. As can be inferred from the figure, the mean transnationalism score is significantly higher in border districts than in the rest of Germany and France. This provides some initial support for Hypothesis 2.5. However, this difference could be due to composition effects. For example, it might be the case that people living close to a national border have a higher socio-economic status or are younger and therefore more transnational. To exclude this possibility, a multilevel regression analysis estimates the effect of living in an intra-European border district while controlling for all other independent variables that have been used in the analyses shown above. In the present multilevel analysis, individuals are nested in districts. The model is displayed in Table 5.2.

The estimation controls for GDP per capita, foreign population, and unemployment rate of each district. A dummy variable is included to account for differences between France and Germany. This analysis shows that the difference in transnationalism between residents of border and non-border districts is also robust when controlling for the individual-level factors that

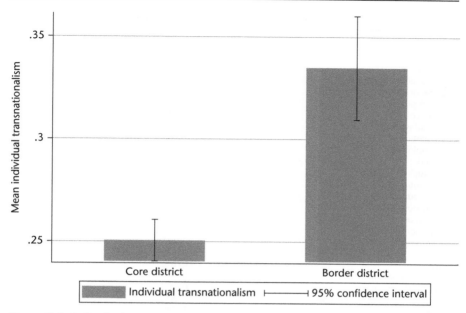

Figure 5.4. Individual transnationalism in French and German core and border districts
Source: Eurobarometer 65.1 (2006)

have been shown to influence transnationalism. In fact, everything else being equal, border residents are 11 per cent more transnational than the rest of the population. The other individual-level variables have similar effects as the previous analyses conducted on the entire European population. It is worth noting that French people are significantly less transnational than Germans.

Let me summarize the findings of the analyses of micro-level predictors of individual transnationalism. Whether a person becomes transnationally active or not seems to be strongly determined by the availability of resources and opportunities. The analyses provide strong support for the hypothesis that individual transnationalism is structured along socio-economic differences within national communities. Educational attainment is a powerful predictor of individual transnationalism. The more educated an individual, the more likely he or she is to be transnationally active. Above and beyond the effect of education, occupations seem to channel people into more or less transnational lives. In general, people working in higher-status jobs are more transnational. The influence of age is less straightforward. While younger cohorts are more transnational than older ones, this difference seems to be largely due to educational expansion over the past decades. However, even when accounting for education and occupation, there is a small age effect. In contrast, it does not seem to matter a great deal whether people live in more or

Table 5.2. Effect of border residence on individual transnationalism

	coeff.	se
Border district	.108***	(.017)
Educational attainment	.079***	(.007)
Occupation (manager ref.)		
Self-employed	.010	(.021)
White collar	−.085***	(.019)
Manual worker	−.114***	(.016)
Homemaker	−.103***	(.021)
Unemployed	−.095***	(.020)
Retired	−.105***	(.018)
Age groups (55+ ref.)		
Age group 15–24	.061**	(.021)
Age group 25–39	.052***	(.015)
Age group 40–54	.020	(.014)
Urbanization	.002	(.009)
Foreign-born	.221***	(.033)
Foreign parents	.036**	(.013)
Female	−.051***	(.009)
France	−.078***	(.016)
District unemployment rate	−.030	(.036)
District GDP per capita	.038	(.062)
District share foreign population	.115*	(.045)
Constant	.151***	(.031)
Variance components		
Level 2: Constant	.005***	(.001)
Level 2: Residual variance	.040***	(.010)
Log-likelihood	299.0	
AIC	−553.9	
ICC	.1130	

Note: Figures are coefficients of multilevel regression models with random intercept, standard errors in parentheses. $N = 279$, $n = 2,341$. Two-tailed test; * $p < .05$, ** $p < .01$, *** $p < .001$.

Source: Eurobarometer 65.1 (2006).

less urban areas. The effect of living in a more urbanized area is negligible both in effect size and in explained variance. Finally, analyses in Germany and France show that people living close to an intra-European border are significantly more transnational than the rest of the population.

5.4 Which Societies are More Transnational?

There is not just simply one single perspective on free movement. There are a variety of experiences. Depending on where you are, in which country, in which region, in which city, you face different needs. You face different challenges and different opportunities.[7]

—Viviane Reding, vice-president of the European Commission

[7] Viviane Reding, speech at the Conference for Mayors on EU Mobility at local level, Brussels, February 2014.

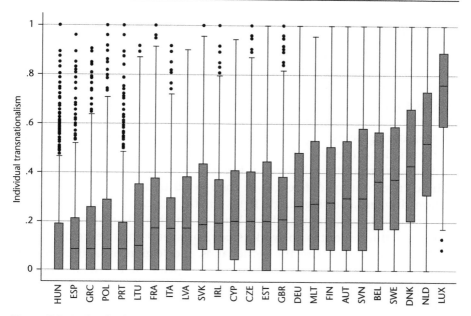

Figure 5.5. Individual transnationalism across member states, sorted by median transnationalism index

Source: Eurobarometer 65.1 (2006)

Having assessed what could make an individual more transnational, the focus of attention now shifts to differences across countries. In essence, the extent to which a person becomes transnational is not only influenced by their individual characteristics, but also by the country they live in.

Figure 5.5 shows box plots of individual transnationalism for each EU member state in 2006.[8] There are substantial differences across EU member states in the extent to which individuals are transnational. Not surprisingly, Luxembourg has a genuinely transnational population: the median transnationalism score of the Luxembourgish population is above the third quartile of any other population, and as high as the outliers in some countries. This is probably due to the small size of the country, which makes cross-border contact more likely.

An additional explanation for the particularly high level of transnationalism of the Luxembourgish society is its important role in international banking, finance, and politics, which attracts workers from abroad and facilitates

---

[8] Each box refers to the inter-quartile range of the distribution: the lower margin of each box indicates the first quartile, while the higher end of the box refers to the third quartile, and the horizontal line in the box indicates the median. The dots refer to outliers, i.e. all observations with a value higher than 150 per cent of the inter-quartile range.

manifold transnational interactions. Moreover, the first and so far only University in Luxembourg was founded as late as 2003 (University of Luxembourg 2013). Until that year, young Luxembourgers had no choice but to complete their university studies abroad. Other countries with highly transnational populations are the Netherlands, Sweden, and Denmark. At the other end of the spectrum are Spain, Portugal, and Hungary. The low incidence of individual transnationalism in these countries might be a relic of their international isolation during fascism and communism, which might be perpetuated in a less transnational lifestyle. Moreover, the Spanish and Portuguese coasts offer plenty of opportunities to holiday at home.

These cross-country differences in the overall transnationalism scale are confirmed when assessing single items on the scale. Figure 5.6 shows the percentage of Europeans who have lived in another EU member state for more than three months to work, study, or spend their retirement. The populations of Luxembourg, the Netherlands, and Belgium are at the forefront of international relocations. About a third of all people living in Luxembourg have lived in another EU member state. The explanations for this high incidence of stays abroad have already been discussed in detail above: the small country size, its important role in international business and politics as well as the long absence of a university at home. While the population of Luxembourg is an extreme case in terms of individual transnationalism, the

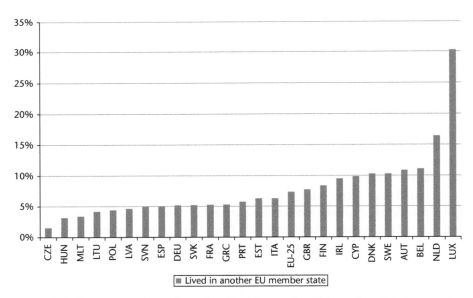

Figure 5.6. Percentage of people having lived in another EU member state by country
Source: Eurobarometer 65.1 (2006)

Dutch and the Belgians are also highly transnational. About 16 per cent of the Dutch have lived in another EU member state, and 11 per cent of Belgians have done so. At the other extreme, only 1.5 per cent of all Czechs reported having lived in another EU member state. Of the eight countries with the lowest incidence of stays abroad, seven are former communist countries, and one is an island (Malta). This highlights the former isolation behind the Iron Curtain and the remoteness of living on an island.

Equally, there are substantial cross-country differences with respect to short-term visits to other European member states. This is illustrated in Figure 5.7. In 2006, 90 per cent of all Greeks had not visited another EU country in the previous year. Similarly, over 80 per cent of all people in Portugal, Poland, Lithuania, Latvia, and Spain had not done so. In contrast, 84 per cent of all Luxembourgers and 74 per cent of all Dutch had visited another EU member state in the previous year. What is more, 60 per cent of the Luxembourgish population had done so on several occasions.

These pronounced differences across EU member states imply the question: what makes some societies more transnational than others? We know very little about the country characteristics that are linked to transnationalism. To date, the only empirical study that has aimed at systematically assessing the macro-level predictors of transnational interaction is the one conducted by

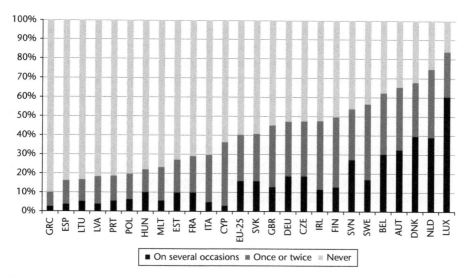

Figure 5.7. Percentage of people having visited another member state in past year by country
Source: Eurobarometer 65.1 (2006)

Mau and Mewes (2012). Using Eurobarometer survey data, they analyse the impact of geographical differences, modernization, and internationalization on two dependent variables: people's likelihood to visit another EU country and the likelihood to socialize with other Europeans. Mau and Mewes (2012) find that Europeanization, modernization, and internationalization play a greater role in influencing short-term trips and socializing with other Europeans than geographic characteristics. In contrast, the analyses presented here relate to the overall transnationalism index. The following section develops a set of hypotheses on which country-level factors could determine individual transnationalism.

5.4.1 *Economic Situation*

Above and beyond individual socio-economic background, a country's economic situation might influence the degree to which people become transnationally active. The relationship between a country's wealth and the transnational interactions of its population is not straightforward. Two competing mechanisms work in opposite directions. On the one hand, migration research has shown that people tend to move from economically weak to wealthy economies (de Haas 2010). If we were to analyse physical and long-term mobility to another country only, we would therefore conclude that the poorer the country, the more inclined its citizens are to move abroad. On the other hand, what is under analysis here is a broader concept of transnationalism that also encompasses short-term visits abroad as well as transnational interactions that happen within the country. Therefore, the link between economic prosperity and transnational interaction is likely to be different. There is good reason to believe that just as on the individual level, the extent to which societies become transnationally active is a question of resources and opportunities. First, a wealthy country attracts international business and a foreign workforce. This increases the opportunities to interact transnationally without leaving one's country. Second, transnational interactions are likely to be less frequent in poorer economies because they come with an economic price. Families have less disposable income to go on vacation, (public) schools might not have the means to nurture the foreign language skills and intercultural competences of their pupils, and states cannot afford to invest in high-speed train connections to other EU member states. In line with this argument, Mau and Mewes (2012) find a strong effect of GDP per capita on the probability to visit another EU member state and on the probability to socialize with other Europeans. This idea is captured in the following hypothesis:

Hypothesis 2.6: People living in richer countries are more transnational.

5.4.2 *EU Membership Duration*

EU membership directly influences the extent to which people interact across EU member states. As Mau and Mewes (2012: 17) put it, 'the European integration process works as an opportunity structure for cross-border inter-actions'. In fact, the provision of opportunities for cross-border transactions was at the heart of Deutsch's idea of security communities, and this objective is one of the driving forces of European integration. On the one hand, it does so by opening borders to other member states and by facilitating free move-ment of goods, services, capital, and people. On the other, a plethora of European policies aims at fostering exchange and cooperation among Euro-pean citizens: in addition to Erasmus and other exchange programmes in the Lifelong Learning Programme that have already been mentioned, initiatives such as town-twinning projects (Falkenhain et al. 2012) provide an institu-tional framework for cross-border interactions among EU citizens.

All countries analysed in this study are EU member states. Hence, adhering to the EU cannot be used as an independent variable in the following analyses. However, while some EU member states belong to the six founding countries, others have joined the EU rather recently. It is to be expected that in countries that have been EU member states for a longer time, citizens have had greater opportunities to establish and institutionalize transnational exchanges. Con-sidering the socializing power of political institutions (Checkel 2005), citizens of old member states have been socialized in a more Europeanized environ-ment than people whose countries have joined the EU only recently. In line with this argument, Mau and Mewes (2012) find, in a multilevel analysis of Eurobarometer data, that the length of EU membership has a significant and positive effect on the propensity to visit another EU member state and to socialize with other Europeans.

> **Hypothesis 2.7**: The longer a country has been in the EU, the more transnational are its citizens.

5.4.3 *Macro-level Transnationalism*

Next, individual transnationalism might be directly influenced by the level of transnationalism of the country of residence. In a highly transnational coun-try, people are more frequently exposed to foreign actors, ideas, and products. Consequently, they can engage more easily in transnational interactions even while staying in their own country. Moreover, interacting transnationally, whether at home or abroad, might seem more natural and normal to them than to citizens of more isolated countries. Finally, more globalized countries provide a better infrastructure to interact across borders. Confirming this expectation, Mau and Mewes (2012) find that economic globalization significantly increases the likelihood of interacting with other Europeans and the likelihood of visiting other European countries.

Countries differ greatly in the degree to which they are transnationalized. Even within the EU, the level of transnationalism varies considerably across member states (Held et al. 1999). According to Mills and Blossfeld (2005), institutional filters determine the degree to which a country is exposed and open to internationalization. The KOF index of globalization (among others) indicates that some European countries, such as the Netherlands, Belgium, and Austria, belong to the most globalized countries worldwide, while others range in the upper quarter of all countries considered (Dreher et al. 2008). For these reasons, the next hypothesis states:

Hypothesis 2.8: The more transnational a country, the more transnational are its citizens.

5.4.4 Country Size

In an early attempt to empirically analyse the scope and scale of transnational interactions, Deutsch (1960) studied historical data on international trade and international mail. His analyses showed that the exchange in trade and mail dropped with the size of a country. Citizens of smaller countries might be more transnational for at least two reasons. First, in small countries, there might be a similar mechanism at work as in small towns: smaller countries offer less choice in terms of professional and private opportunities. People living in these countries might therefore feel compelled to move abroad in pursuit of professional advancement, or in order to live in a cosmopolitan city. For instance, several Dutch actors and entertainers, such as Linda de Mol or Rudi Carrell made careers in German show business, where the market is much bigger than in the Netherlands. In line with this argument, Favell (2008) found that many of the 'Eurostars'—young professional intra-European migrants—moved abroad in order to circumvent obstacles in career paths in their own country. Second, in smaller countries, the average distance to the national border is shorter. When living in a small country, it is therefore, on average, easier to travel across the border than when living in a big country (Mau and Mewes 2012). This renders shopping, working, and studying across the border feasible for a greater share of the population. I therefore formulate the following hypothesis:

Hypothesis 2.9: People living in smaller countries are more transnational.

5.5 Empirical Analysis of Macro-Level Predictors

To empirically test Hypotheses 2.6–2.9 on the macro-level predictors of individual transnationalism, the following operationalizations are used. A country's economic prosperity is measured by the per-capita GDP in Purchasing Power Standards (PPS) expressed in relation to the EU-27 average, which is set at 100. The country with the lowest GDP per capita in PPS (51) in 2006 is Latvia, while Luxembourg is the wealthiest member state with a per capita GDP in PPS of 270. Luxembourg remains at the top in 2007 with 275, while the two newest member states Bulgaria and Romania are poorest, with a GDP per capita in PPS of 40 and 42, respectively. Two measures capture the length of EU membership. The first indicator is calculated by subtracting the year when a country joined the EU from the years 2007 and 2006, respectively. In the case of the six founding states, the Treaty of Rome (European Union 1957) is used as a starting point. Second, a dummy variable distinguishing between the EU-15 and the newer member states is included in another model.[9] Globalization is measured using the economic dimension of the KOF index of globalization (Dreher 2006). This dimension was chosen rather than the overall index because it avoids the risk of endogeneity—in particular, the social dimension of the KOF index is very close to the measure of individual transnationalism. The economic globalization indicator refers to actual economic flows such as trade, as well as restrictions, such as taxes on international trade and hidden import barriers. The country with the lowest level of economic globalization in 2006 is Italy (72.11), while Ireland scores highest with 93.17. In 2007, Romania is least economically globalized, with an index of 71.88, and Luxembourg is the most economically globalized member state, with an index of 94.35.

The size of a country is measured both in terms of geographic territory and in terms of its total population. For the former, data were obtained from the CIA World Factbook (CIA 2013) and are measured in terms of total land and water surface in square kilometres. Data on population size are taken from Eurostat (2006f, 2007f) and refer to all inhabitants registered in a country on 1 January 2006 and 2007, respectively. The natural logarithm of both variables is taken as well so as to ascertain whether a potential effect is due to extreme cases. In order to readily compare the effect sizes, all continuous independent variables have been standardized to run from 0 to 1. Thus, all coefficients shown in Table 5.3 refer to the change of an independent variable from 0 to 1.

In view of the risk of multicollinearity, each hypothesis is analysed in a separate model rather than including them in one and the same estimation.

---

[9] In additional analyses that are not shown here, dummies for prior enlargement rounds are included in separate models. No significant difference was found.

Table 5.3. Effect of macro-level predictors on individual transnationalism

Model	Macro variable	Eurobarometer 65.1			Eurobarometer 67.1		
		coeff.	(se)	ICC	coeff.	(se)	ICC
1				.231			.217
2	GDP per capita	.332***	(.058)	.107	.312***	(.069)	.136
3	EU-15	−.087*	(.035)	.088	−.057	(.034)	.129
4	Years of membership	−.053	(.045)	.099	−.070	(.042)	.128
5	Economic globalization	.119*	(.051)	.091	.105**	(.040)	.113
6	Population size	−.109*	(.046)	.091	−.104*	(.044)	.117
7	Population size (log)	−.035**	(.012)	.082	−.144***	(.041)	.098
8	Territory size	−.124**	(.048)	.087	−.064	(.049)	.133
9	Territory size (log)	−.206***	(.052)	.068	−.185***	(.052)	.097
N; n		25; 21,898			27; 24,975		

Note: Multilevel regressions with random intercept. All models control for educational outcome, occupation, age, gender, transnational background, urbanization. Models 3–11 control for GDP per capita. Control variables not shown. Two-tailed test, * $p < .05$, ** $p < .01$, *** $p < .001$.

The only exception is GDP per capita, because, as will be discussed in detail below, it has a very strong and robust effect on individual transnationalism and also influences the effects of the other independent variables. Rather than presenting the entire models, Table 5.3 shows the coefficients, significance, and model fit of each estimation. In all models, education, occupation, age groups, gender, and urbanization are included as individual-level control variables. The entire models can be conferred in Tables A2 and A3 in the appendix.

To begin with, I test the hypothesis that people living in wealthier countries are more transnational. Before turning to the multivariate statistical models, it is instructive to have a look at Figure 5.8. This figure presents the mean transnationalism score for each country by GDP per capita in purchasing power parity. The figure shows that countries with higher levels of GDP per capita generally have a more transnational population. Clearly, Luxembourg is an outlier with respect to transnationalism and with respect to GDP per capita. Therefore, the relationship is depicted once with Luxembourg in the analysis, and once without. Excluding Luxembourg from the analysis does not excessively influence the gradient. This relationship is confirmed in the multivariate analyses. As indicated in Model 2 (Table 5.3), a country's wealth measured in per-capita GDP has a strong, significant, and positive effect on individual transnationalism in both years. At the highest level of GDP, people are over 30 per cent more transnational than at the lowest level. Including this variable in the analysis decreases the intra-class-correlation by 12 per cent in Eurobarometer 65.1 and by 8 per cent in Eurobarometer 67.1. Additional analyses show that the effect of GDP per capita remains strong and significant when Luxembourg is excluded from the analysis, indicating that the strong

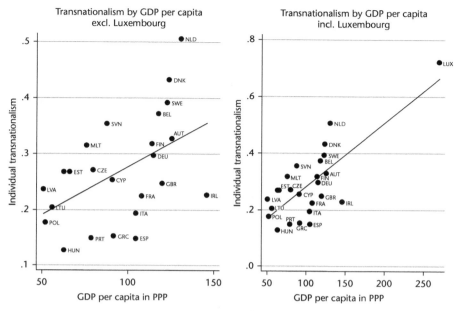

Figure 5.8. Mean individual transnationalism score by GDP per capita
Source: Eurobarometer 65.1 (2006)

effect is not only due to Luxembourg. As can be seen in further detail in Tables A2 and A3 in the appendix, the effect remains robust and highly significant throughout all other models estimated.[10] What is more, further analyses reveal that the effects of other independent variables are highly sensitive to whether or not GDP per capita is accounted for. Therefore, per-capita GDP is included as the only macro-level control variable in all other models presented. All in all, the analyses provide strong and robust support for the hypothesis that people living in richer member states are significantly more transnational.

According to Hypothesis 2.7, people should be more transnational the longer their home country has been in the EU. The analyses do not provide support for this hypothesis. Duration of membership has been operationalized in several ways: first, in Model 4, a dummy variable for belonging to the EU-15 countries (as opposed to being from one of the new member states) is included in the analysis. In 2006, this variable has a significant effect, but it runs counter to the expected direction. Other things being equal, people living

---

[10] Also when taking the natural log of GDP per capita as an independent variable, it has a strong and significant effect.

in old member states are significantly *less* transnational than people in the countries that have joined in 2004 and 2007. When conducting the same analysis using the data for 2007, no significant effect is found. Moreover, when operationalizing membership duration in terms of years since having joined the EU (Model 5), no significant effect can be found. Nor is there a significant relationship with other operationalizations of membership duration, such as dummy variables for each enlargement round (estimations not shown).

The finding that in 2006, people living in the EU-15 are significantly less transnational than people in the new member states is surprising at first sight. However, this relationship might be explained by the reaction to the EU accession of these countries in 2004. The eastern enlargement spurred migration from new member states to the EU-15 (Benton and Petrovic 2013). Thus, the positive effect found in the analyses might reflect the fact that many newly minted Europeans have taken advantage of their new freedom of mobility across the EU. Moreover, when excluding GDP per capita, the effect becomes insignificant. To conclude, however, the analyses contradict the commonly held assumption that European institution building and border removal promote transnationalism, but also the analyses by Mau and Mewes (2012) that found a positive relationship between membership duration and trips to other EU member states as well as socializing with other Europeans.

In turn, the findings of this chapter show that economic globalization of a country significantly increases the level of transnationalism among its population. Everything else being equal, people living in member states that are highly integrated into the global economy, such as the Netherlands or Denmark, are 11–12 per cent more transnational than people living in less economically integrated countries. The effect size of economic globalization is about a third of the effect size of GDP per capita. Thus, the economic prosperity of a country is more important than its degree of economic transnationalization.

Finally, the analysis turns to the geographic and demographic characteristics of a country to test the hypothesis that people living in smaller countries are more transnationally active than residents of large nations. As shown in Models 6–9, the analyses provide support for this expectation both with respect to a country's physical size and its population. Model 6 reveals that population size significantly decreases the extent to which people are transnational. In other words, people living in more populous countries tend to be less transnational than people living in smaller societies. This relationship is further supported when taking the natural log of population size. Analyses on territory size (Models 8 and 9) echo these results. Model 8 finds a negative relationship between territory size and individual transnationalism in 2006, thus indicating that people living in bigger countries are less transnational than people in small countries. In contrast, no significant relationship is found for the data in 2007. When including the natural logarithm of territory size as a predictor, the effect size becomes even greater in 2006, and significant in 2007. This suggests that the effect applies in the first case to the smallest member states, while there are less pronounced differences between big and medium-sized countries.

All in all, these findings suggest that while the size of a country in terms of its physical scale and population is significantly related to transnationalism, the effect mainly applies to the smallest member states in Europe. In very small countries, such as Luxembourg, a large share of the population lives close enough to a national border to be able to regularly cross the border. At the same time, due to their small size, these countries might offer fewer professional and private opportunities within their own geographic and cultural borders, such that their citizens are more inclined to look elsewhere.

In a nutshell, the findings regarding the macro-level predictors of transnational interactions can be summarized as follows. While the result of an individual decision-making process, the extent to which a person becomes transnationally active, is strongly influenced by the country they live in. In the first place, a country's economic wealth, measured in terms of GDP per capita, is a strong and robust predictor of individual transnationalism. The richer a country, the more transnational are its citizens. Controlling for GDP per capita, people living in one of the twelve new member states are more transnational than people in the EU-15. A country's level of economic globalization matters as well: people living in highly globalized countries interact more regularly on a transnational basis. Finally, individual transnationalism is also influenced by the physical and population size of a member state.

It is worth reiterating that all the analyses presented here control for a country's economic wealth when assessing the effect of the other macro-level predictors, which strongly influences their statistical significance. This is done because GDP per capita has strong predictive power both in terms of statistical significance and in terms of explained variance, and is very robust across all model specifications. Moreover, considering that individual income cannot be accounted for, it seems crucial to measure economic differences at least at the aggregate level. Leaving this variable out of the analysis runs the risk of omitted variable bias.

5.6 Conclusion

This chapter aimed at advancing our knowledge on who the highly transnational Europeans are, and how they differ with respect to the rest of the population. The short answer to this question is that only a small, privileged elite from wealthy member states is highly transnational, while the rest of the European population remains largely within their national boundaries. The longer answer to this question points at the role of resources and opportunities as underlying mechanism. This will be discussed in further detail in what follows.

The statistical analyses of this chapter have shown that a person's educational attainment strongly influences their transnationalism. Highly educated people are more transnational. One potential explanation for this relationship is that formal education provides manifold opportunities to interact across countries. In fact, most of the EU's policy instruments aiming at promoting cross-border interactions in the EU take place in education, and disproportionately so in higher education (Anheier and Falkenhain 2012; Kuhn 2012b). Thus, highly educated people have more opportunities to interact across countries—and to establish lasting transnational networks—simply by staying longer in education. Second, formal education provides certain skills that are useful, if not essential, in transnational interactions. While foreign language skills are a major asset in a political Union which now has twenty-four official languages (Gerhards 2012), a number of transferable skills further ease cross-cultural communication and guide the way through a highly complex and diverse society. Finally, people with a high educational outcome are more likely to find a good job, which in turn provides them with the resources to become transnationally active. In fact, the analyses show that above and beyond the effect of education, managers and white-collar workers are significantly more transnational than people in less prestigious jobs, or people outside of the workforce. This indicates that certain jobs provide important opportunities to interact across countries.

Next, the study reveals that younger people are more transnational than older people. Both a life cycle and a cohort effect could be underlying this relationship: younger people might be more transnational because they are at a point in their lives where transnational interactions are more likely to happen, or because they grow up in a more transnational society and therefore adopt a more transnational lifestyle than older people whose lives have been structured primarily by national institutions. Relying on cross-sectional data only, the empirical analysis presented here cannot fully answer this question. However, taking into consideration that the effect of age considerably decreases when controlling for education, and considering the educational expansion that has taken place over the last five decades, it seems plausible that the differences across age groups are due to a cohort effect: younger cohorts are more transnational because a larger proportion is highly educated. If this is indeed the case, Europeans should become increasingly transnational in the coming decades. Perhaps surprisingly, urbanization plays a relatively small role. While people living in more urban areas are indeed slightly more transnational, this effect is rather small and it contributes only slightly to the explained variance of the model. In contrast, the analyses on intra-European border districts in Germany and France show that people living close to a national border are significantly more transnational than the overall population.

In addition to individual differences, there is also remarkable cross-country heterogeneity. Some societies, such as the Benelux countries, have become largely transnational. In these countries, transnational interactions seem to be an everyday experience for a considerable number of citizens. In contrast, in some other member states, such as Portugal and Spain, people generally engage very little in transnational interaction. Again, these differences seem to be explained primarily by resources and opportunities. The most important aspect here is a country's economic wealth, as measured by its GDP per capita. People living in richer countries are significantly more transnational. This effect is remarkably robust across all analyses, and it helps to explain about 10 per cent of the country variance in transnationalism. In a similar vein, people living in economically globalized countries are more transnational. Moreover, the size of a country also plays a role. People living in bigger member states (both in terms of territory and population) are less transnational. Due to their size, these countries provide their citizens with better opportunities and resources at home than do smaller countries. At the same time, people living in smaller countries are on average closer to the next national border and therefore have better opportunities to interact across borders.

The findings of this chapter have a number of important implications. First, they highlight the incomplete state of European society formation. Over six decades of European integration have yet to make a visible mark on people's social interactions. Contrary to Deutsch's expectations, the formation of the European security community has not resulted in proliferated transactions among the entire European population. Rather, a small minority of Europeans leads a genuinely transnational life.

Second, this chapter illustrates the social stratification of transnational interactions in the European Union. Both within and across European member states, socio-economic aspects largely determine the extent to which people interact across borders. In a nutshell, transnational practices and 'being European' remain relatively limited to a highly educated, young elite in wealthy member states. This paints a relatively bleak picture with respect to the EU's effectiveness in forging a genuinely transnational society in Europe. It seems that, contrary to Deutsch's expectations, the majority of Europeans have not yet adopted a European way of life, but remain rather nationalized.

However, there is some reason to believe that individual transnationalism will gradually spread to a broader proportion of society. Higher education has been shown to be a major predictor of individual transnationalism. With educational expansion taking place in European societies, increasing numbers of people will become more transnational. Closely related to that, there are good reasons to believe that the significant differences across age groups are in the first place due to a cohort effect—younger people are more transnational because they grew up in a more transnational environment. It is therefore plausible that future generations will be more transnational, and that transnationalism will spread to a broader share of the European population.

While this chapter emphasized the first qualification to Deutsch's transactionalist theory presented in this book, the next chapter deals with the second qualification, namely that not all transnational interactions are equally effective in nurturing EU support and European identity.

6

Transactionalist Theory under Further Empirical Scrutiny

Purpose and Scope of Interactions

> *One must pay detailed attention to intervening factors, however, to evaluate whether an increase in the density of individual interactions will deepen shared identity. Examples of increasing interaction leading to hostility rather than integration...suggest that no objective function links social/economic/political transactions to identity.*[1]
>
> —Gary Marks

Chapter 4 has shown that highly transnational Europeans are significantly more likely to endorse EU membership and to identify themselves as Europeans than people whose score is low on the transnationalism index. The evidence for this relationship was very robust: individual transnationalism is significantly related to EU support and European identity. Under all conditions analysed, it has a highly significant and strong effect. Moreover, the analyses show that each dimension of individual transnationalism (transnational background, practices, and human capital) on its own exerts a significant effect on the dependent variables. Separate analyses for each country show that the effect of individual transnationalism is robust across most EU member states.

As such, this evidence strongly supports Deutsch's conjecture that transnational interactions foster EU support and identity. Moreover, the findings presented in Chapter 5 that individual transnationalism is highly stratified and limited to a highly educated and young minority helps explain why we do not observe a rise in aggregate EU support in spite of proliferating transnational activity: increased interactions are limited to a small portion of

---

[1] Marks 1999: 82.

the public. These individuals might well develop EU support in response to increased transnational interactions, while the majority of Europeans do not take an active part in transnational networks and mobility, and therefore fail to be prompted to support European integration.

However, this is only one part of the story. To fully understand the discrepancy between increased interactions and orientations towards European integration, Deutsch's theory needs to be further qualified. It seems highly unlikely that all transnational encounters are per se conducive to positive evaluations of European integration. In fact, some transnational interactions might have quite the opposite effect by evoking reserved or even hostile orientations towards European integration. This is likely to be the case if people do not experience transactions in a positive way. Furthermore, individuals might not link their transnational activity to the European integration process. Such a scenario is realistic if transactions are framed in a binational rather than a European context, or if non-European actors are involved.

It is therefore crucial to empirically study the conditions under which transnational interactions generate EU support and European identity. The answer to this question has important implications for theory building and policymaking. On a theoretical level, it is highly relevant with respect to the mechanisms underlying the relationship between individual transnationalism and orientations towards European integration. It also provides crucial information for policy makers who aim at strengthening pro-European attitudes and identities through policies such as the Erasmus programme or town-twinning projects. Knowing how, when, and why interactions trigger EU support and identity helps them to effectively design their policies.

Therefore, this chapter focuses on the dimension of transnational practices and disaggregates it into different forms of interactions. Clearly, the extent to which one can break down the data used in this book into different forms of interactions is limited. It is also not possible to directly study how respondents experience and interpret their transnational interactions. This task is performed better using qualitative methods, such as in Favell's (2008) in-depth qualitative interviews with sixty European migrants in Amsterdam, Brussels, and London. Therefore, the present chapter limits itself to analysing two crucial aspects of transnational interactions, namely their main purpose and their geographic scope. The main argument of this chapter is that these factors influence the extent to which interactions are effective in triggering EU support. Thus, while Chapter 4 assessed the impact of the entire transnationalism scale, this chapter zooms in on certain aspects of transnational activity in order to differentiate between sociable and instrumental forms of interactions, as well as between binational, genuinely European, and extra-European transactions. It then analyses the extent to which these factors are decisive in predicting EU support and European identification. The chapter concludes by discussing the implications for social science and for policy makers.

6.1 Purpose: Instrumental vs. Sociable Interactions

The motivations that underlie transnational interactions are likely to influence how people experience and interpret transnational interactions, and consequently whether they react by becoming more supportive of European integration. In other words, transnational interactions can be framed in very different ways, depending on what the people involved intend them to achieve. It is therefore crucial to study the motivations behind transnationalism, and to analyse which motivations are most conducive to stimulating EU support and European identity.

Europeans interact across borders for a plethora of reasons. When assessing the main motivations for moving to another EU country, Santacreu and colleagues (2009: 59) found that primarily three factors motivate Europeans to do so: the quality of life, the search for a new job, and the wish to live with one's partner or family. Also Verwiebe (2014) found that economic reasons play a decreasing role in motivating migration to Germany, while social and cultural aspects are becoming ever more important.[2] With respect to short-term visits abroad, Mau found that Germans travel chiefly for leisure and vacation. Further prominent motivations were visits to family and friends abroad, other private reasons, and occupational reasons (Mau 2010: 67). As discussed in more detail in Chapter 3, the purpose of cross-border interactions may influence their effectiveness in generating EU support.

It would be a moot point to try and capture each and every single purpose of transactions. A crucial distinction has been proposed by Roose (2010). He categorizes interactions into 'instrumental' and 'sociable' interactions. The latter are mainly intrinsically motivated, that is, people interact for the sake of interacting. The motivation behind the former is the prospect of (material) benefits gained by interaction. Instrumental interactions are thus dominantly interest-led and include activities such as cross-border shopping or trade.

This distinction relates to the two most prominent approaches to explain attitudes towards European integration. According to the utilitarian approach, people base their evaluations of European integration on rational cost–benefit analyses (Eichenberg and Dalton 1993; Gabel 1998c). The 'winners' of European integration, that is, people who obtain (material) benefits from European

---

[2] It should be noted, however, that Verwiebe analyses migration to Berlin. The unemployment rate in the German capital is above the German average, and there is relatively little industry. Migrants seeking employment in Germany might therefore not end up in Berlin.

integration, are expected to endorse the integration process simply because it is in their interest. This hypothesis has been tested mainly with respect to EU membership support (Eichenberg and Dalton 1993; Gabel 1998b; McLaren 2007), but there is also evidence that the relationship holds with respect to European identity (Duchesne and Frognier 1995; Fligstein 2008). If one follows the logic that orientations towards European integration are predominantly driven by utilitarian considerations, one would expect instrumental interactions to be especially effective in triggering EU support and European identity. After all, by executing instrumental transactions across Europe, people directly reap the benefits arising from European integration. This expectation was formulated in Chapter 3 as Hypothesis 3a, 'Instrumental interactions have a stronger effect on EU support and European identity than sociable interactions.'

The other central explanatory approach of orientations towards European integration places emphasis on questions of collective identity (Carey 2002; Hooghe and Marks 2004; McLaren 2006). According to this approach, European integration poses a perceived threat to national communities and thus causes resentment among those who exclusively identify with their nation. However, this does not mean that people who hold a strong national identity automatically reject European integration. Hooghe and Marks (2004) show that only those who perceive themselves *solely* as members of their national community might feel threatened by the supranational polity. As argued in intergroup contact theory, people maintaining relations with members of other groups tend to lower their group boundaries and may develop a common identity (Howard 2000). Arguably, these identity changes are likely to happen more easily if the contact involves sociable interactions. In line with this argument, sociable interactions should be more decisive in triggering EU support and European identity. This idea was specified in Hypothesis 3b in Chapter 3: 'Sociable interactions have a stronger effect on EU support than instrumental interactions.'

The following section empirically tests this hypothesis with respect to EU membership support using Eurobarometer 65.1. It is not always easy to distinguish between instrumental and sociable interactions. In fact, as highlighted by the ubiquitous term 'networking', socializing can be an activity with expected material gains. Moreover, while interacting for utilitarian reasons, people might also develop sociable networks and make friends. This difficulty also arises when operationalizing the two purposes for the analyses of this chapter. Most items in the transnationalism index used in Chapters 4 and 5 cannot be clearly classified into one category or the other. Consequently, only a selection of items is used to distinguish between instrumental and sociable interactions. In the analyses using Eurobarometer 65.1, the following item operationalizes instrumental interactions: having made a

Table 6.1. Effect of instrumental and sociable interactions on EU membership support

	Model 1		Model 2		Model 3	
	b	se	b	se	b	se
Socializing	.426***	(.041)			.414***	(.041)
Cross-border shopping			.218***	(.063)	.116	(.064)
Female	−.190***	(.033)	−.194***	(.032)	−.189***	(.033)
Age groups (55+ ref.)						
Age group 15–24	.082	(.082)	.105	(.082)	.082	(.082)
Age group 25–39	−.107*	(.053)	−.100	(.053)	−.109*	(.053)
Age group 40–54	−.228***	(.049)	−.226***	(.049)	−.228***	(.049)
Educational attainment	.706***	(.051)	.763***	(.051)	.705***	(.051)
Occupation (manager ref.)						
Self-employed	−.270***	(.076)	−.282***	(.076)	−.270***	(.076)
White collar	−.262***	(.066)	−.299***	(.066)	−.263***	(.066)
Manual worker	−.479***	(.059)	−.526***	(.059)	−.478***	(.059)
Homemaker	−.404***	(.075)	−.461***	(.074)	−.405***	(.075)
Unemployed	−.613***	(.078)	−.666***	(.077)	−.612***	(.078)
Retired	−.325***	(.067)	−.388***	(.067)	−.323***	(.067)
Student	−.251*	(.110)	−.273*	(.109)	−.251*	(.110)
Ideology	.449***	(.063)	.448***	(.063)	.449***	(.063)
Ideology squared	−.134*	(.052)	−.133*	(.052)	−.134**	(.052)
Household situation	1.013***	(.092)	1.057***	(.091)	1.013***	(.092)
Attitudes towards immigrants	.568***	(.055)	.588***	(.055)	.568***	(.055)
Convince others	.053	(.053)	.084	(.053)	.051	(.053)
Discuss politics	.435***	(.057)	.510***	(.056)	.434***	(.057)
Urbanization	.156***	(.040)	.182***	(.040)	.159***	(.040)
T1	−.906***	(.108)	−.977***	(.107)	−.897***	(.108)
T2	.969***	(.108)	.891***	(.107)	.979***	(.108)
Log-likelihood	−15,862.5		−15,912.6		−15,860.7	
McFadden's pseudo r-square	.077		.074		.077	

Note: Figures are coefficients of ordinal logit models with country-fixed effects, robust standard errors in parentheses. Country coefficients not shown. Two-tailed test, * $p < .05$, ** $p < .01$, *** $p < .001$. $n = 17,292$.
Source: Eurobarometer 65.1 (2006).

shopping trip to another member state in the past twelve months. An item referring to frequent socializing with citizens of other EU member states captures sociable interactions. This is the only item that allows the isolation of purely sociable forms of interaction in Eurobarometer 65.1.

Are sociable or instrumental interactions more decisive in structuring EU support? To answer this question, Models 1 and 2 in Table 6.1 estimate the effect of socializing with other Europeans and cross-border shopping, respectively. Model 3 includes both the cross-border shopping item and the socializing variable in the same model predicting EU membership support. As in Chapter 4, EU support is operationalized with the item, 'EU membership of our country is a bad / neither good nor bad / good thing.' The models include the same control variables as in the models predicting EU support presented in Chapter 4.

As shown in Table 6.1, both cross-border shopping and socializing with other Europeans are positively and significantly related to EU support. In other words, both people who buy products in another EU member state, and people who socialize with other Europeans are significantly more likely to support EU membership. However, when comparing the coefficients of the two independent variables, it becomes clear that cross-border shopping exerts a smaller effect on EU membership support than socializing. What is more, the effect of cross-border shopping becomes insignificant (and decreases in substantive terms) when including both variables in the analysis. In contrast, the coefficient of socializing with other Europeans remains robust.

We can further examine this relationship by calculating the predicted probabilities of EU support based on Model 3. For the calculations of these predictions, all control variables are set to their mean or mode, while the values of the independent variables are changed in order to ascertain their impact on the outcome variable. The predicted probabilities are shown in Table 6.2. The 'base-line model' refers to the predicted probabilities of EU membership support for people having neither done cross-border shopping nor having socialized with other Europeans. It serves as the benchmark from which to calculate the increase in predicted probability of EU membership support for both forms of interactions. When comparing the predicted probability for the base-line model to the predicted probability under cross-border shopping, it appears that cross-border shopping increases the probability of EU membership support by 3 per cent. However, the predicted probability under cross-border shopping falls within the bounds of the confidence intervals of the base-line model. Hence, this difference is not statistically significant. In contrast, having socialized with other Europeans increases the probability of EU membership support by nine percentage points, and this difference is statistically significant.

These results support Hypothesis 3b, that sociable forms of transnational interactions play a greater role in generating EU support than instrumental

Table 6.2. Changes in predicted probability of EU membership support due to instrumental and sociable interactions

	Predicted probability	95% confidence interval lower bound	95% confidence interval higher bound
Base-line model	.60	.56	.64
Instrumental interactions: cross-border shopping	.63	.58	.68
Sociable interactions: socializing with other Europeans	.69	.65	.73

Note: Coefficients are predicted probabilities of answering 'EU membership is a good thing' based on ordinal logit models with country-fixed effects. All control variables set to mean or mode.

Source: Eurobarometer 65.1 (2006).

Table 6.3. Effect of instrumental and sociable interactions on European identification

	Model 1		Model 2		Model 3	
	coeff.	(se)	coeff.	(se)	coeff.	(se)
International friendships	.878***	(.063)			.832***	(.063)
International job			.486***	(.058)	.315***	(.057)
Female	−.146***	(.042)	−.137**	(.042)	−.136**	(.042)
Age groups (55+ ref.)						
Age group 15–24	.212	(.136)	.243	(.145)	.209	(.137)
Age group 25–39	.301**	(.095)	.307**	(.099)	.294**	(.095)
Age group 40–54	.220**	(.077)	.224**	(.080)	.217**	(.077)
Educational attainment	.928***	(.072)	1.011***	(.073)	.918***	(.072)
Occupation (manager ref.)						
Self-employed	−.161*	(.064)	−.149*	(.067)	−.136*	(.065)
White collar	−.065	(.090)	−.080	(.092)	−.037	(.091)
Manual worker	−.318***	(.075)	−.321***	(.075)	−.273***	(.077)
Homemaker	−.271***	(.073)	−.257***	(.072)	−.212**	(.076)
Unemployed	−.319**	(.113)	−.289*	(.116)	−.262*	(.117)
Retired	−.417***	(.062)	−.398***	(.065)	−.355***	(.063)
Student	−.099	(.126)	−.025	(.129)	−.045	(.128)
Ideology	.770*	(.312)	.661*	(.301)	.772*	(.309)
Ideology squared	−.809*	(.327)	−.731*	(.316)	−.813*	(.324)
Household situation	.521***	(.121)	.535***	(.123)	.513***	(.121)
Urbanization	.298***	(.057)	.341***	(.061)	.293***	(.056)
Constant	−.358***	(.122)	−.331*	(.129)	−.413***	(.121)
Log-likelihood	−11,662.3		−11,784.5		−11,648.8	
McFadden's pseudo r-square	.101		.091		.102	

Note: Figures are coefficients of logit models with country-fixed effects, robust standard errors in parentheses. Country coefficients not shown. Two-tailed test, * p < .05, ** p < .01, *** p < .001. n = 18909.
Source: Eurobarometer 67.1 (2007).

forms of interactions. Does this relationship also hold with respect to European identification? An analysis of Eurobarometer 67.1 sheds further light on this question. Results are shown in Table 6.3. In this case, instrumental interactions are captured by the fact of having a job that involves contact with organizations and people in other countries. Sociable interactions are operationalized on an ordinal scale using the following two items: having friends in another EU member state, and having friends in non-European countries.[3] The control variables included in this analysis are the same as the ones used in the models predicting European identification in Chapter 4.

Overall, the results of this analysis echo the findings with respect to EU membership support. The effect of sociable interactions in Model 1 is almost twice as strong as the effect of instrumental interactions in Model 2, and this difference even increases in the full model (Model 3).

[3] Loevinger's coefficient (HjK) of .55.

Table 6.4. Changes in predicted probability of European identification due to sociable and instrumental transactions

	Predicted probability	95% confidence interval lower bound	95% confidence interval higher bound
Base-line model	.56	.54	.59
Instrumental interactions: international job	.64	.61	.67
Sociable interactions: international friends	.75	.72	.78

Note: Coefficients are predicted probabilities of European identification based on logit models with country-fixed effects. All control variables set to mean or mode.
Source: Eurobarometer 67.1 (2007).

To further interpret these results, the predicted probabilities of identifying as European are displayed in Table 6.4. The predictions are based on Model 3 in Table 6.3; all control variables are set to their mean or mode. The baseline model shows the predicted probability of European identification for people who have reported neither sociable (international friends) nor instrumental (international job) interactions. When comparing the predictions of this model to the other predictions, it appears that both variables significantly increase the probability of considering oneself as European. However, while having an international job increases the probability by eight percentage points, having international friends does so by nineteen percentage points.

All in all, these findings strongly support Hypothesis 3b, that sociable interactions have a greater impact on EU support and European identity than purely instrumental ones. This is informative with respect to the mechanism that links individual transnationalism to orientations towards European integration. In Chapter 3, two alternative mechanisms were proposed. Highly transnational people might be more pro-European because by interacting across borders, they benefit from intra-European border removal, or they might be more pro-European because by interacting across borders they acquire a more inclusive, cosmopolitan self-concept and collective identity. The findings suggest that the latter mechanism is more powerful.

Beyond the scope of this question, these results contribute to the scholarly debate on whether utilitarian considerations or group identity prevail in explaining attitudes toward European integration. To be sure, both forms of transnational interactions—sociable and instrumental—exert a significant effect on European identity. This suggests that both utilitarian and identitarian aspects influence public evaluations of European integration (McLaren 2006). However, the effect of instrumental interactions on EU membership support is not significant. Moreover, the fact that sociable interactions have a stronger and more robust effect confirms earlier studies suggesting that exclusive national identities are a more powerful predictor of EU support (Hooghe and Marks 2004).

6.2 Scope: Binational and European Interactions

We now turn to the scope of transnational interactions in Europe. Whether cross-border interactions are limited to a single country, cover the EU, or extend themselves beyond European borders, it is argued, influences how individuals experience and interpret them, and ultimately, whether they relate them to attitudes towards European integration. The present section focuses on the first distinction—binational and European interactions—whereas the subsequent section differentiates between intra- and extra-European interactions.

Not all transnational interactions in Europe are genuinely European, nor are they necessarily perceived as such. For a number of reasons, some Europeans predominantly interact with one other European member state. Europeans might have relatives living in another country, their own country might have established a special relationship with another member state, or they might just live very close to a national border and therefore have the opportunity to interact with their neighbouring country on a daily basis.

This last scenario is examined in the following analyses. As was stated in Hypothesis 4, interactions among people living in intra-European border districts are expected to be less effective in fostering EU support than interactions among other Europeans. Considering the immediate proximity of their neighbouring country, border residents are likely to primarily interact with people and institutions across the border, and to frame their transnational activity in a binational rather than genuinely European context.

Analysing EU support and transnationalism among border residents also seems to be fruitful beyond the narrow focus of the questions asked above. Chapter 5 has shown that transnational interactions and networks are a niche phenomenon in Europe today. This might be different in intra-European border districts. After all, national border districts are deemed to be the places where the consequences of European integration are most directly felt in everyday life (Dürrschmidt 2006). Border residents can more easily engage in transnational networks and mobility than the rest of the population. Due to their exposure to foreign cultures, border districts have also been perceived as unique laboratories of societal integration and of a supranational identity in the making (Delhey 2004). As O'Dowd (2001: 95) puts it, 'the study of what is happening to, and at, state borders is a *sine qua non* for an adequate understanding of the EU as an emergent transnational polity'. This explains the strong scholarly interest in collective identities (Meinhof 2003; Dürrschmidt 2006; Eigmüller and Vobruba 2006; Rippl et al. 2010; Roose 2010) and EU support (Schmidberger 1997; Gabel 1998b; Díez Medrano 2003) among people living close to a national border. The following analysis aims at contributing to this vivid scholarly debate.

Existing research mainly emphasizes the 'direct' effect of living in a border district on attitudes towards European integration, and expects border residents to be more pro-European. The main argument is that by living close to another European member state, border residents can more frequently benefit from resources beyond their own country, and therefore should endorse intra-European border removal (Gabel 1998b). Analysing pooled Eurobarometer data for twelve EU member states from 1975 to 1992, Gabel finds that people living in a region bordering another country show significantly more EU support than the rest of the population (Gabel 1998b). In an analysis of Eurobarometer data of 1999, Díez Medrano (2003) confirms these findings. Examining border regions in Spain, France, Germany, and Italy, Schmidberger (1997) obtains similar results. However, using a more precise operationalization of border residence, an analysis of German and French border districts shows that the border effect on EU support holds only for German border districts, and that this effect is in fact mediated by transnational interaction (Kuhn 2012a). In other words, living in a border district is not enough; one needs to also actively engage in cross-border interactions.

This chapter tackles the relationship between border residence, transnationalism, and EU support from a different angle. Rather than asking whether border residence or transnationalism make people more pro-European, it asks whether transnational interactions are equally effective in border districts and in non-border districts. The underlying argument is that people living close to another European member state are likely to primarily interact with that state, and to frame their interactions in a binational rather than European context. They might thus less readily link their transnationalism to their attitudes towards European integration.

To test the hypothesis that transnational interactions in border districts are less effective in triggering EU support, the following analysis relies on Eurobarometer survey 65.1 for Germany and France. While Germany is highly federalized, France is the prototype of a centralized nation state. Using these two cases thus allows the impact of vertical division of powers on the border effect to be controlled. Moreover, Germany and France are sufficiently large for a sensible distinction between border and core districts to be made, and their statistical offices provide structural indicators at the regional level.

The information on respondents' residence usually provided by Eurobarometer limits itself to the NUTS-1[4] and NUTS-2 level (Roose 2010). Thus, the most detailed information on where German and French respondents live refers to the sixteen German federal states and the twenty-two French *régions*. This is a rather imprecise basis for distinguishing between border and non-border residents. Therefore, previous research on EU attitudes among border residents was forced to make a relatively crude distinction between regions or provinces bordering another country and those in the centre of the country. For example, when relying on the NUTS-2 level, the German city of Göttingen, as far as 300 kilometres away from the next national border, is coded as a border district.

In contrast, for the present analysis, access to respondents' residential data on the NUTS-3 level for Eurobarometer 65.1 has been granted. This level refers to the over 400 German administrative districts[5] (*Landkreise und Kreisfreie Städte*), and to the 100 French *départements*.[6] A unique dataset has been created, including survey data from the Eurobarometer wave 65.1 (2006) as well as structural indicators on the NUTS-3 level. This makes it possible to distinguish more precisely between border districts and non-border districts and to control for other contextual effects at this level. A dichotomous variable identifies all border districts at the NUTS-3 level. Only those districts that directly border another state are included in the category of border districts.[7] This procedure is in line with Gabel's (1998b: 155) operationalization of border regions. This procedure yields twenty-eight German and twenty-one French border districts.

At the individual level, the same factors are controlled for as in previous analyses using Eurobarometer 65.1 in this book. To ascertain that a discovered effect of border residence is not spurious to other regional characteristics, a number of district-level control variables are included. These indicators are drawn from the Regional database of the German Statistical Offices of the Federation and the Länder (2006a–2006c) as well as from the French Institute of Statistics and Economic Studies (INSEE 2005, 2006, 2007). Control variables included in the analyses refer to unemployment rate, GDP per capita, and the ratio of foreign residents in a region. In the German case, a dichotomous variable accounts for living in the former GDR.

To test the hypothesis that transnational interactions in border districts are less effective in generating EU support, the border variable is interacted with the individual transnationalism scale. For the hypothesis to be confirmed, the

---

[4] The nomenclature of territorial units system (NUTS) is a coherent categorization of territorial units across Europe. It has three levels, the smallest of which is the NUTS-3 level.

[5] Note that only 192 German administrative districts are represented in the dataset. Thus, the higher-level units are a sample rather than the full population.

[6] The number of *départements* in the sample drops to ninety-four as the French overseas departments and Corsica are not included.

[7] For more information on the coding, see Chapter 5.

coefficient of the interaction needs to significantly decrease the effect of transnationalism on EU support.

Given the nested structure of the data and the macro-level predictor, all findings presented in the following section are based on two-level ordinal logit models with a random slope for individual transnationalism using the GLLAMM package available for Stata (Rabe-Hesketh and Skrondal 2005).

Table 6.5 presents the results of the empirical analyses. Model 1 includes the individual transnationalism scale and the border variable. In Model 2, the

Table 6.5. Effect of individual transnationalism and border residence on EU membership support

	Model 1		Model 2	
	coeff.	(se)	coeff.	(se)
Individual transnationalism	1.706***	(.285)	2.100***	(.317)
Border district	.044	(.152)	1.205**	(.418)
Individual TN * border district			−.712**	(.236)
Female	−.230*	(.098)	−.224*	(.099)
Age groups (55+ ref.)				
Age group 15–24	−.117	(.240)	−.124	(.241)
Age group 25–39	−.418*	(.170)	−.424*	(.171)
Age group 40–54	−.346*	(.154)	−.343*	(.155)
Educational attainment	.533***	(.152)	.525***	(.153)
Occupation (Manager ref.)				
Self-employed	−.253	(.236)	−.254	(.237)
White collar	−.157	(.205)	−.161	(.206)
Manual worker	−.337	(.174)	−.344*	(.175)
Homemaker	−.229	(.229)	−.247	(.230)
Unemployed	−.531*	(.222)	−.530*	(.223)
Retired	−.123	(.202)	−.121	(.203)
Student	.053	(.351)	.010	(.353)
Ideology	−.232	(.218)	−.213	(.219)
Ideology squared	−.171	(.187)	−.168	(.187)
Household situation	.738**	(.266)	.766**	(.268)
Attitudes towards immigrants	−.391	(.212)	−.381	(.213)
Discuss politics	.521**	(.173)	.520**	(.174)
Convince others	.272	(.166)	.264	(.166)
Urbanization	−.190	(.170)	−.218	(.172)
Unemployment rate	.069	(.416)	.068	(.423)
GDP per capita	.725	(.487)	.671	(.492)
France	−.196	(.138)	−.223	(.141)
East Germany	−.069	(.216)	−.079	(.219)
T1	−.281	(.390)	−.216	(.393)
T2	.428	(.390)	.497	(.393)
Variance components				
Level 2 variance (constant)	.220	(.125)	.262*	(.133)
Level 2 variance (individual transnationalism)	.004	(.049)	.026	(.136)
Log-likelihood	−1896.5		−1892.0	
AIC	3853.1		3846.0	

Note: Figures are coefficients of multilevel ordinal logit models with random slope for individual transnationalism. Standard errors in parentheses. Two-tailed test, * p < .05, ** p < .01, *** p < .001. N = 276, n = 2,020.

Source: Eurobarometer 65.1 (2006).

interaction effect is added. As shown in Model 1, individual transnationalism has a strong positive effect on EU membership support, while there is no direct effect of living in a border district.[8] However, the interaction effect in Model 2 is negative and significant. In other words, border residence significantly decreases the effect of individual transnationalism. In districts not bordering another country, individual transnationalism has an effect size of 2.1 on EU support. By subtracting the coefficient of the interaction effect, one can calculate the effect of individual transnationalism in border districts (Brambor et al. 2006): The effect size drops to 1.388. This indicates that attitudes towards European integration among border residents are less dependent on their transnational interactions than among people living further away from the border.

Figure 6.1 shows the change in predicted probabilities of EU membership support for border residents and people not living close to another EU member state. In border districts, people with the highest level of individual transnationalism are about twenty percentage points more likely to support European integration than people not interacting across borders. However, individual transnationalism has a much greater impact in districts further

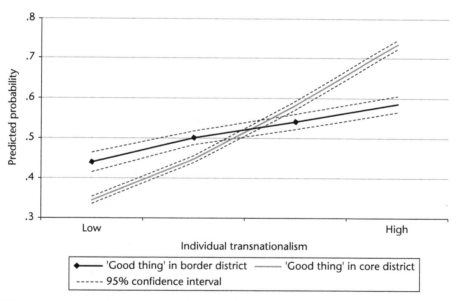

Figure 6.1. Change in predicted probability of EU membership support due to individual transnationalism in border and core districts

---

[8] Further analyses of the border effect show that it is indeed significant in German border districts, but not in French border districts. See Kuhn 2012a.

away from a border. Here, the most transnational individuals are twice as likely to endorse EU membership as the least transnational individuals.

All in all, these findings strongly support Hypothesis 4 that transnational interactions in border districts are less effective in generating EU support than transnational interactions in non-border districts. Assuming that border residents mainly interact with the neighbouring country, this analysis suggests that people living close to another European border frame their transnational interactions in a binational context rather than a European context. When crossing the border to go to work or meet friends, border residents might not have the EU but a binational community in mind. Again, to be more transnational does not necessarily imply being more pro-European.

6.3 Scope: Interactions within Europe and beyond

Deutsch expected transnational interactions to remain within the boundaries of a security community. In other words, when encouraging increased transactions across borders, he implied that these transactions overcome national borders but not those of the security community itself. From today's perspective, this assumption is unrealistic. In the wake of global market integration and massive immigration flows from non-European countries, intra-European transactions go hand in hand with transactions that reach beyond the European borders. Europeans holiday in Northern Africa, do business with South-East Asia, and study in the United States. These experiences might have very different effects on attitudes and identities than intra-European transactions. First, people interacting with institutions and individuals outside of Europe might not link their transnational activity to the European Union at all (Savage et al. 2005). What is more, as intra-European boundary removal has been accompanied by the strengthening of external borders, people frequently travelling to third countries might actually perceive stricter external European border control as an obstacle to their transnationalism. As already indicated in Hypothesis 5 in the theoretical framework of this book, intra-European transactions are expected to have a significantly stronger effect on EU support than transactions that reach beyond the borders of Europe.

The following analyses therefore separate intra-European interactions from interactions that reach beyond European borders and test their respective association with EU support. While the items used in Eurobarometer 65.1 do not allow the making of such a distinction, Eurobarometer 67.1 specifically asks respondents about their friendships with other Europeans and about friendships with people who hail from outside Europe. These two items operationalize intra-European and non-European interactions for the purpose of this analysis. The findings of the analyses are depicted in Table 6.6.

Table 6.6. Effect of intra- and non-European interactions on European identification

	Model 1		Model 2		Model 3	
	b	se	b	se	b	se
European friends	.659***	(.038)			.602***	(.040)
Non-European friends			.451***	(.050)	.217***	(.053)
Female	−.142**	(.044)	−.155***	(.041)	−.143***	(.043)
Age groups (55+ ref.)						
Age group 15–24	.209	(.135)	.238	(.143)	.207	(.134)
Age group 25–39	.303**	(.095)	.311**	(.098)	.301**	(.095)
Age group 40–54	.223**	(.077)	.223**	(.079)	.221**	(.077)
Educational attainment	.937***	(.072)	.991***	(.072)	.925***	(.072)
Occupation (Manager ref.)						
Self-employed	−.165*	(.065)	−.178**	(.065)	−.161*	(.064)
White collar	−.077	(.089)	−.099	(.091)	−.067	(.089)
Manual worker	−.322***	(.074)	−.368***	(.074)	−.314***	(.074)
Homemaker	−.285***	(.071)	−.319***	(.070)	−.272***	(.072)
Unemployed	−.329**	(.111)	−.354**	(.115)	−.320**	(.112)
Retired	−.424***	(.064)	−.468***	(.063)	−.414***	(.063)
Student	−.101	(.122)	−.106	(.129)	−.099	(.123)
Ideology	.765*	(.310)	.696*	(.310)	.777*	(.311)
Ideology squared	−.814*	(.324)	−.747*	(.325)	−.819*	(.326)
Household situation	.502***	(.121)	.554***	(.122)	.507***	(.121)
Urbanization	.316***	(.059)	.321***	(.060)	.304***	(.058)
Constant	−.344**	(.124)	−.288*	(.126)	−.359**	(.122)
Log-likelihood	−11,657.8		−11,767.5		−11,647.5	
McFadden's pseudo r-square	.101		.093		0102	

Note: Figures are coefficients of logit models with country-fixed effects, robust standard errors in parentheses. Country coefficients not shown. Two-tailed test, * p < .05, ** p < .01, *** p < .001. *n* = 18,909.
Source: Eurobarometer 67.1 (2007).

Models 1 and 2 show the separate effects of intra-European interactions in the form of European friendships, and interactions beyond Europe in the form of friendships to non-Europeans, respectively. Both forms of interactions have a highly significant and positive effect on European identity, but the effect of having European friends is stronger. This difference becomes even more pronounced when including both predictors in Model 3.

The changes in predicted probabilities of categorizing oneself as European (Table 6.7) provide further support for the hypothesis that intra-European interactions play a stronger role in structuring European collective identity than non-European interactions. The predictions are based on Model 3 in Table 6.6. While all control variables are set to their mean, the independent variables are allowed to vary. The predictions show that having non-European friends increases the probability of European identification by five percentage points. However, the bounds of the confidence intervals slightly overlap, indicating that this difference is not significant. On the other hand, having European friends boosts the probability of European identification by 14 per cent. People with European friends have a likelihood of 70 per cent to

Table 6.7. Changes in predicted probability of European identification due to having (non-) European friends

	Predicted probability	95% confidence interval lower bound	95% confidence interval higher bound
Base-line model	.56	.54	.59
Having non- European friends	.61	.58	.64
Having European friends	.70	.67	.73

Note: Coefficients are predicted probabilities of European identification based on logit models with country-fixed effects. All control variables set to mean or mode.
Source: Eurobarometer 67.1 (2007).

consider themselves as Europeans, while people without foreign friends have a predicted probability of 56 per cent. As indicated by the confidence intervals, this difference is statistically significant.

In sum, the evidence provided strongly suggests that intra-European inter-actions play a more important role in structuring European identity than interactions that reach beyond the borders of Europe. In fact, the results suggest that non-European interactions alone do not significantly increase the probability of considering oneself as European. Policy makers aiming at strengthening pro-European orientations should therefore focus on promot-ing intra-European transactions rather than cross-border transactions in gen-eral. Nonetheless, it is worth noting that friendships with non-Europeans do not *decrease* the likelihood of identifying as European. The expectation that frequent interactions with third countries might have a negative impact on EU support, as these people might actually see European integration as an obstacle to their transnational interactions, could therefore not be supported.

6.4 Conclusion

A core conjecture of Deutsch's transactionalist theory posits that increased transnational interactions generate support for further European integration and promote a European 'we-feeling'. However, some theories and empirical findings challenge this expectation. Consequently, this chapter argued that not all transnational encounters necessarily generate EU support, but that their effectiveness depends on their purpose and scope. It therefore distinguished between sociable and instrumental interactions, between transnational inter-actions among border residents and among the rest of the population, and between intra-European and non-European interactions. The effects of these different types of interactions were analysed using data from Eurobarometer survey waves 65.1 and 67.1 for the EU-25 and EU-27, respectively.

The analyses of this chapter provided strong support for Hypothesis 3b by showing that sociable forms of interacting across borders have a stronger effect on EU support and European identity than purely instrumental interactions. Instrumental cross-border interactions such as buying petrol at the cheaper filling station across the border, or finding a job in a high-wage country, may have many advantages for the people involved, but they do not seem to trigger the 'learning effects' expected by Deutsch's transactionalist theory. Rather, people seem to approximate themselves to European integration by becoming emotionally closer to other Europeans. This finding bears important theoretical implications. It gives some indication of what the underlying mechanism linking individual transnationalism and EU support may be. According to the analyses carried out in this chapter, highly transnational Europeans are more pro-European due to sociable connections with other Europeans rather than due to the benefits accrued by interacting across borders. In a broader context, this finding suggests that questions of collective identity—rather than utilitarian considerations—are key to understanding orientations towards European integration (Laffan 1996; Hooghe and Marks 2004; McLaren 2006). While European policy makers are increasingly promoting non-economic networks and mobility across member states (Laffan 1996), they are well advised to strengthen their efforts even more in that direction.

Drawing on the example of border residents, the findings of this chapter suggested that, if experienced in a binational rather than a European context, transactions are less effective in prompting EU support and European identity. It was shown that—with regard to developing EU membership support— border residents react less strongly to transnational interactions than people living further away from the border. In addition, the analyses of this chapter provided support for the hypothesis that intra-European transactions are more decisive for orientations towards European integration than transactions that reach beyond the borders of Europe. Arguably, people frame their extra-European transactions quite differently to those that are intra-European. This is an important finding when one considers that increased European transactions go in tandem with an increase in global interconnectedness. What is more, some European countries maintain strong links to their former colonies. In short, Europeans might lead increasingly transnational, but not necessarily more European lives. This might be another explanation for the puzzling discrepancy between soaring transnational interactions and aggregate EU support and identity. While the data used in this analysis do not allow the operationalization of cosmopolitan orientations, it is likely that people who frequently engage in extra-European interactions see themselves as citizens of the world rather than as citizens of Europe. Moreover, these findings might add to the explanations of the low level of EU support among the British population. British citizens tend to have strong transnational links to the Commonwealth (Savage et al. 2005). While highly transnational, their transnationalism might thus fail to generate EU support and European identity.

To conclude, the analyses in this chapter suggest that the 'learning effects' set forth by transnational interactions are linked to identity change rather than to purely utilitarian considerations. Furthermore, to be effective, they ought to be experienced and framed in a genuinely European rather than binational or global frame of reference.

Chapter 7 goes a step further by arguing that increased transnational interactions are likely to generate negative externalities with respect to people with low levels of individual transnationalism. In highly globalized countries, Europeans that do not themselves interact on a transnational plane might react even more negatively to the transnationalization of their realm. This hypothesis is tested in multilevel analyses of Eurobarometer survey data.

7

The Janus Face of Increased Transactions

> *Globalization has to be understood as a dialectical phenomenon, in which events at one pole of a distanciated relation often produce divergent or even contrary occurrences at another.*[1]
>
> —Anthony Giddens

This book aims at further developing Deutsch's transactionalist theory by proposing and testing three major qualifications to it. In line with the first qualification, Chapter 5 has shown that individual transnationalism is greatly stratified within and across EU member states, and that only a relatively small elite of highly educated, young professionals from predominantly rich countries frequently interacts across countries. Next, Chapter 6 provided empirical support for the second qualification that not all cross-border transactions are equally successful in triggering EU support. In fact, transactions which are merely instrumental, as well as transactions within a binational or global context, are less effective than sociable transactions, or transactions with a genuinely European scope.

In turn, this chapter focuses on the third qualification to Deutsch's transactionalist theory, namely that increased transactions at the macro-level lead to negative externalities in the form of increased economic insecurity and cultural competition. People who do not interact across borders are especially concerned by these developments. They therefore react negatively to the transnationalization of their realm by adopting eurosceptic attitudes. This expectation is formalized in Hypothesis 6 in Chapter 3: the more transnationalized a country, the stronger the relationship between individual transnationalism and orientations towards European integration. The aim of this chapter is to further develop this idea and to put it under empirical scrutiny.

[1] Giddens 1991: 22.

By doing so, this chapter delivers two contributions to scholarly knowledge. First, it helps to answer the puzzle motivating this book: why, in the wake of increased transnational interactions, and given the clear correlation between individual transnationalism and pro-European orientations, do we observe low levels of EU membership support and European identity? Second, it sheds further light on a broader research question concerning recent increases in xenophobia and nationalism in several European member states, and the electoral success of right-wing populist parties that cater to such orientations. In light of the increased interconnectedness of European societies, and the 'learning processes' that such transactions are expected to generate, this development might appear paradoxical. However, this chapter shows that quite the contrary is the case—rather than representing a paradox, increasing euroscepticism is inherent to the transnationalization of European domestic societies. Euroscepticism is, in other words, a product of the current globaliza-tion[2] process.

The rest of this chapter is organized as follows. The next section discusses existing literature on the consequences of macro-level transnationalization on attitudes and identities, and explains how increased globalization could influ-ence EU support and European identity. Using the same data sources as in the previous chapters, a multilevel analysis tests the hypothesis that the effect of individual transnationalism is stronger the more globalized a country. Finally, results and their theoretical and policy implications are discussed.

7.1 Backlash or Embrace of Transnationalization?

In Chapter 4, we saw that the extent to which Europeans engage in trans-national activities in the EU is strongly and positively correlated with support for European integration and European identification. Highly transnational people are more likely to see themselves as Europeans and to think that EU membership is a good thing. This is in line with what was expected by Deutsch's transactionalist theory, and what many EU policy makers hope for when promoting intra-European transactions.

Consequently, one may jump to the conclusion that this relationship also holds on the aggregate level: if there are more transnational interactions in a country, its population should also be more likely to support European inte-gration and to feel European. In a broader perspective, this expectation relates to a lively scholarly debate concerning the impact of globalization on indi-vidual attitudes, identities, and behaviour (Guillén 2001; Norris and Inglehart

---

[2] Globalization and macro-level transnationalism are used interchangeably.

2009; Kaya and Karakoc 2012). The intensification of cross-border connectedness has provoked deep-seated societal changes and 'may in turn induce individual-level attitudinal changes as well' (Jung 2008: 579). What these attitudinal changes comprise is not clear, however. Two opposing views have been formulated. Some authors highlight the destructive forces of transnationalization, and predominantly conceive of it as a threat to the social and political cohesion of a country that induces subjective and objective insecurities in society. This is expected to spark a political backlash against globalization (Chomsky 1998; Swank and Betz 2003; Burgoon 2009). In contrast, the 'civilizing / integrative' research strand sees increased international interconnectedness as a trailblazer for economic prosperity and social welfare that brings people all over the world closer together (for a discussion, see Norris 2000; Bhagwati 2004; Kaya and Karakoc 2012: 26). As Norris puts it,

> we can expect the globalization of markets, governance, and communications to strengthen a cosmopolitan orientation, broadening identities beyond national boundaries to a world community, and increasing awareness of the benefits of transnational collaboration within regional associations and international institutions (Norris 2000: 157).

Why should this be the case? The reasoning behind this expectation is rather straightforward. By reducing or even eliminating barriers to international trade and foreign investment, globalization gives rise to more economic opportunities and offers a greater cultural variety. In the 'civilizing/integrative' research strand, people are expected to appreciate these new opportunities and to consequently embrace the transnationalization of society. World system analysis even goes a step further and expects people to internalize certain values that are inherent to globalization and modernization. According to this theory, rising interconnectedness constructs and generates highly rationalized, articulated, and 'surprisingly consensual' universalistic models concerning issues such as citizenship, socio-economic progress, human development, education, and the like (Meyer et al. 1997: 144–5). Following Meyer and colleagues, this leads to a global consensus on what fosters economic development and welfare, and on the best form of governance (Meyer and Hannan 1979; Meyer et al. 1997).

Considering the finding of Chapter 5 that people are more transnational in countries that are more integrated in the global economy, and the finding of Chapter 4 that individual transnationalism is positively related to EU support, one might expect that macro-level transnationalism leads to more EU support. It is striking, however, that especially in the European member states that are most transnationalized, we can observe an increase in eurosceptic and nationalist resentment, and the substantial electoral success of right-wing populist parties. As was discussed in further detail in Chapter 2, European member states differ considerably in the extent to which they are transnationalized. According to the KOF index of globalization (Dreher et al. 2008), in 2007, the most globalized EU member state was Belgium, followed by Austria and the Netherlands. These small open economies are not only at the forefront in the context of the European Union, but belong to the most transnationalized countries worldwide. They are, at the same time, witnessing pronounced conflicts along a demarcation–integration divide (Kriesi et al. 2008). While the Flemish–Walloon relationship in Belgium is a particular case (Deschouwer and Van Parijs 2009), both the Netherlands and Austria have repeatedly made headlines for the electoral success of their eurosceptical and right-wing populist parties. In Austria, the late Jörg Haider's right-wing populist party FPÖ (Austrian Freedom Party) has established itself as a powerful political player since the 1990s (Luther 2009), even forming a coalition government with the Austrian People's Party (ÖVP) from 2000 until 2007. Its success is predominantly based on its aggressive campaign against immigrants, Muslims, and the European Union. Faced with one of the most eurosceptical populations in the EU, other political parties, including the leading Social Democrats (SPÖ) have since decided to follow the anti-European discourse (Bale et al. 2010; Aichholzer et al. 2014).

The Netherlands, once the poster child of multicultural politics, has witnessed a similar trend (Sniderman and Hagendoorn 2007). Right-wing populist politicians Pim Fortuyn, and later Geert Wilders, have provoked a right-wing shift in Dutch party politics (Van Kersbergen and Krouwel 2008) and have stoked anti-immigrant and eurosceptical sentiments among the population. In fact, the biggest increase in euroscepticism all over the EU has been found among the formerly pro-European Dutch population, where people with a low level of education in particular have become increasingly critical of European integration due to a perceived ethnic threat (Lubbers and Jaspers 2011). Also outside of these two countries, we can observe the reification of (sub-)national identities (Buchan et al. 2009; Cram 2009) and an increase in hostile and ethnocentric attitudes (Rippl et al. 2005; Semyonov et al. 2006) that are often understood as negative reactions to globalization (Westle 2003). These observations strongly challenge the expectation that the more transnational a country, the more pro-European its citizens, and they make clear that even in the most globalized countries world-wide, a substantial share of the population is hostile towards further integration.

To better understand this apparent contradiction, it is necessary to consider the individuals that do not interact across borders themselves (either by choice or by fate), but are confronted with the transnationalization of their realm. We have seen in Chapter 4 that a broad share of the European population does not interact across borders at all, or does so to a very limited extent. This book has so far focused on the existing small group of transnationals and has aimed at analysing the extent to which transnational interactions render people more pro-European. Now, the emphasis shifts to the people who do not interact across borders, or do so only to a limited extent. To fully capture the dynamics of increased transactions, it is vital to know how they react to the transnationalization of their domain. As we have seen in Chapter 5, they tend to have a lower socio-economic status and are generally older. They are likely to be the 'losers' in a structural conflict among a demarcation–integration cleavage in post-industrial societies (Kriesi et al. 2008).

Other authors describe these dividing lines even more directly by emphasizing people's differential mobilities (Urry 2000). In Bauman's (1989: 9) view, mobility is 'the most powerful and most coveted stratifying factor; the stuff of which the new, increasingly world-wide, social, political, economic and cultural hierarchies are daily built and rebuilt'. Globalization, according to Bauman (1989: 88), leads to two coexisting realms, the world of the globally mobile and that of the locally tied. In a similar vein, Castells (2000b) opposes the 'space of flows', detached from geographical borders, to the (fixed) 'space of places'. In the context of European integration, Bartolini (2005) speaks of the division between the 'nomadic' and the 'standing'. Rather than physical mobility as such, Bartolini emphasizes the ability to use competing functional and regulative boundaries to one's advantage by transcending national borders (Bartolini 2005).

As argued in Chapter 3, there are good reasons to believe that the relationship between individual transnationalism and EU support is even stronger the more transnational the national society. In highly globalized countries, the structural conflict between integration and demarcation is likely to be more prominent. Globalization not only creates growth and widens economic, political, and social opportunities—it also induces economic risks and threatens the cultural homogeneity of national societies and local cultures. In view of increased economic competition from outside, people's private lives and professional careers have become less predictable and stable (Buchholz et al. 2009). Moreover, as Kriesi and colleagues argue (2008), the increasing presence and institutionalization of immigrant groups gives rise to feelings of threat and cultural competition. To sum up the argument, increased transactions create negative externalities—not only in economic but also in social and cultural terms. These are likely to be most directly felt by people who do not or rarely interact across borders. The proliferation of transactions challenges the status quo, induces socio-economic change and puts pressure on non-transnational members of society to become transnationally active themselves. This challenge is less prominent in more static societies.

Therefore, it is to be expected that, rather than rendering everyone more transnational and pro-European, globalization creates new social tensions that manifest themselves in a more pronounced conflict between pro- and anti-European attitudes. In the wake of this conflict, transnationally inactive Europeans might be more prone to the reification of their national identity, and to turning against any processes that undermine the national society, while highly transnational Europeans embrace the transnationalization of domestic societies. This expectation is in line with existing research that predicts a 'bifurcation of attitudes' (Roudometof 2005) amid globalization. Current comparative survey research on cosmopolitan attitudes provides empirical support for this argument. In a cross-country analysis of ISSP survey data, Haller and Roudometof (2010) find that while Europeans are generally more cosmopolitan than people from other regions of the world, they exhibit quite diverse attitudes on a cosmopolitan–local continuum. Using cross-national data from the European Social Survey, Mewes and Mau (2013) show that globalization exacerbates a socio-economic divide in welfare chauvinism. To cut a long story short, the structuring force of macro-level transnationalization widens the gap between highly transnational Europhiles and local eurosceptics.

Consequently, I specified Hypothesis 6 in Chapter 3: 'The more transnationalized a country, the stronger the relationship between individual transnationalism and orientations towards European integration.'

7.2 Empirical Analysis

The following analysis empirically tests this hypothesis. Just as in the previous chapters, Eurobarometer survey waves 65.1 (2006) and 67.1 (2007) are used to model EU membership support and European identification. A country's level of transnationalism is captured by the KOF index of globalization (Dreher et al. 2008).[3] To recapitulate from Chapter 2, the KOF index consists of three dimensions: economic, political, and social globalization. Economic globalization measures actual economic flows and economic restrictions. The dimension of social globalization captures the spread of ideas, information, images, and people. Finally, political globalization refers to a country's institutional links with the international community (Dreher et al. 2008). For the purpose of this study, the entire index is used. This chapter tests the hypothesis that individual transnationalism has a greater impact on EU support and European identity in more transnationalized countries. Formally, this means that a positive and significant interaction effect between individual transnationalism and globalization is expected (Brambor et al. 2006). Therefore,

---

[3] KOF index 2007 is used for the analyses of Eurobarometer 67.1, while KOF index 2006 is used for the analyses of Eurobarometer 65.1. For more detailed information on the index, see Chapter 2 and Dreher et al. 2008.

the KOF index of globalization is interacted with the individual transnationalism scale and used as a predictor of EU membership support and of European self-identification.

The analyses start out by predicting EU support (cf. Table 7.1). At the individual level, the same control variables as in previous chapters are included on the basis of existing research: a dummy variable accounts for gender; four different age groups capture age differences; educational

Table 7.1. Effect of individual and macro-level transnationalism on EU membership support

	Model 1		Model 2		Model 3	
	coeff.	(se)	coeff.	(se)	coeff.	(se)
Individual transnationalism	1.564***	(.118)	1.550***	(.118)	.617*	(.244)
Globalization index			.158	(.123)	−.321*	(.135)
Individual TN* globalization					1.404***	(.347)
Female	−.178***	(.033)	−.176***	(.033)	−.168***	(.033)
Educational attainment	.605***	(.051)	.595***	(.051)	.607***	(.051)
Age groups (55+ ref.)						
Age group 15–24	.046	(.084)	.051	(.084)	.071	(.084)
Age group 25–39	−.131*	(.054)	−.126*	(.054)	−.113*	(.054)
Age group 40–54	−.220***	(.049)	−.220***	(.049)	−.216***	(.049)
Occupation (manager ref.)						
Self-employed	−.243	(.076)	−.239	(.076)	−.237**	(.076)
White collar	−.231***	(.067)	−.225***	(.067)	−.231***	(.067)
Manual worker	−.389***	(.061)	−.391***	(.061)	−.392***	(.061)
Homemaker	−.331***	(.077)	−.333***	(.077)	−.357***	(.077)
Unemployed	−.515***	(.081)	−.517***	(.081)	−.521***	(.081)
Retired	−.225***	(.068)	−.232***	(.068)	−.229***	(.068)
Student	−.253*	(.110)	−.249*	(.110)	−.270*	(.110)
Ideology	.453***	(.062)	.438***	(.062)	.427***	(.062)
Ideology squared	−.113*	(.051)	−.111*	(.051)	−.123*	(.051)
Household situation	1.007***	(.090)	.985***	(.090)	.953***	(.090)
Attitudes towards immigrants	.523***	(.055)	.520***	(.055)	.515***	(.055)
Convince others	.022	(.054)	.018	(.054)	.029	(.054)
Discuss politics	.337***	(.057)	.340***	(.057)	.379***	(.057)
Urbanization	.133**	(.041)	.132**	(.041)	.147***	(.041)
GDP per capita	.769***	(.192)	.930*	(.365)	.982***	(.285)
Inflation rate	.558***	(.103)	.841***	(.126)	.813***	(.117)
Unemployment rate	.598***	(.094)	.450***	(.108)	.990***	(.091)
Intra-European trade	−.103	(.073)	−.184	(.096)	−.363***	(.089)
T1	.028	(.133)	.081	(.176)	−.220	(.144)
T2	1.861***	(.133)	1.970***	(.177)	1.668***	(.145)
Variance components						
Level 2 variance (constant)	.199***	(.0187)	.196***	(.0180)	.227***	(.021)
Level 2 variance (Ind. transnationalism)	.184*	(.080)	.170	(.119)	.077	(.048)
Log-likelihood	−15,244.5		−15,241.4		−15,233.2	
AIC	30,5471		30,542.8		30,528.5	

Note: Figures are coefficients of multilevel logit models with random slope for individual transnationalism, standard errors in parentheses. Two-tailed test, * p < .05, ** p < .01, *** p < .001. N = 25; n = 16.672.

Source: Eurobarometer 65.1 (2006), Dreher et al. (2008).

attainment and occupational groups account for socio-economic differences. To control for other political orientations that might be correlated with the dependent variables, I include a variable measuring political ideology on a left–right scale and its square, and I control for dissatisfaction with domestic politics and anti-immigrant attitudes. Following Inglehart's (1970) cognitive mobilization hypothesis, the analysis also controls for the skill to convince others and the habit of discussing politics. Finally, respondents' self-assessed economic situation and differences in the level of urbanization of respondents' residence are accounted for.

To capture country-level heterogeneity, controls for unemployment (Eurostat 2006c, 2007c), GDP per capita in purchasing power parities (Eurostat 2006a, 2007a), inflation (Eurostat 2006b, 2007b), and intra-European trade relative to total trade (Eurostat 2006d, 2006e, 2007d, 2007e) are included, as these factors have been shown to influence EU support (Eichenberg and Dalton 1993; Franklin and Wlezien 1997; Eichenberg and Dalton 2007). All independent and control variables are standardized to run from 0 to 1 so as to more easily compare their coefficients and interpret the interaction effects. While previous models accounted for the nested structure of the data by estimating fixed effects models with country dummies and robust standard errors, the following analyses are conducted using multilevel ordinal logit (for EU membership support) and multilevel logit models (for European identification) with random coefficients for individual transnationalism.[4]

Model 1 includes all individual-level variables as well as the macro-level control variables. As can be seen in this model, individual transnationalism has a strong, positive, and highly significant effect on EU membership support. While this has already been established in the previous chapters, the present analysis shows that the effect also remains robust when estimating a multilevel model and when controlling for certain structural differences. Model 2 presents the direct effect of globalization on EU support. As expected, globalization per se does not influence support for EU membership, thus challenging both the 'civilizing/integrative' and 'destructive/globalization as a threat' hypotheses in current research (Kaya and Karakoc 2012). However, the main interest here lies in the interaction between individual transnationalism and globalization. In other words, how does the effect of individual transnationalism vary in highly and less globalized countries? To answer this question, a cross-level interaction (individual transnationalism *globalization) is included in Model 2. The coefficient of the cross-level interaction is positive and highly significant. This means that a country's level of transnationalism

---

[4] Models are estimated using the Gllamm package in Stata.

significantly strengthens the relationship between individual transnationalism and EU support. In other words, in highly globalized countries, individual transnationalism is a stronger predictor of EU support than in less globalized countries.

The coefficients of the constitutive terms of the interaction refer to the marginal effect of this item if all other constitutive terms are held at zero (Brambor et al. 2006). Model 2 reveals a positive and highly significant coefficient for the individual transnationalism scale. Hence, if the index of globalization is held at zero, individual transnationalism has a positive significant effect with an effect size of .617. By adding the interaction term, we obtain the marginal effect of individual transnationalism when the globalization index is held at its maximum. Thus, in a highly globalized country, the marginal effect of individual transnationalism is 2.021. Consequently, in highly globalized countries, transnationalism has the strongest effect in the entire model, and its effect is more than three times as high as in the least globalized countries. This strongly supports the hypothesis that macro-level transnationalization exacerbates the relationship between individual transnationalism and EU support.

Figure 7.1 further clarifies this relation by visualizing the marginal effect of individual transnationalism for the complete observed range of the globalization index following Brambor and colleagues (2006). The solid line in the

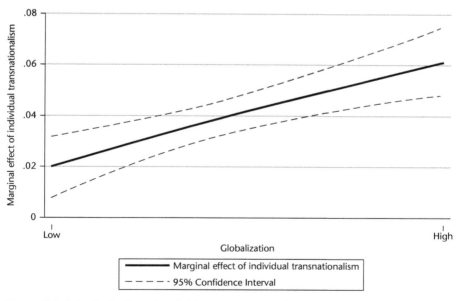

Figure 7.1. Marginal effect of individual transnationalism on EU membership support
Source: Eurobarometer 65.1 (2006), Dreher et al. (2008); control variables set to mean or reference category

figure shows how a one-standard-deviation increase in transnationalism (from its mean) affects the probability of supporting EU membership across the observed range of the globalization index. We can see that individual transnationalism significantly increases the likelihood of EU membership support, and that this effect is stronger with higher levels of globalization. This again supports the hypothesis that globalization exacerbates the relationship between individual transnationalism and EU support.

It is also interesting to obtain further insight on the substantive significance of the relationship. To this aim, Figure 7.2 shows the predicted probabilities of answering that EU membership is 'bad thing' and a 'good thing', respectively. More concretely, the figure on the left compares the change in predicted probability of answering 'good thing' between people living in a highly globalized country and those living in a more isolated country. In both cases, people are less likely to be eurosceptical the more transnational they are. However, the figure shows that the curve for people in a highly globalized country is much steeper. This indicates that transnationalism has greater predictive power on EU support in more transnational countries. What is more, the figure also shows that the predicted probabilities of answering 'EU membership is bad' differ significantly at the lower level of the individual transnationalism index, while there is no significant difference at the higher level of transnationalism. The figure on the right-hand side shows that the same is true with respect to the likelihood of answering that EU membership is a bad

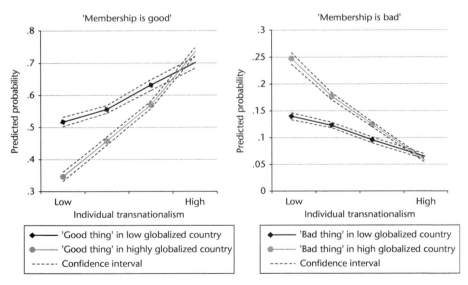

Figure 7.2. Predicted probabilities of answering membership is good/bad in high and low globalized countries

thing. This implies that highly transnational people are equally pro-European, no matter whether they live in a highly globalized country or not. In contrast, people that do not interact across borders but live in a highly integrated country, such as the Netherlands, are even more eurosceptical than people with equally low levels of transnational behaviour living in more isolated countries, such as Portugal. All in all, the analyses thus far provide strong support for the hypothesis that the effect of individual transnationalism on EU support is greater in more globalized countries.

Do we find a similar relationship also with respect to European identity, measured here in terms of identification as European? The following analyses using Eurobarometer 67.1 (2007) provide the answer to this question and are presented in Table 7.2. Again, the KOF index of globalization, this time for the

Table 7.2. Effect of individual and macro-level transnationalism on European identification

	Model 1		Model 2	
	coeff.	(se)	coeff.	(se)
Individual transnationalism	2.891***	(.169)	2.231***	(.348)
Globalization index			.202	(.346)
Individual TN*globalization			1.118*	(.526)
Female	−.120***	(.033)	−.120***	(.033)
Age groups (55+ ref.)				
Age group 15–24	.168*	(.085)	.170*	(.085)
Age group 25–39	.271***	(.054)	.273***	(.054)
Age group 40–54	.222***	(.050)	.222***	(.050)
Educational attainment	.805***	(.053)	.804***	(.053)
Occupation (manager ref.)				
Self-employed	−.106	(.079)	−.106	(.079)
White collar	.011	(.069)	.010	(.069)
Manual worker	−.208***	(.062)	−.209***	(.062)
Homemaker	−.161*	(.080)	−.160*	(.080)
Unemployed	−.218*	(.086)	−.219*	(.086)
Retired	−.281***	(.069)	−.281***	(.069)
Student	−.092	(.118)	−.091	(.118)
Ideology	−.035	(.063)	−.034	(.063)
Ideology squared	−.176***	(.050)	−.176***	(.050)
Household situation	.467***	(.078)	.470***	(.078)
Urbanization	.235***	(.042)	.236***	(.042)
Unemployment rate	.691*	(.338)	.686*	(.334)
GDP per capita	−.015	(.543)	−.171	(.568)
Inflation rate	−.553	(.381)	−.418	(.415)
Intra-EU trade	.094	(.288)	.021	(.302)
Constant	−1.071**	(.327)	−1.147**	(.351)
Level 2 variance (constant)	.144***	(.042)	.140***	(.041)
Level 2 variance (individual transnationalism)	.347***	(.192)	.273***	(.160)
Log-likelihood	−11,526.9		−11,524.3	
AIC	23,101.7		23,100.7	

Note: Figures are coefficients of multilevel logit models with random slope for individual transnationalism, standard errors in parentheses. Two-tailed test, * p < .05, ** p < .01, *** p < .001. N = 27, n = 18,882.

Source: Eurobarometer 67.1 (2007), Dreher et al. (2008).

year 2007, is interacted with the individual transnationalism index and used as a predictor of European identification.

With slight variations due to data availability, the same control variables are used as in the preceding analyses: gender, age groups, educational groups, political ideology and its square, as well as the degree of urbanization account for individual-level heterogeneity, while GDP per capita, intra-European trade as the share of total trade, and inflation rate are included as macro-level control variables.

As shown in Table 7.2, macro-level transnationalization also significantly strengthens the effect of individual transnationalism on European identity, albeit not as much as in the previous analysis. The effect of individual trans-nationalism ranges from 2.231 in a poorly globalized country to 3.349 in a highly globalized country. This means that individual transnationalism is roughly 50 per cent more effective in influencing one's identification as European at the highest observed level of globalization than at the lowest observed level of globalization.

As shown in Figure 7.3, the marginal effect of individual transnationalism is positive and significant across the entire observed range of the globalization index. It is worth noting that the bounds of the confidence interval fan out at both extremes of the globalization index. In fact, while the marginal effect

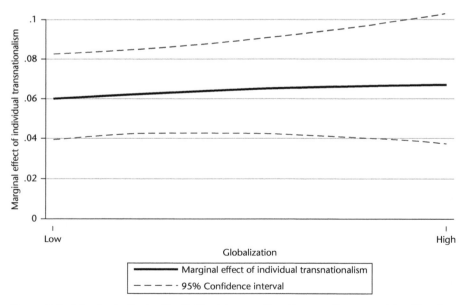

Figure 7.3. Marginal effect of individual transnationalism on European identification as globalization increases

Source: Eurobarometer 67.1 (2007), Dreher et al. (2008); control variables set to mean or reference category

of individual transnationalism slightly increases with each higher level of globalization, the lower bound of the confidence interval decreases as the globalization index reaches its observed maximum. Hence, in statistical terms, I cannot guarantee that the marginal effect of individual transnationalism is in fact greater at the extremes of the globalization index, as suggested by the calculations derived from Table 7.2. However, only a few countries cover the extreme values of the globalization index. It is therefore likely that the 'fanning out' of the confidence intervals is due to the few observations at both ends of the index.

Figure 7.4 presents the predicted probabilities of identifying oneself as European in countries with low, average, and high levels of globalization. The figure confirms that the higher the level of individual transnationalism, the more likely a person is to consider themselves European. It also shows that this relationship is slightly stronger for people living in more globalized countries. This is especially the case for people with low to medium levels of transnationalism, that is, the majority of the European population. However, it should be noted that the differences are not in any way as pronounced as in the previous analysis. While confidence intervals are not shown in this figure, the identification of people with extremely low and extremely high

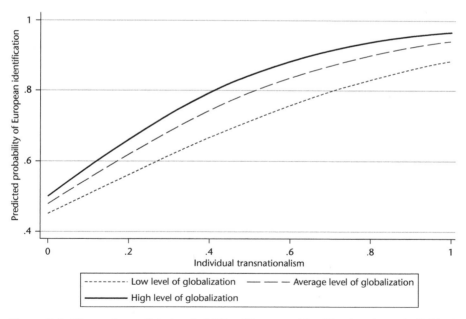

Figure 7.4. Change in predicted probability of European identification due to individual transnationalism in low and highly globalized countries

Source: Eurobarometer 67.1 (2007), Dreher et al. (2008); control variables set to mean or reference category

involvement in transnational interactions and networks does not seem to differ across countries. Thus, while the findings support the hypothesis that individual transnationalism has a stronger impact on European identification in highly transnationalized countries, the evidence provided is clearly weaker than in the case of membership support.

Keeping this caveat in mind, the analyses presented in this chapter suggest that macro-level transnationalization strengthens the relationship between individual transnationalism and EU membership support. They also provide some—albeit weaker—evidence with respect to European identification. Rather than strengthening EU support among the entire population, increased transnational interactions at the macro-level polarize the relationship between highly transnational individuals supporting European integration, and those who do not, or rarely, interact across borders and are critical towards the integration process.

How do we know that it is transnationalization, rather than other structural differences, that ultimately influences the relationship between individual transnationalism and EU support? In order to exclude the possibility that the detected interaction effect is spurious to other relationships, I conducted further analyses with additional macro-level independent variables. I estimated the direct effect and the interaction effect of living in a post-communist country, the percentage of other Europeans living and working in a country, the percentage of third-country nationals living and working in the country, and international air travel. Considering the framing power of political parties, I accounted for the average EU-position in party framing in each country using the Chapel Hill Expert Survey 2006 (Hooghe et al. 2010). These analyses either yielded non-significant effects, or the results were inconclusive because they contradicted each other. This again suggests that it is globalization rather than other country-level differences that polarizes the relationship between transnationalism and public orientations towards European integration.

7.3 Conclusion

The increase of cross-border connectedness is one of the most significant social phenomena of our times. While scholars disagree on whether the increase in transnational interactions of the past decades is something entirely new (Hirst and Thompson 1996; Wade 1996), there is consensus in the literature that it greatly impacts our daily lives. This has motivated a wide array of theories on how globalization changes people's mindsets. At the one extreme, optimists highlight the 'civilizing' nature of globalization and predict that in the wake of increased global interconnectedness, people become increasingly cosmopolitan and open towards different ways of life, which themselves are expected to converge (Norris 2000; Bhagwati 2004). The other extreme position paints a bleak picture of the consequences of globalization. These authors speak of a 'backlash against globalization' and expect chauvinism, nationalism, and out-group-discrimination to increase, mainly because globalization is expected to increase competition and insecurity and to weaken social cohesion (Swank and Betz 2003; Mewes and Mau 2013).

Globalization directly relates to the topic of this book because it entails, among other things, the transnationalization of everyday life. Therefore, this chapter focused on the third qualification to Deutsch's transactionalist theory by emphasizing the negative externalities of increased transactions with respect to the people who do not become transnationally active. In contrast to the small elite of highly transnational Europeans, many people do not interact across borders on a regular basis. They tend to be less educated, worse-off, and older than highly transnational people, and they are likely to perceive the transnationalization of society as a threat to their domain—both in economic and in socio-cultural terms. Consequently, we can observe a structural conflict between the highly transnational 'winners' of globalization and its more rooted 'losers'. This conflict has been described before in several terms, such as 'demarcation–integration' (Kriesi et al. 2008), 'nomadic–standing' (Bartolini 2005), or 'space of flows' vs. 'space of places' (Castells 2000b). However, while previous contributions remained either on a theoretical level (Bauman 1989; Castells 2000b), or link it only to socio-economic differences, this book tackles the question head-on by showing that differences in transnational interactions are structurally linked to differences in attitudes towards European integration, and that this link is stronger the more globalized a society.

The analyses of this chapter showed that macro-level transnationalization exacerbates the effect of individual transnationalism on EU support and European identity. In other words, in highly globalized countries, the extent to which an individual is transnationally active has a stronger effect on public orientations towards European integration than in low globalized countries. Importantly, it has shown that people who do not (or rarely) interact across borders, but who live in a highly globalized country, are among the most eurosceptical members of society. Not only are they more critical towards European integration than people who regularly interact across borders, but also more critical than people with equally low levels of individual transnationalism living in less globalized countries. This last finding highlights once again that increased transactions at the macro-level (measured here with the KOF globalization index) do not directly lead to increased EU support and European identity of the entire population. Rather, they seem to render individual transnationalism even more powerful as a stratifying factor in

141

society. In highly transnationalized countries, there appears to be a clearer dividing line between the individuals who are transnationally active and support European integration, and those who remain within the boundaries of their nation state and are more critical towards European integration. This shows that euroscepticism in the face of growing transnationalism is not a paradox, but rather a product of globalization and European integration itself. In fact, euroscepticism among some members of society is not a relic of less transnational times; rather it is provoked by the transnationalization of society. People who do not interact across borders seem to perceive the transnationalization of their realm as a threat to the world as they know it, and they react by developing negative orientations towards European integration.

What does this chapter tell us with respect to the ongoing debate on the impact of globalization on collective identities and political attitudes? According to the 'civilizing' hypothesis, the integration of markets should render people more open and cosmopolitan (Norris 2000; Bhagwati 2004). In contrast, scholars advocating the 'destructive' hypothesis expect globalization to lead to alienation and a clash between cultures (Scheve and Slaughter 2001; Swank and Betz 2003; Burgoon 2009, 2013). The theoretical argument and empirical findings of this chapter help to reconcile these conflicting positions. They are both correct, but only to a certain extent, and do not provide the full picture. Rather than making everyone more cosmopolitan, or creating an anti-globalization backlash among the entire population, globalization seems to contribute to a 'bifurcation of attitudes' (Roudometof 2005: 127). While highly transnational people become increasingly more cosmopolitan and embrace the transnationalization of their realm, people who do not interact across borders develop sceptical attitudes towards further integration.

To avoid further political polarizations across society, it is advisable to implement policies that cushion the negative consequences of globalization and European integration among the static 'losers' of integration. Considering that Chapter 5 has shown that people with low levels of transnationalism generally have a lower socio-economic status and tend to be from poorer member states, these individuals are already in a disadvantaged situation in society. The removal of national borders and the possibility to interact transnationally further intensifies existing inequalities because being transnational becomes a major asset in today's society. Therefore, it seems useful to promote transnational interactions especially among the lower-educated and poorer members of society. However, for the time being, just the opposite seems to be the case. As Anheier and Falkenhain cogently observe, EU mobility programmes 'systematically exclude those groups among which the rise of Euroscepticism and support for anti-European political parties is the strongest, particularly the less well-educated and the new precariat' (Anheier and Falkenhain 2012: 229). In other words, these policies reify existing patterns of social inequality. Therefore, it seems advisable to further strengthen the social dimension of European integration, for example, to offset the negative consequences of increased international competition for those most exposed to it. This is a daunting task, however: Ironically, the people who might personally benefit from these policies are likely to be critical towards them because their boundaries of solidarity tend not to extend beyond their national community (Van der Waal et al. 2010).

8

Conclusion

Transnational Europhiles, Local Eurosceptics

Speaking from my experience as a person involved for a long time in building the European Union, it is important to have patience and efforts to build a community of nations.

—Giorgio Napolitano, President of the Italian Republic[1]

A major concern of European policy makers has been to integrate national societies by strengthening support for European integration and by promoting a collective European identity. One approach to achieving this goal puts an emphasis on transnational interactions and mobility. By interacting across borders, European citizens are expected to acquire a common identity and to develop support for the integration process. This idea was most famously presented by Deutsch and colleagues, and is at the very heart of the European integration process. It is not just European citizenship rights that enable Europeans to become transnationally active, but also a wide array of policies which actively promote cross-border interactions among Europeans.

After half a century of European integration, can we say that this strategy has been met with success? At face value, there is little evidence for this expectation. While transnational interactions and mobility certainly have increased over the past few decades, Europeans are reluctant in developing a collective identity, and tacit agreement with the integration process has given way to a broader and more critical range of attitudes.

---

[1] Quoted by the Japanese Ministry of Foreign Affairs, September 2009.

8.1 The Incomplete State of European Society Formation

The aim of this book was to engage in the theoretical discussion surrounding this development, and to ask why being and feeling European often drift apart. The presented evidence shows that people who regularly interact across borders in the European Union are indeed more likely to endorse EU membership and to identify themselves as European. However, this is only one part of the story. Taking a closer look at interaction patterns across the European Union by the use of cross-national survey data, it becomes clear that this applies merely to a small group of people and is stratified within and across member states. This book shows that the transnationally active Europeans are a small *avant-garde* of highly skilled young individuals from predominantly rich member states. They regularly cross borders, have international friends and acquaintances, use international media, agree with European institutional integration, and feel European. The overwhelming majority of European citizens, however, predominantly remain within the boundaries of their nation state. They are also less inclined to support EU membership or to identify themselves as Europeans.

This book is the first to systematically analyse the scale and distribution of transnational interactions across the entire European population, and shows that education is the strongest predictor of individual transnationalism. People with higher levels of education are more transnational. Above and beyond the educational effect, certain occupations provide better opportunities to interact across borders, and younger people are generally more transnational. Stratification persists across all aspects of individual transnationalism, but it is especially pronounced with respect to interactions that require more energy and resources, such as long-term stays abroad. In addition to individual differences, there is also considerable cross-country variation. Notwithstanding the mobility rights of European citizens, the duration of EU membership is not associated with higher levels of transnationalism. What really does seem to matter is a country's economic wealth. People living in more prosperous member states are also more transnational. To a lesser extent, a country's level of economic globalization positively influences individual transnationalism. Additionally, populations of smaller member states tend to be more transnational, most probably because smaller distances facilitate cross-border interactions. Moreover, people living in smaller countries might be more inclined to feel the need to exit their country because certain opportunities are not offered at home.

This book has also shown that interacting across borders is not necessarily enough to develop a European mindset. Some forms of cross-border transactions are more effective in promoting EU support and European identity than others. Purely instrumental interactions, such as cross-border shopping, have

145

little to no impact on Europeans' attitudes and identities. In contrast, sociable interactions have the power to instil a European sense of identity. This finding is very insightful with respect to the proposed mechanisms that link individual transnationalism to public orientations towards European integration. From a theoretical perspective, it is plausible that highly transnational individuals are more pro-European because European integration is in their interest, or because interacting across borders alters their self-concept and decreases group boundaries. The findings that sociable interactions have a stronger effect on EU support and European identity suggest that the latter mechanism is more powerful. In a broader perspective, this finding has important implications on the more general debate of what it is that structures EU support and European identification. The fact that sociable interactions outperform instrumental interactions in generating pro-European orientations gives more credence to the proposition that EU support is mainly a question of group identity rather than of material interest (Hooghe and Marks 2004; McLaren 2006, 2007).

The social stratification of transnational interactions represents an important building block for understanding the relevance of another contribution of the book, namely the negative externalities of transnational interactions. The book emphasizes the Janus-faced nature of increased interactions by arguing that macro-level transnationalization can provoke negative externalities among Europeans who are not transnationally active themselves. Macro-level transnationalization leads to greater competition, insecurity, and a need for flexibility, which in turn makes individual transnationalism a stronger stratifying factor in society. In highly transnationalized countries, people who do not interact across borders themselves are thus more likely to turn against these structural changes and become eurosceptical. In other words, higher transnationalization at the macro-level leads to a bifurcation of attitudes between highly transnational, pro-European individuals, and people who are not transnationally active and are rather sceptical towards European integration. This argument is sustained in the empirical analysis. Multilevel analyses show that in highly transnational countries, individual transnationalism has a greater impact on EU membership support and, to a lesser extent, on European identity, than in more isolated countries. In other words, higher degrees of macro-level transnationalization intensify the relationship between individual transnationalism and public orientations towards European integration. This finding suggests that in highly globalized societies, the integration–demarcation divide found by Kriesi and colleagues (2008) is even more pronounced, as people who rarely interact across borders might feel overwhelmed and marginalized by the transnationalization of their environment.

8.2 EU Support vs. European Identification

This book has emphasized two aspects of citizens' orientations towards European integration. On the one hand, it has focused on public support for European integration by studying the extent to which people think that EU membership of their country is a 'good thing'. This orientation is likely to be subject to short-term changes in the performance and policy output of European institutions and policy makers. On the other hand, the book has looked at European identity by studying whether people identify as European or not. It is to be expected that this orientation is more stable than the other one. In most analyses, the effect of individual transnationalism has proven to be very robust with respect to both EU membership support and European identification. In the analyses for each country in Chapter 4, however, the effect of individual transnationalism on identification was significant in more countries than the effect on EU membership support. In a similar vein, Chapter 5 showed that instrumental interactions, such as cross-border shopping, have no significant effect on EU membership support, while they significantly increase the likelihood of considering oneself European. Finally, the analyses of Chapter 7 revealed that macro-level transnationalization, measured by the KOF globalization index, has a stronger intervening role in the relationship between individual transnationalism and EU membership than in the relationship between individual transnationalism and European identification. Taken together this evidence suggests that individual transnationalism is a more powerful predictor of European identification than of EU membership support. This might be due to the fact that other aspects, such as policy output, structure EU membership support to a greater extent than European identification.

Having summarized the main argument and core findings of this book, the discussion now turns to its wider theoretical and practical implications.

8.3 A Layer Cake Model of European Integration

Interestingly, Deutsch himself might have foreseen the stratification of transnationalism and orientations towards European integration—and its consequences for integration—in a contribution that does not directly relate to supranational integration (Deutsch 1953b), and that has received little attention in European studies so far (but see Wiener 2011). Assessing 'the growth of Nations', Deutsch speaks of a 'layer cake' of national integration. Deutsch argues that when local communities become integrated into a larger political unit, social groups take part in this process to varying degrees. He argues that European nation states were preceded by less integrated 'layer cake societies'.

These were characterized by 'a high degree of cultural assimilation and participation in extended social communication among the top layers of society; a lesser degree on the intermediate levels; and little to no assimilation or participation among the mass of the population' (Deutsch 1953b: 170). This analysis sits surprisingly well with the empirical findings of this book: a small group of highly skilled Europeans has become Europeanized, while the majority of Europeans do not have frequent European experiences, and some remain completely nationalized. Deutsch pointed out that societies at this rather loose level of integration were never as successful as nation states (Deutsch 1953b: 191).

One should add that at the top of this layer cake is a highly transnational political elite (Kauppi and Madsen 2013). While this book has emphasized the general public, it is important to note that the EU is governed by people who generally tend to be more transnational and more pro-European than their electorates. Among famous examples of highly transnational politicians are Daniel Cohn-Bendit, who acted as an MEP for both Germany and France, or Helle Thorning-Schmidt, former MEP and current Danish Prime Minister, who is the daughter-in-law of Neil Kinnock, formerly British Labour leader and European Commissioner. In fact, it is practically impossible not to interact transnationally when working for a European institution. What is more, highly transnational individuals self-select into European careers and are therefore likely to be more pro-European from the outset. A study among top permanent European Commission officials reveals that their support for supranational norms is generally high (Hooghe 2005). Via the Council, national officials are also socialized in a European realm. Best (2012) shows that frequent contact with EU actors and institutions significantly increases national political elites' attachment to Europe and their support for integration. A study among German decision makers shows that they are significantly more cosmopolitan than the public, although the authors ascribe this difference to higher levels of postmaterial values and their ideological environment (Helbling and Teney forthcoming). All in all, these studies suggest that national and European political elites are generally more transnational and supportive of integration than the overall public.

This underpins the prominent criticism that European integration is a project for and by elites (Best et al. 2012). From its inception, European integration has been an elite-driven process, and data for 1986 show that already at that time, political elites in all member states were decisively more supportive of European integration than their electorates (Hooghe and Marks 2009a). It seems that the gulf between the elites and the public is widening rather than closing. Moreover, the 'estrangement between the Europe of citizens and the Europe of elites' (Best et al. 2012) is more problematic today than in the early days of integration for two reasons. First, with each step of widening and deepening of the European Union, decisions taken at the European level have gained greater impact on people's everyday lives. The gap between the elites and the public thus concerns policy areas that are of direct concern to citizens. As Hooghe and Marks observe, public support for European integration was not much lower in 2005 than twenty years earlier. However, '[i]n 1985, the public could be ignored; in 2005, this was no longer an option' (Hooghe and Marks 2009a: 9). Second, a number of European member states have witnessed an increase in socio-economic inequality (Hoffmeister 2009; Kuhn et al. forthcoming), thereby increasing social distances across society. Thus, the public–elite gap, the social stratification of transnational behaviour, and orientations towards European integration, as well as the increasing inequalities in domestic societies, combine to create a strong divide between 'winners' and 'losers' of European integration.

8.4 The European Sovereign Debt Crisis: Challenge or Promise for European Identity?

There are good reasons to believe that the aftermath of the European sovereign debt crisis might have the potential to promote European societal integration and identity formation by triggering increased interactions across borders. Soaring levels of unemployment in some member states such as Spain have led people to seek jobs elsewhere. This might proliferate transnational interactions between migrants and natives. However, the overall picture is more complex than that, and it is too early to say that the crisis has spurred transnational interactions and mobility across the European Union. In a nutshell, the crisis has led to an increase in migration from the crisis-hit countries (though not necessarily to other EU member states), but has also considerably slowed down east–west migration flows (Benton and Petrovic 2013).

To fully understand this pattern, it is necessary to consider the pre-crisis situation in the member states. In 2004 and 2007, the EU experienced its greatest enlargement rounds thus far, with a total of twelve new member states, the majority of which are former communist states, and underwent a considerable economic transition over the past two decades. While some of these newly minted Europeans had only limited mobility rights in some old member states, the 2004 and 2007 enlargements set the stage for major migration flows from the east to the west (Triandafyllidou and Maroufof 2013). Between 2004 and 2008, the number of new-member-state citizens living in the old member states has risen by more than a million (Benton and Petrovic 2013). The main destination countries were the United Kingdom and Ireland, to where a great number of Polish and Baltic citizens moved, and

Spain and Italy, which witnessed soaring numbers of newly arriving Romanians and Bulgarians (MobilityLab 2012; Benton and Petrovic 2013). Before the crisis, Spain was a particularly popular destination for European and non-European migrants. Between 2000 and 2007, an average of 730,000 migrants arrived each year in Spain, a third of which were European citizens (Deutsche Bank Research 2011). Equally, pre-crisis Ireland attracted a high number of migrants. Between 2000 and 2008, its migrant population increased from 3 per cent of the overall population to 13 per cent (Deutsche Bank Research 2011).

In the wake of the sovereign debt crisis, these migration flows from new member states to the EU-15 dried up, not only with regard to the crisis-hit countries, but also to other old member states (MobilityLab 2012). In the United Kingdom in particular, the new arrivals of migrants from new member states dropped considerably (MobilityLab 2012). Moreover, a great number of young migrants from the new member states returned to their home countries (Benton and Petrovic 2013). Not surprisingly, many people left Greece in the crisis. Between 2008 and 2010, the outflow of European citizens from Greece (both natives and mobile Europeans) increased by 207 per cent. In 2011, the number of recently arrived Greek migrants to other EU member states was 26 per cent higher than in 2008 (Benton and Petrovic 2013). However, with the exception of Greece, all crisis-ridden countries still have a small migration surplus (meaning that more people arrive than leave). In Spain, this surplus has shrunk from 700,000 in 2007 to 63,000 in 2010 (Deutsche Bank Research 2011). Between 2008 and 2010, the outflow of migrants from Spain rose by 70 per cent (Benton and Petrovic 2013). Importantly, however, more than half of Spanish-born migrants went to a non-European country, most notably to Central America (Benton and Petrovic 2013).

To sum up the argument, rather than resulting in a unidirectional emigration boom from the crisis countries to more economically stable member states, the crisis has considerably decreased migration to Spain, Ireland, and Italy, which had attracted a large number of migrants before its onset. What is more, people who left the countries hardest hit by the crisis did not necessarily resettle in another EU member state. To many migrants, countries outside of the EU are more attractive destinations. This is particularly the case for Spanish migrants, more than half of which left the EU. Therefore, one cannot say that the European sovereign debt crisis has triggered an upsurge in transnational interactions and mobility across the European Union.

However, in the wake of this crisis, a strong collective identity is more relevant to European integration than ever before. The development of a relatively integrated European society was rightly a non-issue as long as European institutional integration limited itself to increased cooperation in order to solve collective action problems via economic cooperation and market building. At that time, European policy makers could rely on the permissive consensus (Lindberg and Scheingold 1970) of a relatively indifferent public. Things have changed dramatically, however. In the past two decades, European integration has had an increasing and tangible impact on people's everyday lives. European institutions have acquired important policy competences that for a long time had been the exclusive domain of the nation state. Consequently, the integration process has become ever more contentious, and the creation of economic benefits does not suffice to legitimize the project. This is when collective identity came in. Citizens came increasingly to perceive European integration as a threat to their national identity, and developed eurosceptical attitudes (Hooghe and Marks 2004; McLaren 2006). In other words, there is a widening gulf between community and scope of government (Hooghe and Marks 2009b).

While we have been witnessing this development for roughly two decades now, and the Treaty on European Union in 1992 has been identified as a turning point in public support for European integration (Eichenberg and Dalton 2007), one may expect that the recent sovereign debt crisis constitutes a second turning point. Until the crisis, it was enough for Europeans not to perceive European integration as a threat to their national identity for them to endorse the integration process (Hooghe and Marks 2004; McLaren 2006). While it is too early to predict the long-term consequences of the sovereign debt crisis, it seems that amid the crisis, people need to have a genuinely European identity—to be 'Europeans at heart'—to legitimize the integration process. An analysis of the factors predicting support for European economic governance in the sovereign debt crisis showed that the typical indicators of utilitarianism have no impact whatsoever on support for European economic governance (Kuhn and Stoeckel 2014). In contrast, European identification and trust in European institutions significantly increase support for European economic governance.

Thus, the advanced level of European institutional integration and the critical economic situation in some member states render a strong collective identity in the EU highly relevant.

8.5 A Word of Caution: The Dark Side of European Identity Formation

This brings us to the important question of how far European identity building can and should go. The wish to overcome national egotisms and to eliminate the prospect of war by establishing security communities in the true sense of the word was one of the main motivations for European integration. In a continent shattered by two brutal wars within the space of a few decades, the idea of a peaceful union that transcends national borders would have seemed utopian. In fact, establishing lasting peace, trust, and cooperation between formerly belligerent states is often cited as one of the major achievements of the European integration process. Against the backdrop of half a century of peace in Europe, many observers portray the unification of Europe as a cosmopolitan dream come true.

A sizeable share of Europeans see themselves both as European and as members of their national community (Citrin and Sides 2004; Fuchs et al. 2009a). They feel some form of attachment to the European community, and have what Risse (2010: 40) calls 'European identity lite'. It is questionable, however, whether this loose and weak degree of identification is sufficient to legitimize further steps in deepening the European Union, such as developing redistributive policies across the member states (Bartolini 2005: 240). Risse (2010: 60) argues that such an advanced level of European integration might require European patriotism that equals patriotic feelings towards the national community. Similarly, in his seminal contribution, Fligstein (2008: e.g. 125, 137, 156) asks to what extent there exists a 'European national identity'. While Fligstein concedes that the finality of the European Union is controversial, he takes a position in favour of a European nation state (Fligstein 2008: 124 ff.). Going even farther still, Smith (1995: 139) has famously (and rhetorically) asked, 'who will die for Europe?'.

However, while such a strong level of European identification might be necessary to legitimize further steps in European integration, it also entails the risk of repeating the historical mistakes of national communities on a European level. It is in fact highly questionable whether the founders of European integration had in mind the creation of a 'European national identity', or the imbuement of so much European patriotism that citizens would be willing to die for the EU. Both from a social-psychological perspective (Brown 2000; Dovidio et al. 2003), and from a constructivist view of international relations (Wendt 1994; Diez 2004; Risse 2004), scholars agree that collective identity cannot exist without a 'common other' against which the collective can delineate itself. For a long time, the EU successfully constructed the European past as a common other. As Waever (1998: 90) observes, 'Europe's other is Europe's own past which should not be allowed to become its future.' However, the further away the world wars moved, and the closer the EU centre moved to its eastern and southern neighbours, the more salient geographical and cultural others became (Diez 2004). In the context of the eastern enlargement in 2004, observers raised the question of the geographical and cultural borders of 'Europe' to the east. There were also doubts as to whether the EU could bridge the (perceived) cultural differences between eastern and western member states (Fuchs and Klingemann 2002: 20). Othering also comes to the fore in the persistent public debate about whether Islam is part of Europe, and connected to that, whether Turkey should join the European Union (Madeker 2007). As Diez (2004: 328) puts it, 'the construction of Islam as Europe's other is back in the headlines, ironically at a time when a substantial number of EU citizens are Muslim'. In the public debate, Islam is often portrayed as inherently incompatible with democratic principles, the respect of which is a prerequisite to joining the European Union. Still today, a majority of Europeans are against the entry of Turkey into the European Union. While economic considerations play an important role, this opposition is also based on religious differences (De Vreese et al. 2011; Gerhards and Hans 2011).

Also a number of 'common others' inside the European Union exist. A recent example is the public debate around Roma communities, who, as EU citizens, are free to move and settle in member states that until recently did not have Roma communities. Politicians across Europe, such as Hans-Peter Friedrich, at the time German Federal Minister for the Interior, accuse them of migrating only for the sake of obtaining welfare benefits, and argue for restricting mobility and social rights to intra-European migrants (*Frankfurter Allgemeine Zeitung* 2013). Additionally, in the wake of the sovereign debt crisis and the two Greek bailouts, some observers have raised the question of whether Greece is actually European (Gosh 2011), suggesting that the economic and political crisis in Greece is due to a lack of European norms of conduct (Chalaniova 2013). What is more, the establishment of European citizenship rights and the promotion of a common European identity have weakened the position of the millions of third-country nationals living in the EU (Maas 2008). Balibar (2001) speaks of an 'apartheid' in the way that European economies and welfare states rely on the cheap labour of migrants from outside of the European Union, but at the same time exclude these migrants from access to important political and civic rights and restrict their mobility.

Thus, building a strong European collective identity runs the risk of building up new frontiers against internal and external others (Schlenker 2013). In fact, Risse (2010: 50 ff.) argues that two narratives of Europe exist: 'Modern Europe' implies enlightenment, democracy, rule of law, human rights, and market economy, while 'Nationalist Europe' rests on a cultural and ethnic understanding of Europe, highlighting a common European culture, Christian past, and the like. According to the author, this construction of Europe is a counter vision of the modern image of Europe (Risse 2010: 52). Mammone (2015) goes as far as to argue that after World War II, a 'euro fascist' ideology has emerged which unites extreme right politicians and their voters across Europe. Indeed, many of today's political turf wars in Europe reflect a battle between these two visions of Europe.

8.6 Implications for Policymaking

You don't fall in love with a Common Market, you need something else[2]

—Jacques Delors

European policy makers are therefore facing a dilemma. On the one hand, there are good reasons to believe that further steps towards an 'ever closer Union', such as establishing a fully-fledged European social policy, or further integrating the macro-economic policies, require a level of European identification that exceeds the present level. On the other hand, such a strong collective European identity might defeat the very purpose of European integration by replicating national egotisms on a European level. How this dilemma is solved will have important and far-reaching implications for the future of the integration project.

Furthermore, the findings of this book suggest that the future of European collective identity depends on the success of policy makers in fostering transnational interactions that (a) involve a broader share of the European public and (b) are not solely instrumental but also include sociable aspects. Qualification (a) is based on the observation that while people with a low level of education generally do not tend to interact across borders, they are especially responsive to the transnational experience in developing a European identity. In other words, transnational experiences can compensate for low education: in general, poorly educated Europeans tend to be more eurosceptic and less transnational, as indicated by the lower transnationalism scores in Chapter 5, and evidenced by a lower likelihood to support EU membership and to see oneself as European in Chapter 4. However, the few people who have a low education level but nonetheless engage in transnational interactions are very likely to be pro-European. In fact, at high levels of transnationalism, poorly and highly educated people do not significantly differ in their attitudes towards European integration (Kuhn 2012b). This can be explained by the fact that highly educated people tend to be pro-European, no matter whether they have gained transnational experiences or not. Transnational interaction cannot add much to their EU support and identity. In contrast, poorly educated people are usually among the most eurosceptical members of society, and transnational interactions can change their perspective. This suggests that the EU's strategy to foster transnational interaction via (higher) education programmes such as Erasmus or the research framework programmes partly misses its mark by excluding less educated people. Thus, rather than focusing on highly educated people and offering them even more opportunities to interact across borders (as in the Erasmus university exchanges), policy makers

---

[2] Jacques Delors, cited in Laffan 1996: 95.

are well advised to promote transnational interactions and mobility among less well educated people. Further efforts in fostering European wide transnational interaction and mobility should thus specifically address groups of society that so far have been neglected by these policies.

Qualification (b) is based on the finding that purely instrumental transactions, such as cross-border shopping, have little or no significant effect on European identification and EU membership support. In contrast, intrinsically motivated transactions, such as socializing with other Europeans, significantly increase the likelihood of considering oneself as European. This suggests that Europeans require more than purely rational arguments to change their political allegiances. A practical implication of this observation is that policy makers aiming at fostering European identity and EU support should promote sociable interactions, or at least emphasize the sociable aspects of instrumentally motivated interactions. This is at odds with the attempt to convince European citizens of the merits of European integration by highlighting the material benefits of the integration process. European policy makers have long emphasized the instrumental aspects of the integration process—European 'workers' and 'consumers' benefit from the 'Single Market', by profiting from cheaper flights and being able to apply for jobs using their 'European CV' template. However, it seems more promising to encourage sociable interactions. To put it bluntly, marriages, not markets, make European integration.

8.7 Suggestions for Further Research

Based on the findings of this book, further research could go in two main directions. Contributions could assess more thoroughly the causal mechanisms highlighted, and study the extent to which the findings are generalizable. To fully understand the causal mechanisms, I suggest conducting a longitudinal (ideally panel) survey that captures people's transnational behaviour and attitudes over several time points. The added value of such a data source would be twofold. First, the cross-sectional nature of the data used in the empirical analyses of this book does not fully allow for testing the causal relationship between individual transnationalism and EU support. Contrary to Deutsch's expectations, it is possible that the causal direction goes from attitudes to behaviour, that is, that people's orientations towards European integration make them more or less inclined to interact across borders. This book has proposed strong theoretical arguments as to why transactions are expected to impact EU support and identity, and it has shown that also exogenous aspects of transnationalism—such as being born abroad or having foreign parents—significantly impact orientations towards European integration. While this alleviates the criticism, it cannot empirically exclude the possibility that the causal link is reversed. Should this be the case, then the prospect of creating a European society by interaction and mobility is even less promising than argued in this book. Second, using cross-sectional data, it is not possible to ascertain whether the different degrees of transnationalism across age groups are due to a life course or a cohort effect. Are younger Europeans more transnational because they have already been socialized in a more transnational environment, and thus likely to stay transnational throughout their lives? Or is their higher transnationalism due to a life course effect and thus likely to decrease once they get older? The answer to this question would give us a better indication as to whether we can expect European societies to become increasingly transnational over the next decades.

Some longitudinal studies on the effects of participation in an Erasmus exchange exist already. Their findings provide rather limited support for the hypothesis that transactions foster European identity and EU support (Sigalas 2010a, 2010b; Wilson 2011). However, it should be kept in mind that these studies focus on a highly selective group of people—university students—who have been shown to be among the most pro-European members of society, no matter whether they interact across borders or not. Therefore, a ceiling effect might explain the fact that studies on Erasmus students found few, if any, effects of transactions on EU attitudes (Kuhn 2012b). In addition, even longitudinal survey data cannot account for self-selection effects. In other words, some people might self-select very early in life into transnationalism and therefore be consistently more pro-European than others.

Experimental data can help in establishing causality by randomly assigning people into transnationally active and inactive groups and therefore eliminating the effect of other potential explanatory variables. Buchan and colleagues have conducted laboratory experiments in an attempt to understand whether transnational contacts foster cosmopolitanism. They found that the more subjects were exposed to the rest of the world, the more likely they were to cooperate with other subjects in other countries (Buchan et al. 2009). Nonetheless, it is questionable whether the results found in the laboratory environment also hold in the real world, and how sustainable these effects are remains an open question.

Another important question relates to the generalizability of the findings of this book beyond the context of European integration. Transactionalist theory was developed not only with respect to European integration, but in view of establishing security communities more generally. It would therefore be interesting to see whether similar dynamics are at work in other integrating areas of the world, such as UNASUR in Latin America or the African Union. To date, we know very little about the identification with, and support for, regional integration worldwide (but see Roose 2012b; Deutschmann 2013). This lacuna is partly due to the fact that the European integration project is often perceived to be too *sui generis* in character as to allow for meaningful comparison with other examples of regional integration. Consequently, the political and societal effects of European integration have predominantly been studied using 'n=1 approaches' (De Lombaerde et al. 2010). However, since the end of the Cold War, we have witnessed a 'New Wave of Regionalism' (Mansfield and Milner 1999) across the globe. While no other regional integration project has gone as far as the EU, this trend raises the question whether regionalization has given rise to cognitive regions in the sense that these regions 'exist in the consciousness of people' (Väyrynen 2003: 37). Is the general public aware of the integration processes taking place in their region and do they extend their interactions beyond national borders? Do citizens in these regions support integration, and do they ultimately adopt a supranational identity or reify their national identity? Finally, and more closely connected to this book, are there similar relationships between transnational interactions and regional identities as exist in the EU? Answering these questions would provide valuable theoretical insight and it would help to bridge the gap between European studies on the one hand and international relations on the other.

Finally, while the findings of this book suggest that sociable interactions are more effective in triggering EU support and European identity, it would be desirable to know more about the quality of interactions and contacts. Indicators such as 'having visited another country' can refer to a wide range of visits entailing very different degrees and forms of interactions. Obviously, the transnational contacts of notorious German 'Ballermann' tourists on the Balearic Islands and stag partiers in the Baltic States hardly fulfil the criteria of successful group contact established by contact theory (Allport 1954; Pettigrew 1998). These experiences are thus less likely to result in the kind of attitude and identity change that Deutsch was hoping for. Neither do the data indicate whether respondents interact across borders out of their own motivation or are rather forced to do so, for example because they could not find a job in their own country. This might also lower the likelihood of attitudinal and identity change. Furthermore, it would be interesting to know the extent to which people are aware of their own transnationalism, or lack thereof. Do they really frame, for example, cross-border shopping as a transnational experience?

To answer these questions, more sophisticated measures of transnationalism are necessary, pinpointing where, when, and how transnational processes and practices occur. Additionally, as questions of attitudes and identities can hardly be grasped by quantitative research alone, it might be very fruitful to conduct qualitative research, using in-depth interviews or focus groups. Some qualitative contributions on transnational contacts and mobility already exist, such as Favell's (2008) study on highly mobile young professionals in three European cities or Meinhof's (2003) research on border residents, but more systematic research is needed to explore issues that cannot come to the fore using quantitative survey instruments. The findings of this book suggest that such an endeavour would be very beneficial indeed.

Appendix

Table A1. Individual-level predictors of individual transnationalism

	Model 1		Model 2		Model 3		Model 4		Model 5	
	2006 coeff. (se)	2007 coeff. (se)	2006 coeff. (se)	2007 coeff. (se)	2006 coeff. (se)	2007 coeff. (se)	2006 coeff. (se)	2007 coeff. (se)	2006 coeff. (se)	2007 coeff. (se)
Educational attainment	.133*** (.002)	.086*** (.002)	.094*** (.002)	.060*** (.002)			.090*** (.002)	.058*** (.002)	.087*** (.002)	.054*** (.002)
Occupation (manager ref.)										
Student			-.022* (.009)	-.007 (.009)			-.057*** (.010)	-.022* (.010)	-.058*** (.010)	-.024* (.010)
Manual worker			-.142*** (.006)	-.105*** (.005)			-.149*** (.006)	-.108*** (.005)	-.146*** (.006)	-.105*** (.005)
Self-employed			-.054*** (.008)	-.046*** (.007)			-.053*** (.008)	-.045*** (.007)	-.048*** (.008)	-.041*** (.007)
White collar			-.078*** (.007)	-.067*** (.006)			-.084*** (.007)	-.071*** (.006)	-.084*** (.007)	-.070*** (.006)
Homemaker			-.136*** (.007)	-.110*** (.006)			-.135*** (.007)	-.110*** (.006)	-.132*** (.007)	-.106*** (.006)
Unemployed			-.150*** (.008)	-.092*** (.006)			-.158*** (.008)	-.096*** (.006)	-.154*** (.008)	-.092*** (.006)
Retired			-.186*** (.006)	-.123*** (.005)			-.168*** (.007)	-.113*** (.005)	-.165*** (.007)	-.110*** (.005)
Age groups (55+ ref.)										
Age group 15–24					.171*** (.006)	.102*** (.005)	.065*** (.007)	.030*** (.006)	.065*** (.007)	.030*** (.006)
Age group 25–39					.137*** (.004)	.085*** (.003)	.041*** (.005)	.026*** (.004)	.041*** (.005)	.026*** (.004)
Age group 40–54					.089*** (.004)	.049*** (.003)	.011* (.005)	.002 (.003)	.012** (.005)	.004 (.003)

(continued)

Table A1. Continued

	Model 1		Model 2		Model 3		Model 4		Model 5	
	2006 coeff. (se)	2007 coeff. (se)	2006 coeff. (se)	2007 coeff. (se)	2006 coeff. (se)	2007 coeff. (se)	2006 coeff. (se)	2007 coeff. (se)	2006 coeff. (se)	2007 coeff. (se)
Urbanization									.020*** (.002)	.022*** (.001)
Foreign-born	.125*** (.014)	.101*** (.011)	.119*** (.014)	.104*** (.011)	.115*** (.015)	.096*** (.012)	.117*** (.014)	.102*** (.011)	.116*** (.014)	.100*** (.011)
Foreign parent	.068*** (.006)	.096*** (.005)	.067*** (.006)	.094*** (.005)	.072*** (.006)	.099*** (.005)	.067*** (.005)	.094*** (.005)	.062*** (.006)	.089*** (.005)
Female	-.036*** (.003)	-.024*** (.002)	-.035*** (.003)	-.020*** (.002)	-.044*** (.003)	-.028*** (.002)	-.034*** (.003)	-.020*** (.002)	-.035*** (.003)	-.021*** (.002)
Constant	.030*** (.008)	-.031*** (.005)	.227*** (.010)	.106*** (.008)	.231*** (.007)	.102*** (.005)	.215*** (.010)	.100*** (.008)	.178*** (.011)	.061*** (.008)
Log-likelihood	2435.2	7776.2	3191.8	8346.4	1413.6	6960.7	3257.9	8388.8	3317.8	8508.6
Explained variance	.330	.300	.375	.328	.264	.249	.378	.330	.382	.337

Note: Figures are coefficients of OLS models with country-fixed effects, country-robust standard errors in parentheses. Country coefficients not shown. Two-tailed test, *p < .05, **p < .01, p < .001. n (2006) = 21,898; n (2007) = 24,975.

Source: Eurobarometer 65.1 (2006), Eurobarometer 67.1 (2007).

Table A2. Macro-level predictors of individual transnationalism using Eurobarometer wave 65.1 (2006)

	Model 1	Model 2	Model 3	Model 4	Model 5	Model 6	Model 7	Model 8	Model 9
	coeff. (se)	coeff. (se)	coeff. (se)	coeff. (se)	coeff. (se)	coeff. (se)	coeff. (se)	coeff. (se)	coeff. (se)
GDP per capita		.332*** (.058)	.558*** (.086)	.484*** (.091)	.348*** (.074)	.424*** (.067)	.397*** (.064)	.420*** (.066)	.377*** (.059)
EU-15			-.087* (.035)						
Years of membership				-.053 (.045)					
Economic globalization					.119* (.051)				
Population size						-.109* (.046)			
Population size (log)							-.035** (.012)		
Territory size								-.124** (.048)	
Territory size (log)									-.206*** (.052)
Constant	.168*** (.000)	.054** (.019)	.089*** (.023)	.108*** (.023)	.015 (.032)	.092*** (.024)	.068** (.021)	.100*** (.025)	.225*** (.044)
Variance components									
L-2 variance (constant)	.0122 (.004)	.003*** (.001)	.004*** (.001)	.005*** (.001)	.004*** (.001)	.004*** (.001)	.004*** (.001)	.004*** (.001)	.056*** (.009)
L-2 variance (residual var.)	.043*** (.000)	.027*** (.000)	.043*** (.000)	.044*** (.000)	.043*** (.000)	.043*** (.000)	.043*** (.000)	.043*** (.000)	.208*** (.001)
Log-likelihood	3167.2	8295.6	3176.7	3121.1	3176.7	3176.6	3176.5	3177.1	3180.3
ICC	.219	.107	.088	.099	.091	.091	.082	.087	.068

Note: Figures are coefficients of multilevel regression models with random intercept, standard errors in parentheses. Independent variables are standardized to run from 0 to 1. Models control for respondents' age, sex, education, occupation, transnational background, and urbanization of residence. Two-tailed test; *p < .05, **p < .01, *** p < .00. N = 25; n = 21,898.

Source: Eurobarometer 65.1 (2006).

Table A3. Macro-level predictors of individual transnationalism using Eurobarometer wave 67.1 (2007)

	Model 1	Model 2	Model 3	Model 4	Model 5	Model 6	Model 7	Model 8	Model 9
	coeff. (se)	coeff. (se)	coeff. (se)	coeff. (se)	coeff. (se)	coeff. (se)	coeff. (se)	coeff. (se)	coeff. (se)
GDP per capita		.312*** (.069)	.409*** (.089)	.407*** (.088)	.245*** (.067)	.316*** (.064)	.278*** (.059)	.312*** (.068)	.264*** (.059)
EU-15			-.057 (.034)						
Years of membership				-.070 (.042)					
Economic globalization					.105** (.040)				
Population size						-.104** (.044)			
Population size (log)							-.144*** (.041)		
Territory size								-.064 (.049)	–
Territory size (log)									-.185*** (.052)
Constant	.098*** (.019)	.020 (.023)	.027 (.022)	.020 (.022)	-.019 (.025)	.042 (.023)	.109*** (.032)	.036 (.026)	.165*** (.045)
Variance components									
L-2 variance (constant)	.008*** (.002)	.005*** (.001)	.004*** (.001)	.004*** (.001)	.004*** (.001)	.004*** (.001)	.003*** (.001)	.005*** (.001)	.003*** (.001)
L-1 variance (reisudal var.)	.030*** (.000)	.030*** (.000)	.030*** (.000)	.030*** (.000)	.030*** (.000)	.030*** (.000)	.030*** (.000)	.030*** (.000)	.030*** (.000)
Log-likelihood	8347.0	8353.0	8351.9	8352.1	8353.9	8353.4	8355.9	8351.7	8356.2
ICC	.217	.136	.129	.128	.113	.117	.098	.133	.097

Note: Figures are coefficients of multilevel regression models with random intercept, standard errors in parentheses. Independent variables are standardized to run from 0 to 1. Models control for respondents' age, sex, education, occupation, transnational background, and urbanization of residence. Two-tailed test; *p < .05, **p < .01, *** p < .00. N = 27; n = 24,975.

Source: Eurobarometer 67.1 (2007).

References

Articles and Books

Abdelal, R., Herrera, Y., Johnston, A. I., and McDermott, R. (eds) (2009). *Measuring Identity: A Guide for Social Scientists*. Cambridge: Cambridge University Press.

Adler, E. (2002). 'Constructivism in International Relations'. In Carlsnaes, W., Simmons, B. and Risse, T. (eds), *Handbook of International Relations*. London: Sage, 95–118.

Adler, E. and Barnett, M. (eds) (1998a). *Security Communities*. Cambridge: Cambridge University Press.

Adler, E. and Barnett, M. (1998b). 'Security Communities in Theoretical Perspective'. In Adler, E. and Barnett, M. (eds), *Security Communities*. Cambridge: Cambridge University Press, 29–65.

Aichholzer, J., Kritzinger, S., Wagner, M., and Zeglovits, E. (2014). 'How has Radical Right Support Transformed Established Political Conflicts? The Case of Austria'. *West European Politics*, 37 (1): 113–37.

Allport, G. W. (1954). *The Nature of Prejudice*. New York: Doubleday & Company.

Almond, G. A. and Verba, S. (1963). *The Civic Culture*. Princeton: Princeton University Press.

Anderson, B. (1991). *Imagined Communities: Reflections on the Origin and Spread of Nationalism*. New York: Verso.

Anderson, C. J. (1998). 'When in Doubt, Use Proxies: Attitudes toward Domestic Politics and Support for European Integration'. *Comparative Political Studies*, 31 (5): 569–601.

Anderson, C. J. and Reichert, S. (1995). 'Economic Benefits and Support for Membership in the EU: A Cross-National Analysis'. *Journal of Public Policy*, 15 (3): 231–49.

Anderson, J. (2002). *Transnational Democracy: Political Spaces and Border Crossings*. London: Routledge.

Andreotti, A., Le Galès, P., and Moreno Fuentes, F. J. (2013). 'Transnational Mobility and Rootedness: The Upper Middle Classes in European Cities'. *Global Networks*, 13 (1): 41–9.

Anheier, H. K. and Falkenhain, M. (2012). 'Europe's Stratified Social Space: Diagnosis and Remedies'. *Global Policy*, 3 (S1): 52–61.

Aradau, C., Huysmans, J., and Squire, V. (2010). 'Acts of European Citizenship: A Political Sociology of Mobility'. *Journal of Common Market Studies*, 48 (4): 945–65.

Ariely, G. (2012). 'Globalization and the Decline of National Identity? An Exploration Across Sixty-three Countries'. *Nations and Nationalism*, 18 (3): 461–82.

References

Bach, M. (2000). 'Die Europäisierung nationaler Gesellschaften'. *Kölner Zeitschrift für Soziologie und Sozialpsychologie*, 40 (Sonderheft).

Baker, C. (2008). 'Wild Dances and Singing Wolves: Simulation, Essentialization, and National Identity at the Eurovision Song Contest'. *Popular Communication: The International Journal of Media and Culture*, 6 (3): 173–89.

Bale, T., Green-Pedersen, C., Krouwel, A., Luther, K. R., and Sitter, N. (2010). 'If You can't Beat Them, Join Them? Explaining Social Democratic Responses to the Challenge from the Populist Radical Right in Western Europe'. *Political Studies*, 58 (3): 410–26.

Balibar, É. (2001). *Nous, citoyens d'Europe?: les frontières, l'État, le peuple*. Paris: La Découverte.

Bartolini, S. (2005). *Restructuring Europe: Centre Formation, System Building, and Political Structuring between Nation State and the European Union*. Cambridge: Cambridge University Press.

Bauman, Z. (1989). *Globalization. The Human Consequences*. Cambridge: Polity Press.

Beck, U. (2002). 'The Cosmopolitan Society and Its Enemies'. *Theory Culture Society*, 19 (1–2): 17–44.

Beck, U. and Beck-Gernsheim, E. (2009). 'Global Generations and the Trap of Methodological Nationalism. For a Cosmopolitan Turn in the Sociology of Youth and Generation'. *European Sociological Review*, 25 (1): 25–36.

Beck, U. and Grande, E. (2004). *Das kosmopolitische Europa. Gesellschaft und Politik in der Zweiten Moderne*. Frankfurt a.M.: Suhrkamp.

Beckfield, J. (2006). 'European Integration and Income Inequality'. *American Sociological Review*, 71: 964–85.

Beetham, D. (1991). *The Legitimation of Power*. Atlantic Highlands, NJ: Humanities Press International.

Beisheim, M., Dreher, S., Walter, G., Zangl, B., and Zürn, M. (1999). *Im Zeitalter der Globalisierung? Thesen und Daten zur gesellschaftlichen und politischen Denationalisierung*. Baden-Baden: Nomos Verlagsgesellschaft.

Bellucci, P., Sanders, D., and Serricchio, F. (2012). 'Explaining European Identity'. In Sanders, D., Bellucci, P., Tóka, G., and Torcal, M. (eds), *The Europeanization of National Politics? Citizenship and Support in a Post-Enlargement Union*. Oxford: Oxford University Press, 61–90.

Benson, M. (2010). 'The Context and Trajectory of Lifestyle Migration. The Case of the British Residents of Southwest France'. *European Societies*, 12 (1): 45–64.

Bentley, J. (1996). 'Cross-Cultural Interaction and Periodization in World History'. *American Historical Review*, 101 (June): 749–70.

Benton, M. and Petrovic, M. (2013). 'How Free is Free Movement? Dynamics and Drivers of Mobility within the European Union'. *Migration Policy Institute Europe* (March).

Berger, P. and Luckmann, T. (1966). *The Social Construction of Reality: A Treatise in the Sociology of Knowledge*. New York: Doubleday.

Best, H. (2012). 'Elite Foundations of European Integration: A Causal Analysis'. In Best, H., Lengyel, G., and Verzichelli, L. (eds), *The Europe of Elites. A Study into the Europeanness of Europe's Political and Economic Elites*. Oxford: Oxford University Press, 208–33.

Best, H., Lengyel, G., and Verzichelli, L. (2012). *The Europe of Elites: A Study into the Europeanness of Europe's Political and Economic Elites*. Oxford: Oxford University Press.

Bhagwati, J. (2004). *In Defence of Globalization*. New York: Oxford University Press.

Blalock, H. M. (1967). *Toward a Theory of Minority-group Relations*. New York: John Wiley & Sons.

Bläser, K.-A. (2013). 'Europa im Spiegel der öffentlichen Meinung. Bilanz und Perspektiven des Eurobarometers nach 40 Jahren'. *Leviathan. Berliner Zeitschrift für Sozialwissenschaft*, 41 (3): 351–7.

Blumer, H. (1958). 'Race Prejudice as a Sense of Group Position'. *Pacific Sociological Review*, 1 (1): 3–7.

Börzel, T. (2002). 'Member State Responses to Europeanization'. *Journal of Common Market Studies*, 40 (2): 193–214.

Bradley, D. E. and Longino, C. F. (2009). 'Geographic Mobility and Aging in Place'. In Uhlenberg, P. (ed.), *International Handbook of Population Aging*. New York: Springer, 319–39.

Brambor, T., Clark, W., and Golder, M. (2006). 'Understanding Interaction Models: Improving Empirical Analyses'. *Political Analysis*, 14 (1): 63–82.

Brown, R. (2000). 'Social Identity Theory: Past Achievements, Current Problems and Future Challenges'. *European Journal of Social Psychology*, 30: 745–88.

Brubaker, R. (2005). 'The "Diaspora" Diaspora'. *Ethnic and Racial Studies*, 28 (1): 1–19.

Brubaker, R. and Cooper, F. (2000). 'Beyond "Identity"'. *Theory and Society*, 29 (1): 1–47.

Bruter, M. (2005). *Citizens of Europe? The Emergence of a Mass European Identity*. Houndmills: Palgrave Macmillan.

Bruter, M. (2004). 'Civic and Cultural Components of a European Identity: A Pilot Model of Measurement of Citizens' Levels of European Identity'. In Herrmann, R. K., Risse, T., and Brewer, M. B. (eds), *Transnational Identities. Becoming European in the EU*. Lanham: Rowman & Littlefield, 186–213.

Buchan, N., Grimalda, G., Wilson, R., Brewer, M. B., Fatas, E., and Foddy, M. (2009). 'Globalization and Human Cooperation'. *Proceedings of the National Academy of Sciences of the United States,* 106 (11): 4138–42.

Buchholz, S., et al. (2009). 'Life Courses in the Globalization Process: The Development of Social Inequalities in Modern Societies'. *European Sociological Review*, 25 (1): 53–71.

Burgoon, B. (2001). 'Globalization and Welfare Compensation: Disentangling the Ties that Bind'. *International Organization*, 55 (3): 509–51.

Burgoon, B. (2009). 'Globalization and Backlash: Polanyi's Revenge?'. *Review of International Political Economy*, 16 (2): 145–77.

Burgoon, B. (2013). 'Inequality and Anti-globalization Backlash by Political Parties'. *European Union Politics*, 4 (3): 408–35.

Byrne, D. (1969). 'Attitudes and Attraction'. In Berkowitz, L. (ed.), *Advances in Experimental Social Psychology*. New York: Academic Press, 36–90.

Calhoun, C. (2002). 'The Class Consciousness of Frequent Travellers: Towards a Critique of Actually Existing Cosmopolitanism'. In Vertovec, S. and Cohen, R. (eds), *Conceiving Cosmopolitanism. Theory, Context, and Practice*. Oxford: Oxford University Press.

References

Carey, S. (2002). 'Undivided Loyalties: Is National Identity an Obstacle to European Integration?'. *European Union Politics*, 3 (4): 387–413.

Carlson, S. (2013). 'Becoming a Mobile Student. A Processual Perspective on German Degree Student Mobility'. *Population, Space and Place*, 19 (2): 168–80.

Casado-Díaz, M. A. (2006). 'Retiring to Spain: An Analysis of Differences among North European Nationals'. *Journal of Ethnic and Migration Studies*, 32 (8): 1321–39.

Castells, M. (2000a). *End of Millenium*. Cambridge: Cambridge University Press.

Castells, M. (2000b). 'Materials for an Explanatory Theory of the Network Society'. *British Journal of Sociology*, 51 (1): 5–24.

Chalaniova, D. (2013). 'Turn the Other Greek. How the Eurozone Crisis Changes the Image of Greeks and What Visual Representations of Greeks Tell Us about European Identity'. *Perspectives. Review of International Affairs*, 2013 (1): 5–41.

Checkel, J. (2005). 'International Institutions and Socialisation in Europe'. *International Organization*, 59 (4): 801–26.

Checkel, J. and Katzenstein, P. (eds) (2009). *European Identity*. Cambridge: Cambridge University Press.

Chomsky, N. (1994). *World Orders Old and New*. New York: Columbia University Press.

Chomsky, N. (1998). *Profit over People: Neoliberalism and Global Order*. New York: Seven Stories Press.

Christin, T. and Trechsel, A. H. (2002). 'Joining the EU?: Explaining Public Opinion in Switzerland'. *European Union Politics*, 3 (4): 415–43.

CIA (2013). *The World Factbook* <https://www.cia.gov/library/publications/the-world-factbook/> (accessed 20 December 2013).

Citrin, J. and Sides, J. (2004). 'More than Nationals: How Identity Choice Matters in the New Europe'. In Herrmann, R., Brewer, M., and Risse, T. (eds), *Transnational Identities: Becoming European in the EU*. Lanham: Rowman & Littlefield, 161–85.

Citrin, J., Wong, C., and Duff, B. (2001). 'The Meaning of American National Identity. Patterns of Ethnic Conflict and Consensus'. In Ashmore, R., Jussim, L., and Wilder, D. (eds), *Social Identity, Intergroup Conflict, and Conflict Reduction*. New York: Oxford University Press, 71–100.

Clarke, N. (2009). 'In What Sense "Spaces of Neoliberalism"? The New Localism, the New Politics of Scale, and Town Twinning'. *Political Geography*, 28 (8): 496–507.

Connor, W. (1972). 'Nation-Building or Nation-Destroying?'. *World Politics*, 24 (3): 319–55.

Cram, L. (2009). 'Identity and European Integration: Diversity as a Source of Integration'. *Nations and Nationalism*, 15 (1): 109–28.

Cram, L. (2012). 'Does the EU need a Navel? Implicit and Explicit Identification with the European Union'. *Journal of Common Market Studies*, 50 (1): 71–86.

De Haas, H. (2010). 'Migration and Development: A Theoretical Perspective'. *International Migration Review*, 44 (1): 227–64.

De Lombaerde, P., Söderbaum, F., Van Langenhove, L., and Baert, F. (2010). 'The Problem of Comparison in Comparative Regionalism'. *Review of International Studies*, 36: 731–53.

De Master, S. and Le Roy, M. (2000). 'Xenophobia and the European Union'. *Comparative Politics*, 32 (4): 419–36.

De Swaan, A. (1995). 'Die soziologische Untersuchung der transnationalen Gesellschaft'. *Journal für Sozialforschung*, 35 (2): 121–44.

De Vreese, C. and Boomgaarden, H. (2005). 'Projecting EU Referendums: Fear of Immigration and Support for European Integration'. *European Union Politics*, 6 (1): 59–82.

De Vreese, C., Boomgaarden, H., and Semetko, H. (2008). 'Hard and Soft: Public Support for Turkish Membership in the EU'. *European Union Politics*, 9 (4): 511–30.

De Vreese, C., Van der Brug, W., and Hobolt, S. (2011). 'Turkey in the EU? How Cultural and Economic Frames affect Support for Turkish Accession'. *Comparative European Politics*, 10 (2): 218–35.

De Vries, C. (2007). 'Sleeping Giant: Fact or Fairytale? How European Integration Affects National Elections'. *European Union Politics*, 8 (3): 363–85.

De Vries, C. (2010). 'EU Issue Voting: Asset or Liability?: How European Integration Affects Parties' Electoral Fortunes'. *European Union Politics*, 11 (1): 89–117.

De Vries, C. and Edwards, E. (2009). 'Taking Europe to its Extremes: Extremist Parties and Public Euroscepticism'. *Party Politics*, 15 (1): 5–28.

De Wilde, P. and Zürn, M. (2012). 'Can the Politicization of European Integration be Reversed?'. *Journal of Common Market Studies*, 50 (S1): 137–53.

Delhey, J. (2004). 'Nationales und transnationales Vertrauen in der Europäischen Union'. *Leviathan. Berliner Zeitschrift für Sozialwissenschaft*, 32 (1): 15–45.

Delhey, J. (2005). 'Das Abenteuer der Europäisierung. Überlegungen zu einem soziologischen Begriff europäischer Integration und zur Stellung der Soziologie zu den Integration Studies'. *Soziologie*, 34 (1): 7–27.

Delhey, J. (2007). 'Grenzüberschreitender Austausch und Vertrauen. Ein Test der Transaktionsthese für Europa'. In Franzen, A. and Freitag, M. (eds), *Kölner Zeitschrift für Soziologie und Sozialpsychologie. (Sonderheft) Sozialkapital: Grundlagen und Anwendungen*. Wiesbaden: VS Verlag für Sozialwissenschaften, 141–62.

Deschouwer, K. and Van Parijs, P. (2009). 'Electoral Engineering for a Stalled Federation'. In McEvoy, J. and O'Leary, B. (eds), *Power Sharing in Deeply Divided Places*. Philadelphia: University of Pennsylvania Press, 112–31.

Deutsch, K. W. (1953a). *Nationalism and Social Communication. An Inquiry into the Foundations of Nationality*. New York: The Technology Press of Massachusetts Institute of Technology and John Wiley & Sons.

Deutsch, K. W. (1953b). 'The Growth of Nations: Some Recurrent Patterns of Political and Social Integration'. *World Politics*, 5 (2): 168–95.

Deutsch, K. W. (1956). 'Shifts in the Balance of Communication Flows: A Problem of Measurement in International Relations'. *Public Opinion Quarterly*, 20 (1): 143–60.

Deutsch, K. W. (1954 [1970]). *Political Community at the International Level. Problems of Definition and Measurement*. Garden City: Doubleday & Company, Inc.

Deutsch, K. W. (1960). 'The Propensity to International Transactions'. *Political Studies*, 8 (2): 147–55.

Deutsch, K. W. (1961). 'On Social Communication and the Metropolis'. *Daedalus*, 90 (1): 99–110.

Deutsch, K. W. (1969). *Nationalism and its Alternatives*. New York: Alfred Knopf, Inc.

Deutsch, K. W. and Eckstein, A. (1961). 'National Industrialization and the Declining Share of the International Economic Sector, 1890–1959'. *World Politics*, 13 (2): 267–99.

Deutsch, K. W. and Foltz, W. J. (eds) (1963). *Nation Building*: Atherton Press.

Deutsch, K. W., Burrell, S. A., Kann, R. A., Lee, M. Jr, Lichterman, M., Lindgren, R. E., Loewenheim, F. L., and van Wagenen, R. W. (1957). *Political Community and the North Atlantic Area*. New York: Greenwood Press, Publishers.

Deutsch, K. W., Edinger, L. J., Macridis, R. C., and Merritt, R. L. (1967). *France, Germany and the Western Alliance*. New York: Scribner.

Deutsche Bank Research (2011). 'Arbeitskräftemobilität in der Eurozone'. *EU Monitor*, 85 (August 2011): 1–12.

Deutschmann, E. (2013). 'The Social Stratification of Continental Attachment in Africa, Europe and Latin America.' European Sociological Association 11th Conference. University of Turin.

Diez, T. (2004). 'Europe's Others and the Return of Geopolitics'. *Cambridge Review of International Affairs*, 17 (2): 319–35.

Díez Medrano, J. (2003). *Framing Europe*. Princeton: Princeton University Press.

Díez Medrano, J. (2008). *Europeanization and the Emergence of a European Society*. Barcelona: Universitat de Barcelona.

Díez Medrano, J. (2010a). 'A New Society in the Making. European Integration and European Social Groups'. *KFG Working Paper Series*, 12.

Díez Medrano, J. (2010b). 'Unpacking European Identity'. *Politique Européenne*, 30 (1): 45–66.

Díez Medrano, J. and Gutiérrez, P. (2001). 'Nested Identities: National and European Identities in Spain'. *Journal of Ethnic and Migration Studies*, 24 (5): 753–78.

Dovidio, J., Gaertner, S., and Kawakami, K. (2003). 'Intergroup Contact: The Past, Present, and the Future'. *Group Processes and Intergroup Relations*, 6 (1): 5–21.

Dreher, A. (2006). 'Does Globalization Affect Growth? Evidence from a New Index of Globalization'. *Applied Economics*, 38 (10): 1091–110.

Dreher, A., Gaston, N., and Martens, P. (2008). *Measuring Globalisation—Gauging its Consequences*. New York: Springer.

Duchesne, S. and Frognier, A.-P. (1995). 'Is there a European Identity?'. In Niedermayer, O. and Sinnott, R. (eds), *Public Opinion and Internationalized Governance*. Oxford: Oxford University Press, 193–225.

Dürrschmidt, J. (2006). 'So Near yet so Far: Blocked Networks, Global Links and Multiple Exclusion in the German-Polish Borderlands'. *Global Networks*, 6 (3): 245–63.

EACEA (2013). 'Youth in Action Programme 2007–2103'. <http://eacea.ec.europa.eu/youth/programme/about_youth_en.php> (accessed 20 December 2013).

Easton, D. (1975). 'A Re-Assessment of the Concept of Political Support'. *British Journal of Political Science*, 5 (4): 435–57.

Eberwein, W.-D. and Ecker-Ehrhart, M. (2001). *Deutschland und Polen: Eine Werte- und Interessengemeinschaft*. Opladen: Leske & Budrich.

Edmunds, J. and Turner, B. (2005). 'Global Generations: Social Change in the 20th Century'. *British Journal of Sociology*, 56 (4): 559–77.

Eichenberg, R. C. and Dalton, R. J. (1993). 'Europeans and the European Union: the Dynamics of Public Support for European Integration'. *International Organization*, 47 (4): 507–34.

Eichenberg, R. C. and Dalton, R. J. (2007). 'Post-Maastricht Blues: The Transformation of Citizen Support for European Integration, 1973–2004'. *Acta Politica*, 42 (2–3): 128–52.

Eigmüller, M. (2013). 'Europeanization From Below: The Influence of Individual Actors on the EU Integration of Social Policies'. *Journal of European Social Policy*, 23 (4): 363–75.

Eigmüller, M. and Vobruba, G. (2006). *Grenzsoziologie. Die politische Strukturierung des Raumes*. Wiesbaden: VS Verlag für Sozialwissenschaften.

Eilstrup-Sangiovanni, M. (2006). *Debates on European Integration*. Houndmills: Palgrave Macmillan.

European Commission (1985). 'Completing the Internal Market—White Paper from the Commission to the European Council'. *COM(85) 310 final*.

European Commission (2008). 'Sharing for Tomorrow's Europe: Thematic Networking of Twinned Towns'. <http://ec.europa.eu/citizenship/pdf/doc321_en.pdf> (accessed 15 May 2014).

European Commission (2011). 'Outgoing Erasmus Students from 1987/1988 to 2009/2010.' <http://ec.europa.eu/education/library/statistics/aggregates-time-series/table1_en.pdf> (accessed 15 May 2014).

European Commission (2013a). *Co-Creating European Union Citizenship, A Policy Review*. Luxembourg: Publications Office of the European Union.

European Commission (2013b). 'Erasmus+ Frequently Asked Questions'. *MEMO/13/1008*.

European Commission (2013c). 'EU Youth Programmes 1988–2013'. <http://www.injuve.es/sites/default/files/2013/19/noticias/25ansEUYouth.pdf> (accessed 20 December 2013).

Falkenhain, M., Hoelscher, M., and Ruser, A. (2012). 'Twinning Peaks—Potential and Limits of an Evolving Network in Shaping Europe as a Social Space'. *Journal of Civil Society*, 8 (3): 229–50.

Falkner, G. (2003). 'Comparing Europeanisation Effects: From Metaphor to Operationalisation'. *European Integration Online Papers*, 7 (13).

Favell, A. (2008). *Eurostars and Eurocities: Free Movement and Mobility in an Integrating Europe*. Malden, MA: Blackwell.

Favell, A. and Guiraudon, V. (2009). 'The Sociology of the European Union: An Agenda'. *European Union Politics*, 10 (4): 550–76.

Favell, A. and Guiraudon, V. (2011). *Sociology of the European Union*. London: Palgrave Macmillan.

Favell, A. and Recchi, E. (2009). 'Pioneers of European Integration: An Introduction'. In Recchi, E. and Favell, A. (eds), *Pioneers of European Integration. Citizenship and Mobility in the EU*. Cheltenham: Edward Elgar, 1–25.

Favell, A. and Recchi, E. (2011). 'Social Mobility and Spacial Mobility'. In Favell, A. and Guiraudon, V. (eds), *Sociology of the European Union*. Basingstoke: Palgrave Macmillan, 50–75.

Favell, A., Recchi, E., Kuhn, T., Jensen, J. S., and Klein, J. (2011). 'The Europeanisation of Everyday Life: Practices and Transnational Identifications Among EU and Third-Country Citizens. State of the Art Report'. *EUCROSS Working Paper* # 1.

Ferrera, M. (2004). 'Social Citizenship and the EU. Toward a Spacial Reconfiguration?'. In Ansell, C. and Di Palma, G. (eds), *Restructuring Territoriality. Europe and the United States Compared*. Cambridge: Cambridge University Press, 90–121.

Finger, C. (2011). 'The Social Selectivity of International Mobility among German University Students'. *WZB Discussion Paper*, SP 1 2011–503.

Fiske, S. (2000). 'Stereotyping, Prejudice, and Discrimination at the Seam between the Centuries'. *European Journal of Social Psychology*, 30 (3): 299–322.

Fligstein, N. (2008). *Euroclash: The EU, European Identity, and the Future of Europe*. Oxford: Oxford University Press.

Fligstein, N. (2009). 'Who Are the Europeans and How Does This Matter for Politics?'. In Checkel, J. and Katzenstein, P. (eds), *European Identity*. Cambridge: Cambridge University Press, 132–66.

Fligstein, N. and Mérand, F. (2002). 'Globalization or Europeanization? Evidence on the European Economy since 1980'. *Acta Sociologica*, 45 (1): 7–22.

Foreign Policy (2007). 'The Globalization Index'. *Foreign Policy*, 163: 68–76.

Frändberg, L. (2009). 'How Normal is Travelling Abroad? Differences in Transnational Mobility between Groups of Young Swedes'. *Environment and Planning*, 41: 649–67.

Franklin, M. and Wlezien, C. (1997). 'The Responsive Public. Issue Salience, Policy Change, and Preferences for European Unification'. *Journal of Theoretical Politics*, 9 (3): 347–63.

Fuchs, D., and Klingemann, H.-D. (2002). 'Eastward Enlargement and the Identity of Europe'. *West European Politics*, 25 (2): 19–54.

Fuchs, D., Guinaudeau, I., and Schubert, S. (2009a). 'National Identity, European Identity and Euroscepticism'. In Fuchs, D., Magni-Berton, R., and Roger, A. (eds), *Euroscepticism. Images of Europe among Mass Publics and Political Elites*. Opladen: Barbara Budrich, 91–112.

Fuchs, D., Magni-Berton, R., and Roger, A. (eds) (2009b). *Euroscepticism: Images of Europe among Mass Publics and Political Elites*. Opladen: Barbara Budrich Publishers.

Fuchs, D., Roger, A., and Magni-Berton, R. (2009c). 'Introduction'. In Fuchs, D., Magni-Berton, R., and Roger, A. (eds), *Euroscepticism. Images of Europe among Mass Publics and Political Elites*. Opladen: Barbara Budrich Publishers, 9–32.

Fürstenau, S. (2004). *Mehrsprachigkeit als Kapital im transnationalen Raum*. Münster: Waxmann Verlag.

Gabel, M. (1998a). 'Economic Integration and Mass Politics: Market Liberalization and Public Attitudes in the European Union'. *American Journal of Political Science*, 42 (3): 936–63.

Gabel, M. (1998b). *Interests and Integration: Market Liberalization, Public Opinion, and European Union*. Ann Arbor: University of Michigan Press.

Gabel, M. (1998c). 'Public Support for Europe: An Empirical Test of Five Theories'. *Journal of Politics*, 60: 333–54.

Gabel, M. (2000). 'European Integration, Voters, and National Politics'. *West European Politics*, 23 (4): 52–72.

Gabel, M. and Palmer, H. (1995). 'Understanding Variation in Public Support for European Integration'. *European Journal of Political Research*, 27 (1): 3–19.

Gabel, M. and Whitten, G. (1997). 'Economic Conditions, Economic Perceptions, and Public Support for European Integration'. *Political Behavior*, 19 (1): 81–96.

Gerhards, J. (2012). *From Babel to Brussels. European Integration and the Importance of Transnational Linguistic Capital.* Berlin: FU Berlin.

Gerhards, J. and Hans, S. (2011). 'Why not Turkey? Attitudes towards Turkish Membership in the EU among Citizens in 27 European Countries'. *Journal of Common Market Studies*, 49 (4): 741–66.

Gerhards, J. and Hans, S. (2013). 'Transnational Human Capital, Education, and Social Inequality. Analyses of International Student Exchange'. *Zeitschrift für Soziologie*, 42 (2): 99–117.

Giddens, A. (1990). *The Consequences of Modernity.* Cambridge: Polity Press in association with Basil Blackwell, Oxford.

Giddens, A. (1991). *Modernity and Self-Identity.* Stanford: Stanford University Press.

Glick Schiller, N. and Fouron, G. (2001). *Georges woke up Laughing: Long-distance Nationalism and the Search for Home.* Durham: Duke University Press.

Gosh, P. (2011). 'Are Greeks Really European?'. *International Business Times*, 9 September 2011.

Goudappel, F. (2010). *The Effects of EU Citizenship. Economic, Social and Political Rights in a Time of Constitutional Change.* The Hague: T.M.C. Asser Press.

Guarnizo, L. E. and Smith, M. P. (1998). 'The Location of Transnationalism'. In Smith, M. P. and Guarnizo, L. E. (eds), *Transnationalism from Below.* New Brunswick: Transaction, 3–34.

Guillén, M. (2001). 'Is Globalization Civilizing, Destructive, Or Feeble? A Critique of Five Key Debates in the Social Sciences'. *Annual Review of Sociology*, 27: 235–60.

Gustafson, P. (2001). 'Retirement Migration and Transnational Lifestyles'. *Ageing and Society*, 21 (4): 371–94.

Gustafson, P. (2009). 'More Cosmopolitan, no Less Local—The Orientations of International Travellers'. *European Societies*, 11 (1): 25–47.

Haas, E. (1970). 'The Study of Regional Integration: Reflections on the Joy and Anguish of Pretheorizing'. *International Organization*, 24 (4): 607–46.

Hainmueller, J. and Hiscox (2007). 'Educated Preferences: Explaining Attitudes Toward Immigration in Europe'. *International Organization*, 61 (02): 339–442.

Hakhverdian, A., van Elsas, E., van der Brug, W., and Kuhn, T. (2013). 'Euroscepticism and Education: A Longitudinal Study of Twelve EU Member States, 1973–2010'. *European Union Politics*, 14 (4): 522–41.

Haller, M. (2008). *European Integration as an Elite Process: The Failure of a Dream?* New York: Routledge.

Haller, W. and Roudometof, V. (2010). 'The Cosmopolitan–Local Continuum in a Cross-National Perspective'. *Journal of Sociology*, 46 (3): 277–97.

Hantrais, L. (2000). *Social Policy in the European Union.* Basingstoke: Macmillan Press.

Harmsen, R. and Spiering, M. (eds) (2004). *Euroscepticism: Party Politics, National Identity and European Integration.* Amsterdam: Rodopi.

Harvey, D. (1990). *The Condition of Postmodernity: An Enquiry into the Origins of Cultural Change*. Cambridge, MA: Blackwell.

Hay, C. (2009). 'Neil Fligstein Euroclash: The EU, European Identity and the Future of Europe'. *Socio-Economic Review*, 7: 535–52.

Helbling, M. and Teney, C. (forthcoming). 'The Cosmopolitan Elite in Germany. Transnationalism and Postmaterialism'. *Global Networks*.

Held, D. (1995). *Democracy and the Global Order. From the Modern State to Cosmopolitan Governance*. Cambridge: Polity Press.

Held, D., McGrew, A., Goldblatt, D., and Perraton, J. (1999). *Global Transformations*. Stanford: Stanford University Press.

Held, D. (2002). 'Culture and Political Community: National, Global, and Cosmopolitan'. In Vertovec, S. and Cohen, R. (eds), *Conceiving Cosmopolitanism. Theory, Context, and Practice*. Oxford: Oxford University Press, 48–58.

Hirschman, A. (1970). *Exit, Voice, and Loyalty. Responses to Decline in Firms, Organizations, and States*. Cambridge, MA: Harvard University Press.

Hirst, P. and Thompson, G. (1996). *Globalization in Question*. London: Polity Press.

Hix, S. and Hoyland, B. (2011). *The Political System of the European Union*. 3rd Edition. Basingstoke: Palgrave Macmillan.

Hobolt, S. (2009). *Europe in Question: Referendums on European Integration*. Oxford: Oxford University Press.

Hoffmeister, O. (2009). 'The Spatial Structure of Income Inequality in the Enlarged EU'. *Review of Income and Wealth*, 55 (1): 101–27.

Hofmeister, H. and Breitenstein, A. P. (2008). 'Contemporary Processes of Transnationalization and Globalization'. *International Sociology*, 23 (4): 480–7.

Hofstede, G. (1994). *Cultures and Organizations: Software of the Mind: Intercultural Cooperation and its Importance for Survival*. London: Harper Collins.

Holland, D., Fic, T., Rincon-Aznar, A., Stokes, L., and Paluchowski, P. (2011). *Labour Mobility within the EU. The Impact of Enlargement and the Functioning of the Transitional Arrangements*. London: National Institute of Economic and Social Research.

Hooghe, L. (2005). 'Several Roads Lead to International Norms, but Few Via International Socialization: A Case Study of the European Commission'. *International Organization*, 59: 861–98.

Hooghe, L. and Marks, G. (2004). 'Does Identity or Economic Rationality drive Public Opinion on European Integration?'. *PS-Political Science & Politics*, 37 (3): 415–20.

Hooghe, L. and Marks, G. (2009a). 'A Postfunctionalist Theory of European Integration: From Permissive Consensus to Constraining Dissensus'. *British Journal of Political Science*, 39 (1): 1–23.

Hooghe, L. and Marks, G. (2009b). 'Does Efficiency Shape the Territorial Structure of Government?'. *Annual Review of Political Science*, 12: 225–41.

Hooghe, L., Bakker, R., Brigevich, A., De Vries, C., Edwards, E., Marks, G., Rovny, J., Steenbergen, M., and Vachudova, M. (2010). 'Reliability and Validity of the 2002 and 2006 Chapel Hill Expert Surveys on Party Positioning'. *European Journal of Political Research*, 49 (5): 687–703.

Höpner, M. and Jurczyk, B. (2012). 'Kritik des Eurobarometers. Über die Verwischung der Grenze zwischen seriöser Demoskopie und interessengeleiteter Propaganda'. *Leviathan. Berliner Zeitschrift für Sozialwissenschaft*, 40 (3): 326–49.

Horst, C. (2004). 'Money and Mobility: Transnational Livelihood Strategies of the Somali Diaspora'. *Global Migration Perspectives*, (9).

Howard, J. (2000). 'Social Psychology of Identities'. *Annual Review of Sociology*, 26: 367–93.

Inglehart, R. (1968). 'Trends and Non-trends in the Western Alliance: A Review'. *Journal of Conflict Resolution*, 12 (1): 120–8.

Inglehart, R. (1970). 'Cognitive Mobilization and European Identity'. *Comparative Politics*, 3 (1): 45–70.

Inglehart, R. (1977). *The Silent Revolution. Changing Values and Political Styles among Western Publics*. Princeton, NJ: Princeton University Press.

Inglehart, R., Rabier, J.-R., and Reif, K. (1991). 'The Evolution of Public Attitudes toward European Integration: 1970–86'. In Reif, K. and Inglehart, R. (eds), *Eurobarometer: The Dynamics of European Public Opinion*. London: Macmillan, 111–31.

Jones, E. and Van der Bijl, N. (2004). 'Public Opinion and Enlargement: A Gravity Approach'. *European Union Politics*, 5 (3): 331–51.

Jung, J. K. (2008). 'Growing Supranational Identities in a Globalising World? A Multilevel Analysis of the World Values Surveys'. *European Journal of Political Research*, 47 (5): 578–609.

Juravle, C., Weber, T., Canetta, E., Fries Tersch, E., and Kadunc, M. (2013). 'A Fact Finding Analysis on the Impact on the Member States' Social Security Systems of the Entitlements of Non-Active Intra-EU Migrants to Special Non-contributory Cash Benefits and Healthcare Granted on the Basis of Residence.' Final report submitted by ICF GHK in association with Milieu Ltd. London. Brussels.

Kaina, V. and Karolewski, I. P. (2013). 'EU governance and European Identity'. *Living Review of European Governance*, 4 (2): 1–41.

Karp, J. A., Banducci, S. A., and Bowler, S. (2003). 'To Know it is to Love it? Satisfaction with Democracy in the European Union'. *Comparative Political Studies*, 36 (3): 271–92.

Katz, D. and Braly, K. W. (1933). 'Racial Stereotypes of One-Hundred College Students'. *Journal of Abnormal and Social Psychology*, 28: 280–90.

Kauppi, N. (ed.) (2013). *A Political Sociology of Transnational Europe*. Colchester: ECPR Press.

Kauppi, N. and Madsen, M. R. (eds) (2013). *Transnational Power Elites. The New Professionals of Governance, Law and Security*. Abingdon: Routledge.

Kaya, Y. and Karakoc, E. (2012). 'Civilizing vs Destructive Globalization? A Multi-Level Analysis of Anti-Immigrant Prejudice'. *International Journal of Comparative Sociology*, 53 (1): 23–44.

King, R., Warnes, T., and Williams, A. (eds) (2000). *Sunset Lives: British Retirement Migration to the Mediterranean*. Oxford: Berg.

Kittilson, M. C. (2007). 'Research Resources in Comparative Political Behavior'. In Dalton, R. J. and Klingemann, H.-D. (eds), *The Oxford Handbook of Political Behavior*. Oxford: Oxford University Press, 865–95.

Klatt, M. and Herrmann, H. (2011). 'Half Empty or Half Full? Over 30 Years of Regional Cooperation Within the EU: Experiences at the Dutch–German and Danish–German Border'. *Journal of Borderlands Studies*, 26 (1): 65–87.

Klingemann, H.-D. and Weldon, S. (2013). 'A Crisis of Integration? The Development of Transnational Dyadic Trust in the European Union, 1954–2004'. *European Journal of Political Research*, 52 (4): 457–82.

Koehn, P. and Rosenau, J. (2002). 'Transnational Competence in an Emergent Epoch'. *International Studies Perspectives*, 3: 105–27.

Kohli, M. (2000). 'The Battlegrounds of European Identity'. *European Societies*, 2 (2): 113–37.

König, J. and Ohr, R. (2013). 'Different Efforts in European Economic Integration. Implications of the EU Index'. *Journal of Common Market Studies*, 51 (6): 1074–90.

Koopmans, R., Erbe, J., and Meyer, M. F. (2010). 'The Europeanization of Public Spheres: Comparisons across Issues, Time, and Countries'. In Koopmans, R. and Statham, P. (eds), *The Making of a European Public Sphere. Media Discourse and Political Contention*. Cambridge: Cambridge University Press, 63–96.

Kriesi, H. (2007). 'The Role of European Integration in National Election Campaigns'. *European Union Politics*, 8 (1): 83–108.

Kriesi, H. (2009). 'Rejoinder to Liesbet Hooghe and Gary Marks, "A Postfunctional Theory of European Integration: From Permissive Consensus to Constraining Dissensus"'. *British Journal of Political Science*, 39 (1): 221–4.

Kriesi, H. and Frey, T. (2008). 'The Netherlands: A Challenge that was Slow in Coming'. In Kriesi, H., Grande, E., Lachat, R., Dolezal, M., Bornschier, S., and Frey, T. (eds), *West European Politics in the Age of Globalization*. Cambridge: Cambridge University Press, 154–82.

Kriesi, H., Grande, E., Lachat, R., Dolezal, M., Bornschier, S., and Frey, T. (eds) (2008). *West European Politics in the Age of Globalization*: Cambridge University Press.

Krotz, U. (2007). 'Parapublic Underpinnings of International Relations: The Franco-German Construction of Europeanization of a Particular Kind'. *European Journal of International Relations*, 13 (3): 385–417.

Krotz, U. and Schild, J. (2012). *Shaping Europe: France, Germany, and Embedded Bilateralism from the Elysée Treaty to Twenty-First Century Politics*. Oxford: Oxford University Press.

Krouwel, A. and Abts, K. (2007). 'Varieties of Euroscepticism and Populist Mobilization: Transforming Attitudes from Mild Euroscepticism to Harsh Eurocynicism'. *Acta Politica*, 42 (2–3): 252–70.

Kuhn, T. (2011). 'Individual Transnationalism, Globalization and Euroscepticism: An Empirical Test of Deutsch's Transactionalist Theory'. *European Journal of Political Research*, 50(6): 811–37.

Kuhn, T. (2012a). 'Europa ante Portas: Border Residence, Transnational Interaction and Euroscepticism in Germany and France'. *European Union Politics*, 13 (1): 94–117.

Kuhn, T. (2012b). 'Why Educational Exchange Programmes miss their Mark: Mobility, Education and European Identity'. *Journal of Common Market Studies*, 50 (6): 994–1010.

Kuhn, T. and Stoeckel, F. (2014). 'When European Integration becomes costly. The Euro Crisis as a Test of Public Support for European Economic Governance'. *Journal of European Public Policy*, 21 (4): 624–41.

Kuhn, T., van Elsas, E., Hakhverdian, A., and van der Brug, W. (forthcoming). 'An Ever Wider Gap in an Ever Closer Union: Rising Inequalities and Euroscepticism in 12 West European Democracies, 1975–2009'. *Socio-Economic Review*.

Laffan, B. (1996). 'The Politics of Identity and Political Order in Europe'. *Journal of Common Market Studies*, 34 (1): 81–102.

Lancee, B. and Dronkers, J. (2011). 'Ethnic, Religious and Economic Diversity in the Neighbourhood: Explaining Quality of Contact with Neighbours, Trust in the Neighbourhood and Inter-ethnic Trust for Immigrant and Native Residents'. *Journal of Ethnic and Migration Studies*, 37 (4): 597–618.

Lindberg, L. and Scheingold, S. (1970). *Europe's Would-be Polity. Patterns of Change in the European Community*. Englewood Cliffs: Prentice Hall.

Lockwood, B. and Redoano, M. (2005). 'The CSGR Globalisation Index: an Introductory Guide'. *Centre for the Study of Globalisation and Regionalisation Working Paper* 155 (04).

Lörz, M. and Krawietz, M. (2011). 'Internationale Mobilität und soziale Selektivität: Ausmaß, Mechanismen und Entwicklung herkunftsspezifischer Unterschiede zwischen 1990 und 2005'. *Kölner Zeitschrift für Soziologie und Sozialpsychologie*, 63 (2): 185–205.

Lubbers, M. and Jaspers, E. (2011). 'A Longitudinal Study of Euroscepticism in the Netherlands: 2008 versus 1990'. *European Union Politics*, 12 (1): 21–40.

Lubbers, M. and Scheepers, P. (2007). 'Explanations of Political Euro-scepticism at the Individual, Regional and National Levels'. *European Societies*, 9 (4): 643–69.

Lubbers, M. and Scheepers, P. (2010). 'Divergent Trends of Euroscepticism in Countries and Regions of the European Union'. *European Journal of Political Research*, 49 (6): 787–817.

Luther, K. R. (2009). 'The Revival of the Radical Right. The Austrian Parliamentary Election of 2008'. *West European Politics*, 32 (5): 1049–61.

Maas, W. (2008). 'Migrants, States, and EU Citizenships's Unfulfilled Promise'. *Citizenship Studies*, 12 (6): 583–96.

McLaren, L. (2002). 'Public Support for the European Union: Cost/Benefit Analysis or Perceived Cultural Threat?'. *Journal of Politics*, 64 (2): 551–88.

McLaren, L. (2006). *Identity, Interests and Attitudes to European Integration*. Houndmills: Palgrave Macmillan.

McLaren, L. (2007). 'Explaining Mass-Level Euroscepticism: Identity, Interests, and Institutional Distrust'. *Acta Politica*, 42 (2–3): 233–51.

Madeker, E. (2007). *Türkei und Europäische Identität. Eine wissenssoziologische Analyse der Debatte um den EU-Beitritt*. Wiesbaden: VS.

Majone, G. (1993). 'The European Community Between Social Policy and Social Regulation'. *Journal of Common Market Studies*, 31 (2): 153–70.

Mammone, A. (2015). *Transnational Neofascism in France and Italy*. Cambridge: Cambridge University Press.

Mansfield, E. D. and Milner, H. V. (1999). 'The New Wave of Regionalism'. *International Organization*, 53 (3): 589–627.

Markowits, A. (2012). 'Karl Wolfgang Deutsch (1912–1992)'. *Czech Sociological Review*, 48 (6): 1131–5.

Marks, G. (1999). 'Territorial Identities in the European Union'. In Anderson, J. J. (ed.), *Regional Integration and Democracy. Expanding on the European Experience.* Landham, Maryland: Rowman & Littlefield, 69–91.

Mau, S. (2007). *Transnationale Vergesellschaftung. Die Entgrenzung sozialer Lebenswelten.* Frankfurt: Campus Verlag.

Mau, S. (2010). *Social Transnationalism: Lifeworlds beyond the Nation-State.* London: Routledge.

Mau, S. and Büttner, S. (2010). 'Transnationality'. In Immerfall, S. and Therborn, G. (eds), *Handbook of European Societies.* New York: Springer, 537–70.

Mau, S. and Mewes, J. (2007). 'Transnationale soziale Beziehungen. Eine Kartographie der deutschen Bevölkerung'. *Soziale Welt*, 57 (2): 2003–222.

Mau, S. and Mewes, J. (2009). 'Class Divides within Transnationalisation—The German Population and its Practices'. In Ohnmacht, T., Maksim, H., and Bergman, M. M. (eds), *Mobilities and Inequality.* Farnham: Ashgate, 165–86.

Mau, S. and Mewes, J. (2012). 'Horizontal Europeanisation in Contextual Perspective: What Drives Interactions within the European Union?'. *European Societies*, 14 (1): 7–34.

Mau, S. and Verwiebe, R. (2009). *Die Sozialstruktur Europas.* Konstanz: UVK.

Mau, S., Mewes, J., and Zimmermann, A. (2008). 'Cosmopolitan Attitudes through Transnational Social Practices?'. *Global Networks*, 8 (1): 1–24.

Meinhof, U. H. (2003). 'Migrating Borders: An Introduction to European Identity Construction in Process'. *Journal of Ethnic and Migration Studies*, 29 (5): 781–96.

Mewes, J. and Mau, S. (2013). 'Globalization, Socio-economic Status and Welfare Chauvinism: European Perspectives on Attitudes Toward the Exclusion of Immigrants'. *International Journal of Comparative Sociology*, 54 (3): 228–45.

Meyer, J. W. (2005). *Weltkultur. Wie die westlichen Prinzipien die Welt durchdringen.* Frankfurt a.M.: Suhrkamp.

Meyer, J. W. and Hannan, M. T. (1979). *National Developments and the World System. Educational, Economic, and Political Change, 1950–1970.* Chicago: University of Chicago Press.

Meyer, J. W., Boli, J., Thomas, G. M., and Ramirez, F. O. (1997). 'World Society and the Nation-State'. *American Journal of Sociology*, 103 (1): 144–81.

Mills, M. and Blossfeld, H.-P. (2005). 'Globalization, Uncertainty and the Early Life Course. A Theoretical Framework'. In Blossfeld, H.-P., Klijzing, E., Mills, M., and Kunz, K. (eds), *Globalization, Uncertainty and Youth in Society.* London: Routledge, 1–24.

MobilityLab (2012). 'Mobility in Europe 2012'. *Employment, Social Affairs & Inclusion*, November 2012. <http://www.mobilitypartnership.eu/Documents/Mobility%20in%20Europe%202012.pdf> (accessed 31 July 2014).

Monti, M. (2010). 'A New Strategy for the Single Market. At the Service of Europe's Economy and Society'. *Report to the President to the European Commission, José Manuel Barroso.*

Nelson, B. and Guth, J. (2000). 'Exploring the Gender Gap: Women, Men and Public Attitudes toward European Integration'. *European Union Politics*, 1 (3): 267–91.

Niedermayer, O. and Westle, B. (1995). 'A Typology of Orientations'. In Niedermayer, O. and Sinnott, R. (eds), *Public Opinion and Internationalized Governance*. Oxford: Oxford University Press, 33–51.

Norris, P. (2000). 'Global Governance and Cosmopolitan Citizens'. In Nye, J. and Donahue, J. D. (eds), *Governance in a Globalizing World*. Washington, DC: Brookings Institution, 155–77.

Norris, P. and Inglehart, R. (2009). *Cosmopolitan Communications. Cultural Diversity in a Globalized World*. Cambridge: Cambridge University Press.

Nye, J. (1968). 'Comparative Regional Integration'. *International Organization*, 22 (4): 855–80.

O'Dowd, L. (2001). 'State Borders, Border Regions and the Construction of European Identity'. In Kohli, M. and Novak, M. (eds), *Will Europe Work?*. London: Routledge, 95–110.

Outhwaite, W. (2008). *European Society*. Cambridge: Polity Press.

Özden, C., Parsons, C., and Schiff, M. (2011). 'Where on Earth is Everybody? The Evolution of Global Bilateral Migration 1960–2000'. *World Bank Economic Review*, 25 (1): 12–56.

Pépin, L. (2007). 'The History of EU Cooperation in the Field of Education and Training: How Lifelong Learning Became a Strategic Objective'. *European Journal of Education*, 42 (1): 121–32.

Petit, I. (2007). 'Mimicking History: The European Commisison and its Education Policy'. *World Political Science Review*, 3 (1): 1–25.

Pettigrew, T. (1998). 'Intergroup Contact Theory'. *Annual Review of Psychology*, 49: 65–86.

Pettigrew, T. and Tropp, L. (2006). 'A Meta-Analytic Test of Intergroup Contact Theory'. *Journal of Personality and Social Psychology*, 90 (5): 751–83.

Puchala, D. (1970a). 'Integration and Disintegration in Franco-German Relations, 1954–1965'. *International Organization*, 24 (4): 183–208.

Puchala, D. (1970b). 'International Transactions and Regional Integration'. *International Organization*, 24 (4): 732–62.

Puchala, D. (1981). 'Integration Theory and the Study of International Relations'. In Merritt, R. L. and Russett, B. (eds), *From National Development to Global Community. Essays in Honour of Karl W. Deutsch*. London: George Allen & Unwin, 145–64.

Putnam, R. D. (2007). 'E Pluribus Unum: Diversity and Community in the Twenty-first Century. The 2006 Johan Skytte Prize Lecture'. *Scandinavian Political Studies*, 30 (2): 137–74.

Raab, M., Ruland, M., Schönberger, B., Blossfeld, H.-P., Hofäcker, D., Buchholz, S., and Schmelzer, P. (2008). 'GlobalIndex: A Sociological Approach to Globalization Measurement'. *International Sociology*, 23 (4): 596–631.

Rabe-Hesketh, S. and Skrondal, A. (2005). *Multilevel and Longitudinal Modeling Using Stata*. College Station, Texas: Stata Press.

Radaelli, C. (2000). 'Whither Europeanization? Concept Stretching and Substantive Change'. *European Integration Online Papers*, 4 (8): 1–25.

Randolph, Jan. (2001). 'G-Index: Globalisation Measured'. *World Market Research Centre.*

Recchi, E. (2008a). 'Cross-State Mobility in the EU: Trends, Puzzles and Consequences'. *European Societies*, 10 (2): 197–224.

Recchi, E. (2008b). 'From Migrants to Movers: Citizenship and Mobility in the European Union'. In Smith, M. P. and Favell, A. (eds), *The Human Face of Global Mobility. International Highly Skilled Migration in Europe, North America and the Asia-Pacific.* New Brunswick, NJ: Transaction Publishers.

Recchi, E. and Favell, A. (eds) (2009). *Pioneers of European Integration. Citizenship and Mobility in the EU.* Cheltenham: Edward Elgar.

Recchi, E. and Kuhn, T. (2013). 'Europeans' Space-Sets and the Political Legitimacy of the EU'. In Kauppi, N. (ed.) *A Political Sociology of Transnational Europe.* Colchester: ECPR Press, 191–222.

Rippl, S., Baier, D., Kindervater, A., and Boehnke, K. (2005). 'Die EU-Osterweiterung als Mobilisierungsschub für ethnozentrische Einstellungen? Die Rolle von Bedrohungsgefühlen im Kontext situativer und dispositioneller Faktoren'. *Zeitschrift für Soziologie*, 34 (4): 288–310.

Rippl, S., Bücker, N., Petrat, A., and Boehnke, K. (2010). 'Crossing the Frontier: Transnational Social Integration in the EU's Border Regions'. *International Journal of Comparative Sociology*, 51 (1–2): 5–31.

Risse, T. (2004). 'Social Constructivism and European Integration'. In Wiener, A. and Diez, T. (eds), *European Integration Theory.* Oxford: Oxford University Press, 159–76.

Risse, T. (2010). *A Community of Europeans? Transnational Identities and Public Spheres.* Ithaca, NY: Cornell University Press.

Ritzer, G. (2004). *The McDonaldization of Society. Revised New Century Edition.* Thousand Oaks: Pine Forge Press.

Roeder, A. (2011). 'Does Mobility Matter for Attitudes to Europe? A Multi-level Analysis of Immigrants' Attitudes to European Unification'. *Political Studies*, 59 (2): 458–71.

Rohrschneider, R. (2002). 'The Democratic Deficit and Mass Support for an EU-wide Government'. *American Journal of Political Science*, 46 (2): 463–75.

Rokkan, S. (2000). *Staat, Nation und Demokratie in Europa. Die Theorie Stein Rokkans aus seinen gesammelten Werken rekonstruiert und eingeleitet von Peter Flora.* Frankfurt a.M.: Suhrkamp.

Roose, J. (2010). *Vergesellschaftung an Europas Binnengrenzen. Eine vergleichende Studie zu den Bedingungen sozialer Integration.* Wiesbaden: VS Verlag für Sozialwissenschaften.

Roose, J. (2012a). 'Die quantitative Bestimmung kultureller Unterschiedlichkeit in Europa. Vorschlag für einen Index kultureller Ähnlichkeit'. *Kölner Zeitschrift für Soziologie und Sozialpsychologie*, 64 (2): 361–76.

Roose, J. (2012b). 'How European is European Identification? Comparing Continental Identification in Europe and Beyond'. *Journal of Common Market Studies*, 51 (2): 281–97.

Rosamond, B. (2005). 'Globalization, the Ambivalence of European Integration and the Possibilities for a "Post-disciplinary EU Studies"'. *Innovation: The European Journal of Social Science Research*, 18 (1): 25–45.

Ross, G. (1998). 'European Integration and Globalization'. In Axtman, R. (ed.), *Globalization and Europe: Theoretical and Empirical Investigations*. London: Pinter.

Ross, G. (2011). 'Postscript: Arriving Late at the EU Studies Ball—Dilemmas, Prospects and Strategies for a Sociology of the European Union'. In Favell, A. and Guiraudon, V. (eds), *Sociology of the European Union*. Basingstoke: Palgrave Macmillan, 215–24.

Rossbach, D. (2010). 'National Identity, Globalization and Attitudes towards European Integration'. *Paper presented at MPSA Annual Conference*.

Rother, N. and Nebe, T. M. (2009). 'More Mobile, More European? Free Movement and EU Identity'. In Recchi, E. and Favell, A. (eds), *Pioneers of European Integration. Citizenship and Mobility in the EU*. Cheltenham: Edward Elgar Publishers, 120–55.

Roudometof, V. (2005). 'Transnationalism, Cosmopolitanism and Glocalization'. *Current Sociology*, 53 (1): 113–35.

Sandholtz, W. and Stone Sweet, A. (1998). *European Integration and Supranational Governance*. Oxford: Oxford University Press.

Santacreu, O., Baldoni, E., and Albert, M. C. (2009). 'Deciding to Move: Migration Projects in an Integrating Europe'. In Recchi, E. and Favell, A. (eds), *Pioneers of European Integration. Citizenship and Mobility in the EU*. Cheltenham: Edward Elgar, 52–71.

Sassen, S. (2001). *The Global City: New York, London, Tokyo*. Princeton, NJ: Princeton University Press.

Sassenberg, K. and Matschke, B. (2010). 'The Impact of Exchange Programs on the Integration of the Hostgroup into the Self-concept'. *European Journal of Social Psychology*, 40: 148–59.

Savage, M., Bagnall, G., and Longhurst, B. (2005). *Globalization and Belonging*. London: Sage.

Scharpf, F. (1999). *Governing in Europe: Effective and Democratic?* Oxford: Oxford University Press.

Scheingold, S. (1971). 'The North Atlantic Area as a Policy Arena'. *International Studies Quarterly*, 15 (1): 32–65.

Scheve, K. and Slaughter, M. (2001). *Globalization and Perception of American Workers*. Washington, DC: Institute for International Economics.

Schild, J. (2005). 'Ein Sieg der Angst—Das gescheiterte französische Verfassungsreferendum'. *Integration*, 28 (3): 187–200.

Schlenker, A. (2013). 'Cosmopolitan Europeans or Partisans of Fortress Europe? Supranational Identity Patterns in the EU'. *Global Society*, 27 (1): 25–51.

Schlueter, E. and Wagner, U. (2008). 'Regional Differences Matter: Examining the Dual Influence of the Regional Size of the Immigrant Population on Derogation of Immigrants in Europe'. *International Journal of Comparative Sociology*, 49 (2–3): 153–73.

Schmidberger, M. (1997). *Regionen und europäische Legitimität. Der Einfluss des regionalen Umfeldes auf Bevölkerungseinstellungen zur EU*. Frankfurt a.M.: Peter Lang.

Schmidt, S. (2007). 'Mutual Recognition as a New Mode of Governance'. *Journal of European Public Policy*, 14 (5): 667–81.

Schmidt, V. A. (2003). 'European Integration as a Regional Variant of Globalization: The Challenges to National Democracy'. In Katenhusen, I. and Lamping, W. (eds), *Demokratien in Europa: Der Einfluss der europäischen Integration auf Institutionenwandel und neue Konturen des demokratischen Verfassungsstaates*. Opladen: Westdeutscher Verlag, 205–28.

Schmitt, M., Spears, R., and Branscombe, N. (2003). 'Constructing a Minority Group Identity out of Shared Rejection: The Case of International Students'. *European Journal of Social Psychology*, 33 (1): 1–12.

Schneider, N. and Meil, G. (eds) (2008). *Mobile Living Across Europe I. Relevance and Diversity of Job-Related Spatial Mobility in Six European Countries*. Opladen: Barbara Budrich Publishers.

Semyonov, M., Raijman, R., and Gorodzeisky, A. (2006). 'The Rise of Anti-Foreigner Sentiment in European Societies, 1988–2000'. *American Sociological Review*, 71 (3): 426–49.

Senghaas, D. (2012). 'Practicing Politics with Alert Senses'. *Czech Sociological Review*, 48 (6): 1135–44.

Shulman, S. (2002). 'Challenging the Civic/Ethnic and West/East Dichotomies in the Study of Nationalism'. *Comparative Political Studies*, 35 (5): 554–84.

Sigalas, E. (2010a). 'Mobility and European Identity: The Effectiveness of Intergroup Contact during the ERASMUS year abroad'. *European Union Politics*, 11 (2): 241–65.

Sigalas, E. (2010b). 'The Role of Personal Benefits in Public Support for the EU: Learning from the Erasmus Students'. *West European Politics*, 33 (6): 1341–61.

Sikorski, R. (2012). 'The Blenheim Palace Speech (on the UK and Europe)'. *Blenheim Palace*, 21 September 2012.

Sinnott, R. (1995). 'Bringing Public Opinion Back In'. In Niedermayer, O. and Sinnott, R. (eds), *Public Opinion and Internationalized Governance*. Oxford: Oxford University Press, 11–31.

Sinnott, R. (2005). 'An Evaluation of the Measurement of National, Subnational and Supranational Identity in Crossnational Surveys'. *International Journal of Public Opinion Research*, 18 (2): 211–23.

Sklair, L. (1991). *Sociology of the Global System. Social Change in Global Perspective*. Baltimore: Johns Hopkins University Press.

Sklair, L. (2001). *The Transnational Capitalist Class*. London: Blackwell Publishers.

Smith, A. (1995). *Nations and Nationalism in a Global Era*. Oxford: Polity Press.

Smith, A. (1998). *Nationalism and Modernism*. London: Routledge.

Smith, P. M. (2001). *Transnational Urbanism. Locating Globalization*. Malden, MA: Blackwell Publishers.

Sniderman, P. M. and Hagendoorn, L. (2007). *When Ways of Life Collide: Multiculturalism and Its Discontents in the The Netherlands*. Princeton, NJ: Princeton University Press.

Snijders, T. and Bosker, R. (1999). *Multilevel Analysis: An Introduction to Basic and Advanced Multilevel Modeling*. London: Sage.

Statistisches Bundesamt (2013). *Statistisches Jahrbuch Deutschland und Internationales 2013*. Wiesbaden.

Steenbergen, M., Edwards, E., and De Vries, C. (2007). 'Who's Cueing Whom?: Mass-Elite Linkages and the Future of European Integration'. *European Union Politics*, 8 (1): 13–35.

Stone Sweet, A. (2004). *The Judicial Construction of Europe*. Oxford: Oxford University Press.

Stone Sweet, A. and Sandholtz, W. (1998). 'Integration, Supranational Governance, and the Institutionalization of the European Polity'. In Sandholtz, W. and Stone Sweet, A. (eds), *European Integration and Supranational Governance*. Oxford: Oxford University Press.

Swank, D. and Betz, H.-G. (2003). 'Globalization, the Welfare State and Right-Wing Populism in Western Europe'. *Socio-Economic Review*, 1 (2): 215–45.

Tajfel, H. (1981). *Human Groups and Social Categories: Studies in Social Psychology*. Cambridge: Cambridge University Press.

Thompson, G. (2005). 'The Limits to Globalization: Questions for Held and Wolf'. In Held, D. (ed.) *Debating Globalization*. Cambridge: Polity.

Threlfall, M. (2003). 'European Social Integration: Harmonization, Convergence and Single Social Areas'. *Journal of European Social Policy*, 13 (2): 121–39.

Tillman, E. (2004). 'The European Union at the Ballot Box? European Integration and Voting Behavior in the New Member States'. *Comparative Political Studies*, 37 (5).

Titunik, R. (2005). 'Democracy, Domination and Legitimacy in Max Weber's Political Thought'. In Camic, C., Gorski, P., and Trubek, D. (eds), *Max Weber's Economy and Society: A Critical Companion*. Stanford: Stanford University Press, 143–63.

Triandafyllidou, A. and Maroufof, M. (2013). 'EU Citizenship and Intra-EU Mobility: A Virtuous Circle Even in Times of Crisis'. In De Witte, B., Héritier, A., and Trechsel, A. (eds), *The Euro Crisis and the State of European Democracy*. Florence: Robert Schuman Centre for Advanced Studies, 370–91.

Tucker, J., Pacek, A., and Berinsky, A. (2002). 'Transitional Winners and Losers: Attitudes toward EU Membership in Post-Communist Countries'. *American Journal of Political Science*, 46 (3): 557–71.

University of Luxembourg (2013). 'About the University.' <http://wwwen.uni.lu/university/about_the_university> (accessed 20 December 2013).

Urry, J. (2000). 'Mobile Sociology'. *British Journal of Sociology*, 51 (1): 185–203.

Van der Waal, J., Achterberg, P., Houtman, D., and De Koster, W. (2010). '"Some Are More Equal Than Others": Economic Egalitarianism and Welfare Chauvinism in the Netherlands'. *Journal of European Social Policy*, 20 (4): 350–63.

Van Hooren, F. (2012). 'Varieties of Migrant Care Work: Comparing Patterns of Migrant Labour in Social Care'. *Journal of European Social Policy*, 22 (2): 133–47.

Van Kersbergen, K. and Krouwel, A. (2008). 'A Double-Edged Sword! The Dutch Centre-Right and the "Foreigners Issue"'. *Journal of European Public Policy*, 15 (3): 398–414.

Väyrynen, R. (2003). 'Regionalism: Old and New'. *International Studies Review*, 5 (1): 25–51.

Vertovec, S. (1999). 'Conceiving and Researching Transnationalism'. *Ethnic and Racial Studies*, 22 (2): 447–62.

Vertovec, S. and Cohen, R. (2002). *Conceiving Cosmopolitanism: Theory, Context, And Practice*. Oxford: Oxford University Press.

Verwiebe, R. (2014). 'Why do Europeans Migrate to Berlin? Social-Structural Differences for Italian, British, French and Polish Nationals in the Period between 1980 and 2002'. *International Migration*, 52 (4): 209–30.

Wade, R. (1996). 'Globalization and its Limits: Reports of the Death of the National Economy are Greatly Exagerated'. In Berger, S. and Dore, R. (eds), *National Diversity and Global Capitalism*. Ithaca, NY: Cornell University Press, 60–88.

Waever, O. (1998). 'Insecurity, Security and Asecurity in the West European Non-war Community'. In Adler, E. and Barnett, M. (eds), *Security Communities*. Cambridge: Cambridge University Press.

Wallace, H. (1996). 'Politics and Policy in the EU: The Challenge of Governance'. In Wallace, H. and Wallace, W. (eds), *Policy-making in the European Union*. Oxford: Oxford University Press, 3–36.

Ward, C., Bochner, S., and Furnham, A. (2001). *The Psychology of Culture Shock*. London: Routledge.

Warnes, A. M. and Williams, A. (2007). 'Older Migrants in Europe: A New Focus for Migration Studies'. *Journal of Ethnic and Migration Studies*, 32 (8): 1257–81.

Weber, M. (1962). *Basic Concepts in Sociology*. New York: Kensington Press Books.

Wendt, A. (1994). 'Collective Identity Formation and the International State'. *American Political Science Review*, 88 (2): 384–96.

Werner, H. (2001). 'Wirtschaftliche Integration und Arbeitskräftewanderungen in der EU'. *Aus Politik und Zeitgeschichte*, 51 (8).

Westle, B. (2003). 'Europäische Identifikation im Spannungsfeld regionaler und nationaler Identitäten. Theoretische Überlegungen und empirische Befunde'. *Politische Vierteljahrsschrift*, 44 (4): 453–82.

Whelan, C. T. and Maître, B. (2009). 'Europeanization of Inequality and European Reference Groups'. *Journal of European Social Policy*, 19 (2): 117–30.

Wiener, A. (2011). 'Cultural Validation: Examining the Familiarity Deficit of Global Governance'. In Bjola, C. and Kornprobst, M. (eds), *Arguing Global Governance*. New York: Routledge.

Wilson, I. (2011). 'What Should We Expect of "Erasmus Generations"?'. *Journal of Common Market Studies*, 49 (5): 1113–40.

Zürn, M. (2000). 'Democratic Governance Beyond the Nation-State: The EU and Other International Institutions'. *European Journal of International Relations*, 6 (2): 183–221.

Zürn, M. (2005). *Regieren jenseits des Nationalstaats*. Frankfurt a.M.: Suhrkamp.

Data Sources

European Commission (2006). 'Eurobarometer 65.1. The Future of Europe, Consumer Protection in Transborder Purchases, Family Planning, and Opinions and Experiences in Transborder Purchases'. February–March 2006. TNS OPINION & SOCIAL, Brussels [Producer]; GESIS, Cologne [Publisher]: ZA4505.

European Commission (2007). 'Eurobarometer 67.1. Cultural Values, Poverty and Social Exclusion, Developmental Aid, and Residential Mobility'. February–March 2007. TNS OPINION & SOCIAL, Brussels [Producer]; GESIS, Cologne [Publisher]: ZA4529.

Eurostat (2006a). 'Gross Domestic Product in Purchasing Power Standards 2006.' <http://epp.eurostat.ec.europa.eu/portal/page/portal/eurostat/home/>.

Eurostat (2006b). 'Harmonised Indices of Consumer Prices 2006.' <http://epp.eurostat.ec.europa.eu/portal/page/portal/eurostat/home/>.

Eurostat (2006c). 'Harmonised Unemployment Rates 2006.' <http://epp.eurostat.ec. europa.eu/portal/page/portal/eurostat/home/>.

Eurostat (2006d). 'Share of Exports in the EU-25 2006.' <http://epp.eurostat.ec.europa. eu/portal/page/portal/eurostat/home/>.

Eurostat (2006e). 'Share of Imports in the EU-25 2006'. <http://epp.eurostat.ec.europa. eu/portal/page/portal/eurostat/home/>.

Eurostat (2006f). 'Total Population 2006'. <http://epp.eurostat.ec.europa.eu/portal/ page/portal/eurostat/home/>.

Eurostat (2007a). 'Gross Domestic Product in Purchasing Power Standards'. <http:// epp.eurostat.ec.europa.eu/portal/page/portal/eurostat/home/>.

Eurostat (2007b). 'Harmonised Indices of Consumer Prices 2007'. <http://epp.eurostat. ec.europa.eu/portal/page/portal/eurostat/home/>.

Eurostat (2007c). 'Harmonised Unemployment Rates 2007'. <http://epp.eurostat.ec. europa.eu/portal/page/portal/eurostat/home/>.

Eurostat (2007d). 'Share of Exports in the EU-27 2007'. <http://epp.eurostat.ec.europa. eu/portal/page/portal/eurostat/home/>.

Eurostat (2007e). 'Share of Imports in the EU-27 2007'. <http://epp.eurostat.ec.europa. eu/portal/page/portal/eurostat/home/>.

Eurostat (2007f). 'Total Population 2007'. <http://epp.eurostat.ec.europa.eu/portal/ page/portal/eurostat/home/>.

Eurostat (2012). 'Foreign and foreign-born population by group of citizenship and country of birth 2012.' <http://epp.eurostat.ec.europa.eu/portal/page/portal/eu rostat/home/>.

INSEE (2005). 'Statistiques locales—Produit Intérieur Brut par habitant par départe- ment'. <http://www.insee.fr/fr/bases-de-donnees/>.

INSEE (2006). 'Statistiques locales - Taux de chômage localisés'. <http://www.insee.fr/ fr/bases-de-donnees/>.

INSEE (2007). 'Statistiques locales—Population étrangère'. <http://www.insee.fr/fr/ bases-de-donnees/>.

Statistical Offices of the Federation and the Länder (2006a). 'Regional atlas—Foreign Population.' <https://www-genesis.destatis.de/gis/genView?GenMLURL=https:// www-genesis.destatis.de/regatlas/AI002-1.xml&CONTEXT=REGATLAS01>.

Statistical Offices of the Federation and the Länder (2006b). 'Regional atlas—GDP per capita.' <https://www-genesis.destatis.de/gis/genView?GenMLURL=https://www- genesis.destatis.de/regatlas/AI002-1.xml&CONTEXT=REGATLAS01>.

Statistical Offices of the Federation and the Länder (2006c). 'Regional atlas— Unemployment rate.' <https://www-genesis.destatis.de/gis/genView?GenMLURL= https://www-genesis.destatis.de/regatlas/AI002-1.xml&CONTEXT=REGATLAS01>.

Treaties

European Union (1957). *Treaty Establishing the European Economic Community*. Luxem- bourg: Office for Official Publications of the European Communities.

European Union (1986). *Single European Act*. Luxembourg: Office for Official Publica- tions of the European Communities.

References

European Union (1992). *Treaty on European Union*. Luxembourg: Office for Official Publications of the European Communities.

European Union (1997). *Treaty of Amsterdam*. Luxembourg: Office for Official Publications of the European Communities.

European Union (2008). *Consolidated Version of the Treaty on the Functioning of the European Union*. Luxembourg: Office for Official Publications of the European Communities.

Newspaper Articles

Frankfurter Allgemeine Zeitung (2013). 'Roma aus Südeuropa: Friedrich will stärker gegen Armutseinwanderung vorgehen'. (18 February 2013).

Die Zeit Online (2013). 'Hartz-IV für Ausländer: Bundessozialgericht wartet Ergebnis des EuGH ab'. (12 December 2013) <http://www.zeit.de/wirtschaft/2013-2012/bundessozialgericht-hartz-iv-eu-arbeitslose> (accessed 31 July 2014).

Index

Index